The American Economy

From the Great Crash to the Third Industrial Revolution

Arthur S. Link
Princeton University
General Editor for History

The American Economy

From the Great Crash to the Third Industrial Revolution

Joseph Finkelstein
Union College

Harlan Davidson, Inc.
Arlington Heights, Illinois 60004

To Sharon, Jonathan, and Neal

Copyright © 1992
Harlan Davidson, Inc.
All rights reserved

Library of Congress Cataloging-in-Publication Data

Finkelstein, Joseph, 1926–
   The American economy from the great crash to the third Industrial Revolution/ by Joseph Finkelstein.
      p. cm.
   Includes bibliographical references and index.
   ISBN 0-88295-873-9
   1. United States—Economic conditions—1918–1945. 2. United States—Economic conditions—1945–   3. United States—Economic policy. I. Title.
HC106.3.F49 1991
330.973'09—dc20   90–48127
                                                                            CIP

Book design: Matthew Doherty
Cover design: DePinto Graphic Design
Cartoons: Page 70-"It's the Multiple Head Re-entry Principle," from Herblock's *State of the Union* (New York: Simon and Schuster, 1972).
Page 105-"All Possible Care Is Taken to Avoid Civilian Casulaties," from Herblock's *The Herblock Gallery* (New York: Simon and Schuster, 1969).

Manufactured in the United States of America
96   95   94   93   92   1   2   3   4   5   BC

CONTENTS

INTRODUCTION

We are, I believe, in the beginning stages of a Third Industrial Revolution which will control and alter our lives for the next fifty years and beyond. Founded on unprecedented scientific knowledge, the new technologies are more powerful than anything we have ever known; and like galaxies they are ever expanding. Our politics, our social and economic institutions, and our familiar and conventional ways of handling change are all being shaken. Beyond the uncertainties, however, lies the prospect of a world largely free from scarcity and far richer in material goods than has ever been known. The United States has been the birthplace of this impending revolution, and the last six decades in particular have created the environment for these explosive changes. Because we always look to history for explanation and understanding, there is a need for a book which examines the American economy from the Great Depression of the 1930s to this Third Industrial Revolution of the present. No current American history interprets this period with such a special emphasis. It is essential to reexamine these decades in detail and demonstrate how they shaped the current changes taking place.

By comparison with the economic transformations of the eighteenth century, the developments of the Third Industrial Revolution are more pervasive and profound. Even the Second Industrial Revolution (1880–1920) which generated the automobile industry, mass production and electricity, and corporate management and which established the economic preeminence of the United States, pales in significance when compared to the scale of present changes. What is happening with microprocessors, communications, biogenetics, bioagriculture, lasers, fiber optics, robotics, CAD/CAM, the office of the future, and other areas today towers over the technological changes of the eighteenth and nineteenth centuries. Although America reaped the largest benefits from the Second Industrial Revolution, from industries founded by men like Edison, Ford, and Eastman, some indicators point to Japan and other Asian countries as the long-term beneficiaries of American science and the potential winners. As Americans we need to stop and examine how we are going to maintain and enhance our economy, institutions, and values as these changes increase.

Students expect a broader and clearer understanding of this half century than they are usually offered. They often have no historical reference that enables them to make sense out of the bewildering pace of global change. Not only do they want to understand the past, but they want to see how that past relates to current problems and prospects for the future. This book hopes to help that process of understanding.

The American Economy from the Great Crash to the Third Industrial Revolution is divided into four major sections. Within each section I have usually, but not slavishly, attended to such topics as agriculture, labor, banking and finance, business management, and government policy, though I have not hesitated to add or subtract material when it seemed to make good sense. Readers may not always agree with the choice of topic or treatment, and there is wide room for disagreement. I have tried particularly to avoid any dogmatic philosophical opinions because I do not believe that the history of this period can be forced into an ideological straitjacket, whether Keynesian, Marxist, or monetarist. This textbook uses a flexible, basically chronological approach in the first ten chapters. The last two chapters provide a glimpse at the coming Third Industrial Revolution and the part the United States economy will play in that global system.

I have chosen not to present economic theory apart from social and political developments since this type of separation is not relevant, appropriate, or helpful to readers of this book. Neither equations nor mathematical formulas are employed, but I have selected relevant statistical data when appropriate to illustrate important trends. This material should easily be grasped by college students and lay readers.

The theme of the book is that the United States, richly endowed by nature, fashioned through its people the most successful consumer society the world has known. Although the nation is flawed by poverty, racial and ethnic discrimination, and great volatility, 80 to 90 percent of the American people are free from the chains of serious scarcity. The largely successful capitalist system that came apart during the Great Depression has recovered impressively and stands on the threshold of a new era. Recounting the story of this recovery is a worthy investigation that should give us a fuller appreciation of how we arrived at our present destination.

ACKNOWLEDGMENTS

Many colleagues and thousands of students, willingly and unwillingly, have listened to these themes and concerns over my four decades of teaching Controlling Forces in U.S. Economic Development, a required course for all graduate M.B.A. students, and a history course entitled Development of the American Economy. The maturity, intelligence, and involvement of many students has made the teaching of this material a continuously innovative and stimulating experience. The undergraduate students of Union College who have taken economic history also should be given their due since without their energy, enthusiasm, and candor this manuscript could not have come into being.

My colleagues in the departments of History and Economics and in the Graduate Management Program have given help, lent me books, suggested changes, even offered me access to their personal collections, and have made me aware of the benefits of a small college and its warm colleagueship. In particular, Stephen Berk, Erik Hansen, Manfred Jonas, Al Thimm (formerly of Union College, now of the University of Vermont), Peter Prosper, and Brad Lewis have been of special help.

Special thanks must be paid to Judy Peck and Carolyn Micklas, and to Rita Michalec for typing chapters many times as they emerged from handwritten yellow pages to final copy. A close friend and former colleague, Malcolm Willison, spent hours reading and commenting on the manuscript. A sociologist by training and profession, he made me aware of so many issues in my treatment that needed rethinking and reworking. I have tried to incorporate the best of these suggestions in my writing. Many assistants and grants-in-aid have helped; Ken Orosz, Paul Gallagher, and Jeff Goldstein deserve my special gratitude.

My wife, Nadia Ehrlich Finkelstein, has been a stalwart supporter, and I am indebted once again for her help, her judgment, and her clarity; without her support this book might never have been completed, and would not have been as sensitive to human problems.

Union College too deserves thanks. Dean Weiner and Dean Butterstein paid for much of the typing. The Department of History and the Graduate Management Institute furnished assistants throughout the years of effort. Above all, the staff of Schaffer Library, Union College, supported me by special effort in interlibrary loans and reference searches to make my work possible. Only their patience, skill, and hard work made research possible in Schenectady; they are wonderful people, wonderful professionals.

My editors, Maureen Hewitt and Michael Kendrick of Harlan Davidson, gave encouragement at the appropriate times and support when I needed it.

Finally in August 1989, I traveled across the country from Orleans on Cape Cod to Berkeley, California with my son. I saw not only the country anew but in a fresh way through his younger and unspoiled view. Economic historians in particular need to return to basics.

I offer the usual disclaimers that I alone stand responsible for the opinions and interpretations in these pages. My final thought is that I hope you, the reader, will enjoy the book.

BOOK I

The New Deal and World War II

1   *The Great Crash and the Great Depression*

THE HISTORICAL SETTING

When Herbert Hoover took the presidential oath of office on March 4, 1929, no one would have predicted that within eight short months the roaring twenties would brusquely end and give way to the Depression of the '30s. Hoover had won a smashing victory over his Democratic opponent Alfred E. Smith; the final electoral vote had given Hoover 444 votes to Smith's 87. The President's credentials were outstanding. A brilliant engineer, he had achieved worldwide status both for his professional and public achievements. His was a household name noted for humanitarian success in Belgium during the First World War and for work, after the war, as chairman of the American Relief Administration which had prevented suffering and starvation in twenty-three countries. As early as 1920, he was mentioned as a Republican presidential candidate. As Secretary of Commerce under Harding, he was active in furthering the needs of American business and supported especially programs of voluntary cooperation among manufacturers and consumers. In 1927, as personal representative of President Coolidge, he directed the relief efforts to aid the victims of the great Mississippi flood. It was believed that the country could not have been entrusted to better hands.

On October 29, 1929, the stock market crash ended the boom market of the twenties and ushered in almost a full decade of unemployment, bank failures, business disasters, and personal hardship and tragedy for one-third of the American people. For three more years, Hoover struggled to restore the country's economic health. How terribly he failed! Ill-equipped to understand the full extent of the economic catastrophe, he failed to halt the downward slide. Even the creation of the Reconstruction Finance Corporation (RFC), which was an outstanding innovation to make available government credits to distressed institutions, came to be associated with his successor and the New Deal. Historians now regard Hoover with more un-

Chronology

1933
March: Congress convened in emergency session; bank holiday; Emergency Banking Act
May: Agricultural Adjustment Act; Emergency Farm Mortgage Act; Federal Emergency Relief Act; London Economic Conference; Tennessee Valley Authority created
June: Glass-Steagall Banking Act; Emergency Railroad Transportation Act; National Industrial Recovery Act; Public Works Administration (PWA) established
1934
January: Price of gold set at $35 per ounce
February: Export-Import Bank established
June: Securities Exchange Act; Reciprocal Trade Agreements Act; Silver Purchase Act; Federal Farm Bankruptcy Act (Frazier-Lemke bill)
1935
February: Connally Act
May: Works Progress Administration (WPA) established; Rural Electrification Administration established; *Schecter Poultry Corporation* v. *United States* nullifies NRA codes
July: National Labor Relations Act (Wagner-Connery bill)
August: Social Security Act; Banking Act; Farm Mortgage Moratorium Act
1936
January: *United States* v. *Butler et al.* makes processing tax on agricultural products illegal
February: Soil Conservation and Domestic Allotment Act
1937
February: "Court-packing" bill sent to Congress
April: *National Labor Relations Board* v. *Jones and Laughlin Steel Corporation* (301 U.S. 1) upholds legality of N.L.R.B.
1938
February: Agricultural Adjustment Act; Federal Crop Insurance Act
June: Fair Labor Standards Act; Food, Drug, and Cosmetics Act

derstanding and sympathy than his countrymen did in those ebb years of his presidency.

On March 4, 1933, Hoover saw his office turned over to a most unlikely successor. Franklin Delano Roosevelt was born at Hyde Park, New York on January 30, 1882 and entered life as part of the "establishment." Educated at Harvard, and with a law degree from Columbia, he practiced law before entering politics. During the First World War he was Assistant Secretary of the Navy, and in 1920 he was the vice presidential candidate on the Democratic ticket. In 1921, he was crippled for life by an attack of infantile paralysis, but by 1928, he had rebounded to win the important governorship of New York.

The election of 1933 was an overwhelming victory for the Democratic party. FDR took 472 electoral votes to Hoover's 59. For the first time since 1919 the Democratic party had control of both legislative and executive branches. Hoover had tried to convince the electorate that the Republicans had done all that could be done safely. A Democratic victory, he warned, would bring even greater economic collapse. The people, however, had voted to risk their futures on a more confident leader.

The presidency of FDR from 1933 to 1945 remains with good reason one of the most exciting and controversial periods in our recent history. The first 100 days of the administration brought a legislative barrage that was meant to restore confidence in the economic system and self-confidence to a very frightened people; it largely succeeded. In Roosevelt's first term the New Deal brought victories such as the passage of Social Security (1935) and defeats, such as the intractability of unemployment. Staunch New Dealers like Harry Hopkins believed by 1936 that the country faced a permanent core of at least four or five million jobless.

The election of 1936 brought the President to the height of his personal and political success. (Not until his death in April 1945 would so many millions of Americans revere him so.) Only Maine and Vermont had voted Republican. Seventy-five Democrats dominated the Senate. But only a year later, Roosevelt "appeared to be a thoroughly repudiated leader."[1] Three crises had undermined the momentum of the New Deal—the emotional and abortive attempt to reform the Supreme Court, the epidemic of sit-down strikes, and the sharp and scary economic recession of 1937. Later, the stalemate at home was offset by the rising threat of Fascism abroad. America would become enmeshed, indirectly at first, in confronting the threat to world peace that Nazism posed. Roosevelt would become the President of a wartime America and a world leader in the fight for freedom until his death in 1945.

THE ONSET OF DEPRESSION

Six months after Thorstein Veblen, the controversial American economist and philosopher, died in California—lonely and unchastened—the American business system came apart. For Veblen, this would not have been a great shock, for he had assumed that an economic system so opposed to fundamental human needs and so contrary to the beneficent forces of technology would run amuck. Veblen had achieved renown as a critic of American life. In 1899, he published *The Theory of the Leisure Class* and coined such phrases as "conspicuous consumption" and "conspicuous waste" to describe the materialistic overindulgence of Americans. Even he would have recoiled, however, at the severity of the crisis, despite his continuing belief in business chicanery described in *The Theory of Business Enterprises* (1904) and ending with *Absentee Ownership and Business Enterprise in Recent Times: The Case of America* (1923). To the left of Veblen, Marxist writers attributed the stock market crash of October to fundamental contradictions within the capitalist system. Marxist theory posited a thesis of recurring cycles of boom and bust culminating with the last cycle which would destroy the system. To their thinking the 1920s was clearly the great boom, thus the crash was both predictable and inevitable.

Both Veblen's and Marxist explanations of the crisis and the resulting Great Depression are, however, excessively simplistic. The long depression of the 1930s resulted from many structural flaws in the economy. By the close of the 1920s, the ebbing of a long cycle of investment and growth and an absence of public policy, especially fiscal and monetary policy, could no longer contain an unmanageable speculative stock market boom. Americans had been taught to believe Adam Smith's promise that each individual who strained to maximize his own interest would produce benefits for the entire society. Our economic institutions were built on this premise, and our industrial growth had benefitted from this wisdom. Could anyone deny that this way of life had succeeded? From the Second Industrial Revolution of the 1880s through the chaos of World War I, the United States had emerged as the world's richest and strongest power. While Europe struggled to rebuild after World War I, the U.S. enjoyed a consumer revolution. Americans of all classes were able to afford consumer durables that were unattainable luxuries to the rest of the world. In the purchase of houses, automobiles, and electrical appliances, the United States reached levels of consumption that were not reached elsewhere on the globe for several decades. America's economic system discriminated against a minority, in contrast to other world economic systems that discriminated against the majority. The stock market frenzy of the 1920s could easily have been curbed without touching the essential strengths and energies of American capitalism. But many people were unable or unwilling to set limits.

The decade of the 1920s was the harvest season of the Second Industrial Revolution. Having grown rich and irresponsible, Americans allowed structural weaknesses to develop in the economic system, particularly in manufacturing, marketing, and finance. American industry was dominated by oligopolies that controlled pricing and turned out homogenous products.[2] The most powerful corporations in the newest and fastest growing economic sectors shared huge markets with a half-dozen or fewer real competitors; what was left of a particular market might then be fought over by a relatively large number of small companies that had carved out a particular niche for themselves. The steel, auto, rubber, and electrical industries followed this general pattern. In a few cases, companies engaged in outright collusion. The evidence suggests, for example, that collusive practices in the electrical industry existed for decades before the government indictments of 1964. The Temporary National Economic Commission (TNEC) reports describe similar cartel-like arrangements in the optical and chemical industries. Much more important, however, than these relatively few outright legal violations was the misconception of the power and size of American industry. Many Americans still believed that large companies operated in much the same way that a corner candy store did, and that opportunity existed for all businesses regardless of size. It was a self-deception of the highest order. Big business had long come of age and had acquired tremendous power in several markets. It was questionable whether the laissez-faire philosophy of the nineteenth century was still desirable, since obviously not all were benefitting from an unregulated free-enterprise system.

American enterprise turned out a flood of consumer goods. The market mechanism, it was assumed, would provide the means and the incentives to absorb these goods. On the whole during the 1920s consumer demand was sufficient to accomplish this absorption only on an increasingly precarious basis. Hence the beginnings of economic recession predated the stock market crash. Although total personal consumption expenditures had fallen briefly in the short post–World War I depression to $56 billion, they had climbed to nearly $81 billion by 1929. The Gross National Product (GNP) rose from about $72 billion to about $104 billion in the same period. These large increases, however, meant that demand, employment, income, and investments had to grow at ever-increasing rates if the economy was not to trip over its own success. No mechanism, either public or private, existed to coordinate these related factors. Economists in the 1920s had not yet developed a body of macroeconomic theory that explained the potential gap between the actual rate of growth and the potential GNP, i.e., the rate of growth necessary to achieve a full employment economy without inflation or deflation.

In the most sophisticated analysis of the Great Depression, Professor Michael Bernstein argues convincingly that the stock market crash and the collapse of the financial markets was not the cause of the depression. The economy, he believes, was in the process of working out a "long-term structural transition involving a change in the composition of final demand."[3] There were, he argues, cyclical events and structural problems of economic transformation which came together as the economy tried to adjust to a new order. However, the development and growth of new industries and new products was too slow "because of a combination of demand-side problems, supply-side shocks, and policy difficulties."[4] Financial upheaval precipitated a decade of crisis as these underlying weaknesses in the economy emerged.

To most Americans, however, Wall Street was the villain. In the seats of banking and finance, the greatest anarchy reigned throughout the twenties. Magic, mysticism, and myth dominated the operation of securities markets. There was much outright and shameless abuse. From the trustees of great New York money houses to the small banker in Babbittsville, guardians had carelessly neglected their responsibilities. The fault lay less in the integrity of bankers and brokers than in the virulence of an epidemic in securities specu- lation. On every level, the financial regulation of our society was still inde- scribably primitive. The Federal Reserve System, established in 1913, neither operated as a system, nor functioned as a central bank, nor used its powers to curb financial excess. In the 1920s, the Fed's policies were a congeries of haphazard activities, frequently administered too little and too late. The Fed had no coherent monetary program except for the restrictive and deflation- ary policies it enacted. But on Wall Street, speculative frenzy dominated the trading. An average day on the New York Exchange saw anywhere from 4 to 6 million shares trade hands, an enormous volume for that time. Virtually nothing existed to guarantee the integrity of stock exchanges or the honesty of these transactions. Newly issued stock without value was thrown to a rav- enous public; old issues were inflated and reinflated by investment maneu- vers. Insiders always won; sometimes the insiders allowed friends to win too. Several of the large investment houses had special lists of important public figures. These men would be allowed to buy shares at a lower price before they were listed on the exchange. In the "permanent" bull market one could gain twice—early and late. As one writer put it in a popular magazine:

If a man saves $15 a week, and invests in good common stocks, and allows the dividends and rights to accumulate, at the end of twenty years he will have at least $80,000 and an income from investment of around $400 a month. He will be rich. And because income can do that, I am firm in my belief that everyone not only can be rich, but ought to be rich.[5]

Although not everyone in the country was in on the shell game, no ma- jor country in modern times can point to such a period of financial self- delusion. If the speculative boom could have gone on forever, there would have been no depression. In real terms, impressive gains had been made in the 1920s, i.e., GNP had risen nearly 50 percent and per capita income from $660 to $875. Nevertheless, there were fundamental problems in the econ- omy, and the worst excesses were bred in the financial canyons of lower Manhattan. Here the break occurred on October 29, 1929:

The big gong had hardly sounded in the great hall of the Exchange at ten o'clock Tuesday morning before the storm broke in full force. Huge blocks of stock were thrown upon the market for what they would bring....Not only were innumerable small traders being sold out, but big ones too.... Again and again the specialist in a stock would find himself surrounded by brokers fighting to sell—and nobody at all even thinking of buying....The scene on the floor was chaotic....Within half an hour of the opening the volume of trading passed three million shares, by twelve o'clock it had passed eight million, by half past one it had passed twelve million, and when the closing gong brought the day's madness to an end, the gigantic re- cord of 16,410,030 shares had been set....The average prices of fifty lead- ing stocks as compiled by the N.Y. Times had fallen nearly forty points.[6]

By the first of the New Year, 1930, the system was beginning its long downward slide. There was no recovery. In place of a short panic, the ensuing decade witnessed a steady liquidation of corporate assets and the deflation of prices nationwide. The drop in national income from $83.3 billion in 1929 to $68.9 billion in 1930 and then to $40.0 billion in 1932 illustrated the magnitude of the crisis. Industrial production measured by the Federal Reserve index fell from 110 in 1929 to 91 in 1930 and stood at 58 in 1937. Unemployment rose almost fivefold over the three years, 1930–1933, and wholesale prices dropped almost one-third from 95.3 in 1929 to 64.8 in 1932.[7]

Between 1929 and the election of FDR in 1932, the depression gained momentum. Commercial and bank failures pulled apart the mastic that held the economy together. Investment virtually ceased. Since prices did not fall as rapidly as wages, unemployment soared. Foreign markets disappeared under a wave of autarchy and protectionism symbolized by the Hawley-Smoot Tariff. Sound banks were destroyed as the abuses of bad banks were uncovered. The consequences of unrestrained economic individualism generated a new kind of disaster that exacerbated every problem. Attempting to cut its budget, the federal government increased the deflationary forces that were wreaking such damage. President Hoover seemed frozen by the fiscal attitudes of the past and panicked as the Bonus Army marched on Washington to ask that Congress pay in advance the war service bonuses Congress had agreed to award in 1945. State and local governments fled from spending. Individual businessmen also adopted deflationary policies as they cut back. To survive, everyone tried to retrench as quickly and as completely as possible, and the depression then became self-fulfilling. In the midst of this hurricane, very few captains let out more sail. Most citizens tried to survive by adopting the same kind of retrenchment policies in their own little way. Typically they cut their spending. In the face of rising unemployment and falling prices, common sense dictated the utmost financial prudence. The sum of all these efforts was the deepest, longest, and most destructive economic catastrophe in our national history.

At his inaugural in March 1933, the new President showed courage and optimism. He told a shattered people:

> The only thing we have to fear is fear itself.... Values have shrunken to fantastic levels; taxes have risen; our ability to pay has fallen; government of all kinds is faced by serious curtailment of income, the means of exchange are frozen in the currents of trade; the withered leaves of industrial enterprise lie on every side; farmers find no markets for their produce; the savings of many years in thousands of families are gone. More important, a host of unemployed citizens face the grim problem of existence.... We must act and act quickly.[8]

Despite the rhetoric, Americans had more than fear to fear. They had to find out how they could salvage their economy and society. For almost a decade, in fits and starts, in bits and pieces, they struggled to break free from this immense deflation-depression. Unemployment and human suffering had to be relieved and legislation introduced to assist the economic institutions that had broken down so overwhelmingly.

The New Deal that Roosevelt initiated in March 1933 mounted no revolution. Every change was deeply embedded in historical antecedents. Our capitalist system was retained, although modified under a great deal of regulatory apparatus. Much innovation was piecemeal, and virtually all the changes were influenced by political considerations. Some New Deal programs were regressive and self-defeating, while many have since outlived their usefulness. But from the vantage of six decades, it is striking how lasting so many of these changes were. These programs have become so much a part of our system that almost sixty years later both major political parties are still beholden to the principles of the New Deal and Social Security systems, federal deposit insurance, securities regulation, and much else; some programs stand almost above the level of controversy. Very few decades in our history have brought so many changes in our national economic environment.

The distance between the experience of the present generation and of those who lived through the 1930s is so great that it is worth recalling what some of these hardships were. In very rough terms the economy was operating at somewhere between one-half and two-thirds of its productive ability. Every industry suffered from excess manufacturing and unused production capacity. Very few companies invested in new plants, machinery, or innovations even if they seemed promising. Though change and growth in such industries as chemicals, airlines, and foods continued, business leadership was totally broken and routed. For long periods in the 1930s businessmen suffered from a kind of ideological schizophrenia. They bewailed the growing spread of government involvement and regulation of economic activities, but they became increasingly eager to depend on government aid and subsidies. Conservative businessmen hated Roosevelt passionately, but they could offer few alternatives. Because they feared Marxism more than the New Deal, they clung anxiously to the latter.

If business suffered during the depression, individuals suffered even more. Perhaps as much as one-third of the work force was actually unemployed for very long periods. Even these figures conceal the real hardships. Lower income groups depended on family income. To survive, most or all family members had to bring home earnings. Although frequently less skilled and lower paid, their marginal increment of income was important to the family's well-being. Those in this category could find scant employment in the 1930s. Women who worked for lower wages frequently replaced male heads of families as breadwinners because the men could find no work. People without jobs often disintegrated psychologically in this environment of hopelessness. For many others the society of the 1930s had no use whatsoever for their skills. Engineers became taxi drivers, college graduates in history, real estate salesmen. Young men destined for the foreign service became corset vendors. Life for many became preoccupied with the small change of existence. Everything could be bought for pennies, nickels, dimes,

Map 1.1 Hardiness Zones and Minimum Temperature Ranges

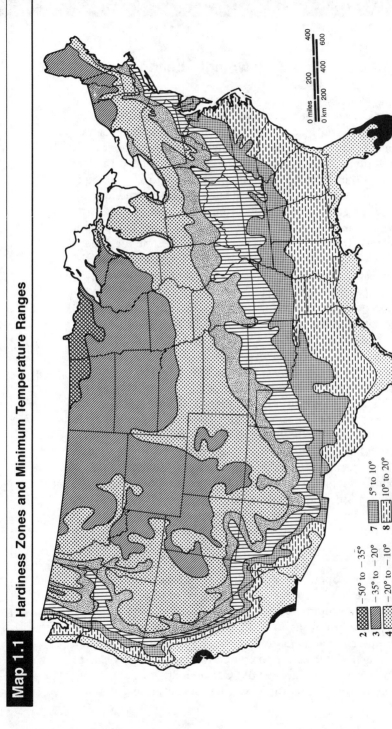

2 — 50° to − 35°
3 — 35° to − 20°
4 — 20° to − 10°
5 — 10° to − 5°
6 — 5° to 5°

7 — 5° to 10°
8 — 10° to 20°
9 — 20° to 30°
10 — 30° to 40°

0 miles   200   400
0 km   200   400   600

Source: United States Department of Agriculture

The Endowment—Land

The United States has the largest viable acreage for farm crops of any major country in the world. Some 300 million acres of farm land, of 1.45 billion available acres of privately owned land, extend through a range of climates and geography. This expanse of land has conditioned the history of the nation and is a sure foundation for its economic future. One should not forget the range of related agricultural assets—climate, water, minerals, timber, fish, etc., which must be added to the overall picture. Throughout history, this rich resource has made it possible for Americans to attain the highest standard of real income at the lowest real cost: they spend comparatively the lowest percentage of their disposable income on food. The agricultural good fortune of the United States is the bedrock of its economic history.

Although there is a tremendous diversity of crops grown in every region of the country, modern specialization of major commercial crops grown by the latest technology has evolved only since the late nineteenth century. This recent agricultural evolution is closely geared to the most sophisticated, up-to-date knowledge of farming; U.S. agriculture may be unique not only in this concentrated specialization but also in its use of scientific knowledge, farm mechanization, and big business techniques. Despite its liabilities—price volatility, farmer indebtedness and dislocation, dependence on government subsidies and price supports, and soil depletion—American agriculture is as innovative and profit-driven as any other American business and has maintained incredibly high rates of productivity.

The country is divided into natural growing zones which extend from the Gulf of Mexico to Canada. Zone 10 is the Subtropical Belt, the Gulf plain that stretches from southeastern Texas to southern Florida. Here is found a unique cultivation pattern of rice, sugar cane, soft fruit and garden vegetables for the winter markets. Next come the southern states, once the old Cotton Belt, which now concentrate on hay, pasture, livestock, soybeans, and peanuts.

Cotton is concentrated in the irrigated regions from Texas to California. Tobacco, once the great southern staple, is much diminished since the Surgeon General's report of 1964, but lighter tobaccos hang on in North Carolina and the heavier burleys in Kentucky. North and west are the corn and winter wheat belts. The Corn Belt itself covers the great central prairies. It stretches from Ohio to southern South Dakota and Nebraska, across much of Iowa, Missouri, and Illinois, as well as parts of Minnesota and Kansas. To its north and east is the great Hay and Dairy Region, which grows large quantities of feed grains. To its west, the Great Plains, stretching from Canada to Mexico, grows wheat—spring wheat in the Dakotas, winter wheat from Nebraska to Texas; grain sorghum is also a widespread crop where conditions in this region permit. Variable rainfall, or the lack of it, determines the agricultural output of the area in a given season—15–25 inches permit reasonably successful crops; beyond the 100th meridian (the north-south line from the Canadian border to Mexico through North and South Dakota, Nebraska, Kansas, Oklahoma, and Texas) however, cropping makes sense only through irrigation. This portion of the Great Plains was, before feedlots, the great grazing area of the country. The Pacific Region of Washington, Oregon, and California is noted for market garden crops, and citrus and soft fruit.

The revolution in American diet since the Second World War has created enormous incentives for market garden crops of all kinds; increasingly they replace traditional staples, for fresh strawberries and fresh tomatoes are more profitable than wheat, and lettuce is a necessity, no matter what the price. We fatten great herds of cattle. Pigs too blend into this system, for they are often the recipients of the vast yields of corn grown in the Midwest. Our agriculture is so highly specialized that some despair of our future. Each year it seems we grow fewer varieties of almost all crops and concentrate only on those that earn the best profit. Upstate New York, for example, at one time grew over one hundred kinds of apples, but today fewer than twenty are grown. Everywhere in the country this pattern is repeated for many crops.

and quarters. Everywhere were queues and handouts. People looked ugly when they were poor and unfed. Thousands lived in shacks and shanty towns. Others rode the rails illegally, hoping to find work elsewhere. Poverty scarred this entire generation permanently, and its children.

The New Deal provided to millions relief on a subsistence level. New Deal policies also attempted to stimulate and encourage economic recovery. Finally, the New Deal passed reform legislation, but only where known and blatant abuses contributed to the breakdown of the economy. In banking, finance, social welfare, and labor relations, the New Deal made permanent contributions. In agriculture, however, stopgap policies provided no permanent resolution of chronic difficulties. In fiscal and monetary policy, and in the domestic cartelization of American business, e.g., the NRA codes, New Deal programs were actually either harmful or regressive.

In the next few pages, we will discuss seven areas that were central to the New Deal strategy of relieving the crisis, initiating recovery, and guiding reform: 1) agriculture, 2) banking, finance, and securities, 3) strategies for business recovery, 4) labor, 5) social welfare, 6) incomes policy, and 7) trade and commerce. In all cases, the New Deal scored highest marks for relief and the lowest for reform.

AGRICULTURE AND THE NEW DEAL

The purpose of the first Agricultural Adjustment Act of 1933 was, in the words of that bill, to "re-establish prices to farmers at a level that will give agricultural commodities a purchasing power with respect to articles that farmers buy equivalent to the purchasing power of agricultural commodities in the base period." (For this law, 1909–1914 was the base period for wheat, cotton, corn, hogs, rice, and dairy products; 1919–1929, for tobacco.) This act and later ones were passed in a continuing hope to bring in balance the prices of agricultural products and manufactured goods.[9] Broad powers were given to the Secretary of Agriculture to reduce productive acreage, to foster market quotas, and to establish land banks and "ever-normal" granaries. Although individual farmers were helped, large farmers benefitted more than small farmers from these activities, and none of these programs freed the agricultural community from grave distress in the 1930s. In 1935, the average price of cotton fell to 8 cents a pound and wheat stood at 50 cents a bushel. In a world suffering from an agricultural depression and falling prices, American farmers were unable to raise the value of their produce even with this legislative help. A thorough reform of U.S. agriculture which would have reduced the number of farmers, thereby bringing agriculture in line with the realities of an overwhelmingly industrial society, was not considered because it would have been enormously costly and socially revolutionary.

No farmer needed to be told in the 1920s that he was odd man out. John Jacob Raskob wasn't talking to the farmer when he wrote in the *Ladies Home Journal* that all one needed to become rich was to invest in good common stocks. The boom of the twenties never got beyond the city limits. In the period from 1926 to 1929, farm prices were only 88 percent of what they had been between 1910 and 1914; from 1938 to 1940, these prices had sunk 10 more points to 78 percent. In the bleak days of 1932, the parity ratio stood at 58 percent. The figures reflect not only the great hardships in agriculture, but also attest to the ongoing revolution—in fact a twofold revolution: of people needing to move from the land, as agriculture became more and more an industry that needed only a small number of people to produce enormous yields at low cost, and of agricultural prices determined increasingly by world markets. Price supports for domestic production proliferated, but were largely for these reasons ineffectual.

The 1920s saw innovative attempts to stop the decline in agricultural prices. As early as 1921, the American Farm Bureau virtually adopted a scheme of agricultural cooperation devised by Aaron Schapiro to market 85 or 90 percent of output in an orderly way, but this domestic program would not alter the world depression in agriculture and the collapse of prices. U.S. government policy relied mostly on tariffs. Three times, in 1921, 1922, and 1924, duties were extended and increased, but these tariffs did not help raise prices for export crops. Although President Coolidge vetoed several McNary-Haugen bills, their scheme for a differentiated price structure between the home and export markets would not have worked anyway because of the disarray in the world markets. The Agricultural Marketing Act of 1929, part of the Hoover program, authorized the Federal Farm Board to provide credit to cooperatives and create corporations that would withhold enough of a crop to stabilize the price of agricultural products. However, the plunge in farm prices (1930–1931) following the Great Crash ended all hopes for raising prices.

The Roosevelt administration's special relief programs greatly buoyed the farm community. Not only was the President deeply concerned about the people who were in such distress, but he was also aware of the possible political damage to the Democrats from a hostile farm bloc. The New Deal moved quickly on three fronts: farm mortgage abatement, farm credit allocations, and restrictions of farm acreage. New legislation was passed that aimed at preventing forced sales and foreclosures. Not every farmer was a land speculator, but many had been easily seduced by the high crop prices of the World War I era. The overextension of indebtedness of the 1920s was anchored more in speculation than in the long-term slump of farm prices. But the government was naturally expected to alleviate the distress—this was nothing new in our capitalistic system. Farm debt and low prices closed off traditional means of credit, so the New Deal made loans available through the Commodity Credit Corporation. The CCC urged producers to hold crops off the market until prices rose. If prices did not rise, farmers could obtain loans against the value of their crops. But these accumulated stores served further to depress prices.

The Agricultural Adjustment Act of 1933 (AAA) restricted the output of six "basic" products through acreage allotments to individual producers. The most interesting feature of the act was the tax levied on food processing industries. The basic commodities of wheat, cotton, corn, hogs, rice, tobacco, and milk products—all of which reached consumers through additional processing—were named in the bill. Furthermore, the federal government was to contract with farmers "for reduction in acreage or reduction in the production for market." Farmers who voluntarily entered into these programs were to be compensated with the funds raised by the processing tax. Some of the "best" brains were behind the legislation: Professors M. L. Wilson of the University of Montana at Bozeman, and Rexford Guy Tugwell from Columbia University; on the periphery were businessmen—George N. Peek, Bernard Baruch, General Hugh Johnson (see the later discussion of the NRA), and Secretary of Agriculture Henry A. Wallace, former editor of an agricultural journal in Iowa and scion of a family that had grown rich from breeding hybrid corn. In 1934 and 1936 drought and dust storms hit the Midwest and Southwest and effectively, if cruelly, balanced supply and demand. Agricultural prices rose in 1937, but by then the Supreme Court (in *U.S.* v. *Butler*) had already declared the processing tax unconstitutional when coupled with the intent to regulate agriculture. "The Act," Justice Roberts said,

> invades the reserved rights of the states. It is a statutory plan to regulate and control agricultural production, a matter beyond the powers delegated to the federal government. The tax, the appropriation of the funds raised, and the direction for their disbursement, are but parts of the plan. They are but means to an unconstitutional end.[10]

Henry Wallace, disillusioned with the processing tax program, had the last word: "God was good to us and the farmer and the country when the Supreme Court destroyed the processing tax."

The American home farm was left behind in this emerging system of commercial, large scale, market-oriented agriculture. Like the hand-loom weavers who were displaced by the machine age, the small farmer was increasingly a relic and could save himself only by growing crops for highly specialized markets. Many choose to leave farming. Unfortunately, the New Deal never addressed the problems of this departing population, though the hardships of this group were apparent to all.

The Agricultural Adjustment Act of 1938 would become the basis for government policy until well after the Second World War. The legislation paid farmers to withdraw acreage from production and encouraged soil conservation practices. The legislation made loans to growers of corn, cotton, wheat, tobacco, and rice when the market price fell below parity, i.e., 52 percent to 75 percent. These parities were raised to 85 percent in 1941, and to 90 percent in 1942 (wheat and corn were excepted, but the parity ratio for cotton was 95 percent). The Steagall Amendment of July 1, 1944, guaranteed 85 percent of parity, then 90 percent for two years after the end of the war. The war itself, much more than the parity level supports, resolved temporarily the economic hardships of the farmer (see Table 1.1).

Other provisions of the second AAA were minutely detailed. One sec-

Table 1.1	U.S. Agriculture, 1930–1980: Selected Statistics					
	1930	1940	1950	1960	1970	1980
Consumer Expenditure for all Farm Products (billions)	$16.2	14.1	44.0	65.9	110.6	264.4
Balance Sheet of Farming Sector Assets and Liabilities (billions)	——	52.9	132.5	311.1	362.8	1005.5
Value of Gross Farm Product in Constant Dollars (billions)	$16.1	17.5	19.4	29.2	31.1	35.0
Net Income of Farm Operations from Farming	$4,528	4,201	12,861	11,500	14,400	21,500

Source: *Historical Abstract: Colonial Times to 1970,* Series K; *Statistical Abstract,* 1983, 1988.

tion set acreage allotments for each staple, beginning with a total national allotment, then state and county allotments, and finally those for the individual farm. If quotas were exceeded, the government could then set marketing quotas if two-thirds of the growers of that crop consented. Surplus could be placed in the federal government's "ever normal granary" and stored. This "ever normal granary," a salient feature of the second AAA, was created to store surplus for lean years and thus maintain stable commodity prices. By 1941, cash receipts from farming had increased 60 percent, although it was hard to say whether government policy had been responsible for the change. Prices continued this upward trend for the entire war period.

BANKING, FINANCE, AND SECURITIES

Immediately after his inauguration, Roosevelt proposed his first banking programs. Faced with growing panic over the collapse of banks (20 percent nationwide by early 1933) and the lack of effective leadership at the Federal Reserve, Roosevelt borrowed a tactic used by state governors, who by March 4, had closed every state bank in the Union for an extended "holiday." On March 6, Roosevelt closed the banks. From March 6 to 9, the country had to get along on makeshift arrangements. Not until the ninth was Roosevelt's action given congressional approval through the Emergency Banking Act. This legislation began the process of allowing certain approved banks belonging to the Federal Reserve System to reopen. Within a week, though thousands of banks remained closed, those controlling 90 percent of the country's deposits were functioning. By mid-month, the immediate banking crisis was over. Widespread banking and securities reforms were established by the Glass-Steagall Act (June 1933). This legislation provided stricter banking supervision and set up the Federal Deposit Insurance Corporation to guarantee the savings deposits of individuals; in retrospect, it was perhaps the most important personal guarantee the New Deal made to distraught families. Other provisions in this law made a start toward securities regulation by preventing banks from making securities investments with depositors' funds. A year later the Federal Securities Act set up the Securities and Exchange Commission (SEC) as the permanent regulatory agency over all stock exchanges. The Federal Reserve System was given power through its Board of Governors to act more quickly and more determinedly in the open market, but the Fed remained on the whole a loosely joined fraternity of twelve regional banks without an overall policy. Certainly the Fed had no mandate for a stimulative monetary program, nor did it see itself as the lender of last resort in a time of emergency. If these changes in American banking and finance were modest, still they marked a recognition that these vital institutions should be subject to sanctions because they had violated the public trust during the late 1920s and the crash.

The immediate crisis which faced Roosevelt in March 1933 was a nonfunctioning and discredited banking system. Architects in the 1920s had designed banks to look like Greek temples, sacred places, unshakable and holy, befitting of course a highly successful capitalist system. But in 1933 banks seemed to be more like Augean stables, places which somehow needed Herculean efforts to clean the abuse from them. For the college professor in Peoria who woke up to find out that his life's savings of $900 had been wiped out and that his bank had closed, he knew that corruption had been to blame. However the banking system was meant to operate, it simply wasn't functioning that gray spring of 1933.

Meanwhile, Roosevelt and Congress moved to implement permanent banking reforms. The doyen of banking legislation was Carter Glass, longtime senator from Virginia, 75 years old in 1933. His views on banking had not changed much since his involvement with the Federal Reserve System twenty years earlier. But if help for banking reform was to come from anyone, Glass was the man, and his support pushed through the needed legislation of June 1933. The Glass-Steagall Act attacked some of the immediate problems. The bill provided for stricter banking supervision, curbed credit for stock market speculation, divorced banks from their security-selling affiliations (which often had been speculating with depositor's funds), approved branch banking in states where permitted, and set up the Federal Deposit Insurance Corporation. This new agency, originally opposed by both Glass and Roosevelt, guaranteed individual deposit accounts to $5,000. The FDIC, much criticized today, quickly restored a great deal of faith in the banking system and encouraged depositors to bring their money back out of the teapots and other safekeeping places. The Banking Act of 1935 further extended the FDIC, but more crucially, drastically rearranged the Federal Reserve Board. In short, the bill gave the Board of Governors greater power and control over the discounting and open market operations of its member banks.

The bursting of Wall Street's "golden bubble" and the revelations of the investigatory commissions about stock market highjinks led Congress to pass the Federal Securities Act (1933) and establish the Securities and Exchange Commission, with general control over the issuance of stock and the protection of the investor. A half century later the SEC today is much under criticism for being behind the times and unable to meet its obligations in a new investment environment dominated by pension funds and large institutional investors. But after the crash and for much of the sixty years since, the SEC performed its duties in a largely unpoliticized, professional manner. Surely it played a major role in restoring the faith and credit of the securities markets.

Another problem, that of how to raise prices, bedeviled the makers of the New Deal. Abandoning the gold standard was believed to be one solution. By doing so, Roosevelt hoped to increase the money in circulation and encourage consumer spending. He also advocated the purchase by the government of gold reserves; by announcing daily the price the government would pay for gold, he hoped that such action would stabilize the currency. Prices were determined in informal "seance" breakfast sessions with trusted advisors. Choosing lucky numbers on hunches was often Roosevelt's method for determining the daily gold price.

Accordingly, the U.S. was taken off the gold standard on March 6, 1933. Later, Roosevelt was criticized for his closely related decision not to back any international plan for currency stabilization because of his belief that such action might impair economic recovery. The repeated calumny that FDR scuttled the World Economic Congress by unilaterally abandoning gold overlooks the worldwide departure from the gold standard that country after country found necessary in order to gain more complete control over domestic prices. On June 5, 1933, a joint resolution of Congress abrogated the payment of all debts in gold. In the fall of that year the Reconstruction Finance Corporation (RFC), which had been established by Hoover, was authorized to buy gold at $35 an ounce as a means of raising prices through devaluing the currency. The Gold Revenue Act of January 1934 authorized citizens to turn in all gold except jewelry and small gold coins and set the gold content of the dollar at 59.06 cents. These efforts did not have the desired effect because no great leap in prices occurred, not even after further manipulations of silver purchases were thrown in.

STRATEGIES FOR BUSINESS RECOVERY

On September 13, 1933, one-quarter million people, arms locked and the NRA Blue Eagle banners flying in the wind, marched down Fifth Avenue in New York City to launch the National Industrial Recovery program (NRA). It was called "a great spontaneous cooperation to put millions of men back in their regular jobs this summer." The NRA required employers to "hire more men to do existing work by reducing the hours of each man each week while at the same time paying a larger wage for the shorter week." Prodded by grim statistics (see the figures for 1933 in Table 1.2), the inspiration for the NRA came from many sources. Most supporters, like FDR himself,

Table 1.2	Selected Economic Statistics, 1929–1939					
	1929	1931	1933	1935	1937	1939
GNP (billions of 1959 dollars)	$203.6	$169.3	$141.5	$169.5	$203.2	$209.4
Index of manufacturing production (1947 = 100)	56	40	35	46	58	57
Employment in non-agricultural businesses (millions)	31.3	26.6	23.7	27.0	31.0	30.6
Unemployment (% of labor force)	3.2	15.9	24.9	20.1	14.3	17.2
Wholesale prices index (1967 = 100)	49.0	37.6	34.0	41.3	44.5	39.8
Earnings of production workers in manufacturing (dollars)	$.56	$.51	$.44	$.54	$.62	$.63
Corporate profits before taxes (billions of dollars)	$10.0	$ – .4	$1.0	$3.6	$6.8	$7.0
Federal debt (billions of dollars)	$16.5	$18.5	$24.3	$34.4	$39.2	$42.6

Source: *Historical Statistics of the United States—Colonial Times to 1970*, U.S. Department of Commerce, Bureau of Labor Statistics.

merely wanted to do something dramatic; a few were idealogues with left-wing collectivist tendencies; and maybe one or two even believed that Mussolini's corporate state made some sense. Thus the New Deal in 1933 instituted a makeshift cartelization of American business. The NRA encouraged the self-regulation of business and industry through the formulation of codes of fair competition drafted by the representatives of major industries. Some 578 national industrial codes plus 200 supplements eventually were promulgated. Section 7, which later became the basis for the Wagner Act (National Labor Relations Act) of 1935, covered 22 million workers. This code appeased Bill Green, the president of the AFL, by granting employees "the right to organize and bargain collectively through representatives of their own choosing." But there was something for everybody. Prosecution under the antitrust statutes was to be set aside (or at least businessmen interpreted the codes in this way). The cotton textile industry had the first code ready by June 1933. Its NRA provision guaranteed a minimum wage of ten dollars a week in the South and eleven dollars in the North, a forty-hour week, and no more than two shifts a day.

From the beginning, the codes did not work well. Some employers refused to bargain either with their competition or their workers. Consumers did not like the price increases that resulted from the codes, and there was wide evidence of cheating. And General Hugh Johnson, who headed the NRA, was a disaster as an administrator. By 1935, a sick chicken in the Schechter Poultry Corporation resulted in a lawsuit that got this mischievous and misguided experiment declared unconstitutional. Every single justice found that the NRA violated some provision of the Constitution though not all cited the same reasons. In the main the justices took the high ground in arguing that not even the Depression could destroy the distinction between intrastate and interstate commerce and that the regulation of hours and wages of employees in the defendant's slaughterhouse markets went too far. Chief Justice Hughes stated:

> Without in any way disparaging the motive [stimulating economic activity], it is enough to say that the recuperative efforts of the federal government must be made in a manner consistent with the authority granted by the Constitution.[11]

Fortunately for all, the NRA was dead.

LABOR

The Wagner Act of 1935 recognized free collective bargaining and set precedents for a "pluralist model of labor relations" in which negotiating for wages, hours, and working conditions was legitimized.[12] Previously Section 7 of the NIRA had won the support of union leaders by supporting workers' right to organize and bargain collectively. When the Supreme Court declared the NRA unconstitutional in 1935, Senator Robert Wagner of New York moved swiftly to guarantee these union rights. Two months after the Schechter decision, the National Labor Relations Act (NLRA) became law. Two years later, in a five-to-four opinion, Chief Justice Charles Evans Hughes declared the Wagner Act within the bounds of the Constitution. In a startling turnabout from the Schechter case, the Court held that the stoppage of a steel company's operations by strikes

> would have a most serious effect upon interstate commerce. . . . It is obvious that the effects would be immediate and might be catastrophic. . . . When industries organize themselves on a national scale, making their relation to interstate commerce the dominant factor in their activities, how can it be maintained that their industrial labor relations constitute a forbidden field into which Congress may not enter when it is necessary to protect interstate commerce from the paralyzing consequences of industrial war?[14]

Nine old men had seen the wisdom of changing their legal opinions! When the Supreme Court upheld the Wagner Act in the case known as the Jones & Laughlin Steel Co. decision of 1937, labor relations entered a new era. For more than a hundred years, virtually all efforts to build collective labor organizations in the United States had faced a degree of hostility, from both management and law, almost unparalleled in the Western industrial world. Even the most established craft unions had to make their way through the thicket of injunctions, lockouts, and personal violence. Our country's background of rugged individualism sanctioned an antipathy toward collective labor efforts that has been enormously long-lived, and these feelings still thrive in both management and labor. We continue to pay an enormous price in the workplace for the historic legacy of distrust and confrontation.

The Depression, the Democratic majority in Congress, the wave of sit-ins and mass organizing, and the sense that the President was sympathetic to organized labor all contributed to the new respect for workers. As early as 1932, Congress had passed the Norris-LaGuardia Act, which affirmed the right of an individual to join a union and drastically limited the granting of injunctions, permitting them only if a "substantial and irreparable injury to the complainant's property [would] be unavoidable." The creation of the National Labor Relations Board (NLRB) in 1935 was the capstone. Its board of three members was given wide powers to assist workers who were organizing and to mediate disputed elections in companies whose workers had voted for collective bargaining. If a company or union rejected this "administered" justice, it could bring the matter into the courts, but this alternative was both time-consuming and expensive. Rightly or wrongly, businessmen believed that the NLRB was more sympathetic to labor than to business. Although many businessmen continued to hate the NLRB, on the whole they obeyed its rulings. What resulted was a surge of union recognitions and the emergence of the CIO (Congress of Industrial Organizations) as the major voice of industrial unionism. In June 1938 the Congress, prodded by President Roosevelt, passed the Fair Labor Standards Act. This bill created a minimum wage of 25 cents an hour, which would rise over a seven-year period to 40 cents. By 1940 the work week was to be set at forty hours, with time-and-a-half pay for overtime. Further, the act outlawed labor for children under eighteen under most conditions, although agriculture and retail trade were specifically excepted. With the advent of World War II many of the immediate provisions became irrelevant as wages climbed rapidly beyond the minimum. But the concept of a minimum wage was heartily welcomed by liberals as a forward step toward social justice, though today the idea of a minimum wage has come under increasing attack because employers are less likely to hire the unskilled and/or minority youth. Much of the postwar history of American labor-management relations has been about management's attempt to whittle away at this New Deal legislation. Moreover, the NLRB, like all bureaucratic organizations, over the years developed its own interests and standards, not always to the liking of either business or labor.

SOCIAL WELFARE

The Social Security Act of August 1935 marked the beginning of modern social welfare legislation in the United States. At least twenty nations had similar programs, some dating back to 1875, but we had persisted in denying the need for social insurance. Vested interests, particularly the American Medical Association, spent millions to warn of the dire effects on American character if the legislation passed. Nevertheless, the federal government agreed to match contributions to state old-age programs dollar for dollar, up to $40 a month, to each eligible person. In 1935, only seven million workers were covered; today virtually all workers must belong. Other social welfare provisions allocated federal funds to families with dependent children, to the blind, and to those needing vocational rehabilitation. All of this was to be administered under a federal-state matching grant program. Employers of eight or more persons were required to pay into an unemployment insurance fund, and 90 percent of this federal tax would be returned to those state unemployment schemes that came up to federal standards. Despite all the limitations of this very modest legislation, the Social Security Act marked a new age in the history of American society. The federal government recognized its obligation to moderate the worst economic hardships and to help care for people in their old age. For the century and a half after the American Revolution, as the United States grew to the world's greatest industrial power, Americans relied almost entirely on private voluntary methods to deal with social problems caused by the up and down cycles of American capitalism. In the 1880s Chancellor Bismarck of Germany had sponsored legislation that provided disability and old age benefits to workers, but we waited until the Great Depression to act on this problem of devising a meaningful social insurance plan.

Everyone in the 1930s could see the long pitiful lines of workers looking for jobs that frequently did not exist. Some states, including New York under then-Governor Franklin Roosevelt, had favored schemes to provide unemployment relief. By the summer of 1935, the Congress was considering an omnibus bill to cover unemployment insurance, old-age pensions, aid to the handicapped, and job retraining. New Deal policy makers already had tried to provide a scattered measure of relief; now they moved toward a more comprehensive contributory social insurance.

> This Social Security measure gives at least some protection to 30,000,000 of our citizens who will reap direct benefits through unemployment compensation, through old-age pensions and through increased services for the protection of children and the prevention of ill health. . . . We can never insure 100 percent of the population against 100 percent of the hazards and vicissitudes of life, but we have tried to frame a law which will give some measure of protection to the average citizen and to his family against the loss of a job and against poverty-ridden old age.[15]

The federal government levied a payroll tax on employers to induce states to set up unemployment schemes. At first, this tax was applied only to those workers receiving an hourly wage or salary in traditional industries and commercial businesses. Ninety percent of the revenue from this payroll tax would go to approved state unemployment agencies, while the other ten percent would go to the federal government. In general these schemes provided benefits of approximately half-wages, though not to exceed $15 a week for a maximum period of 12 to 16 weeks. Both the original coverage and the pay benefits have, of course, been increased many times since 1935.

Of greater interest, then and now, was the system of old-age annuity payments which was legislated by Congress. The incentive for creating this pension plan was not only the dire need of the elderly, but also the threat of the Townsend movement which was creating a veritable fire under the politicians. Dr. Francis Townsend, a former physician, had devised a scheme whereby the government would give older retired workers two hundred dollars of "purchasing power" per person per month. In some states, notably California, the movement had won political victories. As the election of 1936 came closer, Roosevelt felt politically threatened. Almost two-thirds of the states (29) had some form of pension law, and by introducing the Social Security Act Roosevelt tried to rationalize these varied plans. Persons over sixty-five would receive payments directly through a system of federal matching grants paid to the states, except that initially the federal government's share could not exceed $20 a month. This contributory old-age insurance scheme was to be paid beginning in 1937 with a 1 percent income tax on employees and a 1 percent payroll tax on employers; each year this tax would increase until it reached 3 percent in 1948, when the system in theory would be self-financing. The monthly retirement payment was expected to range between $10 and $85. Some economists who drafted the bill never assumed that Social Security would be more than a small piece of retirement income. However, since 1935, taxes, payments, and eligibility have all been increased many times.

INCOMES POLICY

The Depression crisis brought many gifted advisers to Washington—Paul Douglas, Harry Hopkins, Bernard Baruch, A. A. Berle, Arthur Burns, and Thurman Arnold to name a few. They constituted the so-called "brain trust" in the first New Deal. Some had ideological sympathies, and a few could even be called somewhat leftist. But the responsibility for evaluating the content of the New Deal started and ended at the top. The President was not interested in radical thinking. Roosevelt was an aristocrat, politician, and pragmatist, but not an intellectual. We know that one of his favorite means of resolving conflicts in the cabinet, and of setting policy, was to have two advocates, each championing a particular position, present their cases. The President then ordered the two to work out a solution. Sometimes the method worked, and sometimes the attempt to force agreement between two drastically different opinions failed. FDR's mind was constantly exploring new possibilities. Perhaps that is one of the reasons that we will never know, for instance, if he disliked or really approved of the Supreme Court's decision to void the NRA.

Strangely, the most important vehicle of industrial policy during the New Deal was not an innovation of Roosevelt's. It was the Reconstruction

Finance Corporation (RFC) created by Herbert Hoover in January 1932, begun with a capital of $500 million and the right to incur indebtedness of $1.5 billion. Originally the RFC's purpose was to aid financial institutions, banks, trust companies and, with approval of the ICC, faltering railroads. Six months after its inception, the RFC's lending powers were enlarged to $1.8 billion, and it could loan to both public and private agencies for self-liquidating projects (i.e., projects of public benefit that would make enough money to repay the loan—housing, bridges, dams, military installations). The New Deal further increased the RFC's capital and lending powers; in the first eighteen months of FDR's term, the RFC loaned $3 billion. For just over twenty years, the RFC was a major conduit of funds from the United States Treasury to farms and industries. The RFC was ordered in May 1935, for example, to make available $500 million for emergency relief to the states as part of the attack on unemployment. The RFC lent $1.5 billion to states and municipalities for self-legislating public works. Title II of the NIRA established the Public Works Administration (PWA) with an appropriation of $3.3 billion to promote construction of public interest projects, such as post offices, and in 1935 a second public works program, the Works Progress Administration (WPA), was hastily set up to tap the reserves of the largely unskilled unemployed. The PWA spent a total of $7 billion, while the WPA spent $10.5 billion plus $2.7 billion in contributions from local governments. PWA left a legacy of public buildings, and even the WPA, much criticized in its time, gave jobs to millions of the neediest. In 1938, the WPA employed 3.8 million; over the seven years of its existence it gave employment to 8.5 million. One estimate assesses that it indirectly benefitted 25 million people, including dependents. Some WPA projects consisted of removing streetcar tracks brick by brick and rail by rail, but a great deal of necessary work was done in building and restoring parks, playgrounds, and reservoirs. The WPA constructed 122,000 public buildings, 664,000 miles of new roads, 77,000 new bridges, 285 new airports, and 24,000 miles of storm and water sewers. These additions to the infrastructure were useful and worthwhile, though critics argued that the costs were excessive.

The New Deal efforts to increase demand and thus reinvigorate the economy were pushed on multiple fronts. Housing subsidies were managed by the USHA (United States Housing Authority), youth employment by the CCC (Civilian Conservation Corporation) and the NYA (National Youth Administration), rural electrification by the TVA (Tennessee Valley Authority). Also important were the NRA, the Wagner Act, Fair Labor Standards Act, and Social Security. These programs were all similar in that they tried to encourage economic demand. More employment, higher prices created by a devalued dollar, public spending—all were goals of this early version of incomes policy. Still, the New Deal did little to take advantage of new innovations and technologies born in the twenties and furnished scant direct aid for private business investment. If many businessmen hated Roosevelt and the New Deal, they did so instinctively and with reason; their greatest gains were reaped only with the coming of World War II.

Today's fashion in economics dictates a severe censure of the New Deal's monetary and fiscal policy. In a celebrated article, "Fiscal Policy in the Thirties: A Reappraisal," Cary Brown argued that the effective federal tax rate increased by 700 percent from 1932 to 1939. However, if we use full employment GNP as the base, e.g., the GNP that would have been reached if we had full employment, New Deal tax policies were modest. From 1932 to 1936 federal expenditures rose by about $5 billion, certainly a far cry from the fiscal spending of the post–World War II period. But Brown's conclusion is most apt—fiscal policy did not fail because it was not tried.[16] Milton Friedman and Anna Schwartz have done a seminal analysis of monetary policy during this period, and they too condemn the New Deal. According to them, Roosevelt's fiscal and monetary attempts failed. The Federal Reserve's policies were either passive or counterproductive or both. For instance, between 1929 and 1933 and again in 1937 the Fed contracted the currency supply, exacerbating the economic downturn. Intent on preserving conventions such as balanced budgets and financial stability, the Fed's orthodoxy did great damage. Schumpeter reminds us, however, of the futility of demanding that previous generations act with the knowledge and hindsight that we possess decades later. Had the Fed done everything suggested by modern economists, the depression would still have persisted. Had Roosevelt done everything suggested by present day theorists, he would not have been reelected.

THE KEYNESIAN REVOLUTION

The emergence of Keynes's General Theory took a long time. Keynes's thinking matured in the 1920s. In his limited articles and in *The General Theory of Employment, Interest and Money* (1936), he was still primarily concerned with reaching trained economists. Despite the severity of depression in England and the United States, the adoption of the Keynesian model made slow progress. In the 1930s, Alvin Hansen, professor of economics at Harvard University, was the first major American scholar to recognize Keynes's contribution and use the economist's models in his seminars. But President Roosevelt was too pragmatic and concerned with immediate issues to embrace a new economic theory. Keynes and his wife visited FDR in 1934, but the visit was not a success. The two aristocrats seemed to dislike each other.

In 1948, Professor Paul Samuelson of the Massachusetts Institute of Technology published his first edition of *Principles of Economics*. This elementary text ushered in a new chapter in the history of economics education in the United States. For the first time in this country, the Keynesian model was used to discuss the basic economic questions. Tens of millions of American students in the 1950s and 1960s would be taught this new outlook. However, in the 1930s, only crisis and desperation were pushing New Deal advisors like Marriner Eccles toward approaches which were Keynesian. Economic orthodoxy never lost its primacy, however, and balancing the budget was always a greater goal than stimulating economic growth through deficit spending.

Keynes and the Economics of Depression

The economic crisis of the 1930s in the United States seemed to fit ideally the type of economic analysis that Keynes had been working on since the long-run decline of the British economy after the First World War. Initially Keynes did not have the United States in mind in his early articles, but increasingly he felt that the Depression crisis was imbedded in the structure of unregulated capitalistic systems everywhere. Depression America thus offered a potential laboratory for trying out his ideas; in this regard, he was to be disappointed by the unsympathetic response of Roosevelt.

The underlying assumption of Keynes's model was the dominant force of uncertainty—uncertainty of individual and business decisions in regard to consumption and investment. This uncertainty made it necessary for economists and policymakers to rely on macro factors and overall data rather than follow the neoclassical emphasis on micro conditions. Keynes examined the marginal propensities of consumption and saving, the multiplier effect linked to the accelerator principle, the volatility of private investment, and the overwhelming necessity for fiscal and monetary policies. Without government involvement, the capitalist system, inherently unstable, would tend either toward too much or too little growth in its efforts to maintain full employment. Keynes's theory and policy were closely linked through a simple interchange.

If income must equal total output, then the following formulae could summarize national income:

1. $Y = C + I$ where Y stands for national income, C for consumption, and I for investment.
2. $Y = C + S$ where Y stands for national income, C for consumption and S for savings. By definition $I = S$.

Keynes's concern was that the economy would tend to underconsume because of a propensity to save at a higher rate than the level of new investment, resulting in a more serious lower level of growth than necessary for a full employment economy. Only fiscal policy carried out by the federal government could reverse this deflationary drag.

In order to maintain steady growth at full employment levels without inflation or deflation, a level of investment sufficient to this end had to be maintained. Investment was the key to the problem, since it worked simultaneously to generate income and increase capacity. However, this increased capacity could result in greater output or greater unemployment, depending on the behavior of income. We could, Keynes argued, determine the condition for the behavior of income that would allow full employment to be maintained. This equilibrium rate of growth depends on the size of the multiplier (the magnified effect that changes in investment spending have on total income) and the productivity of new investment. Under capitalism the actual rate of economic growth may differ over time from the rate of growth necessary for full employment. If the actual rate of growth was less than the warranted rate of growth, as was the case in the '30s, chronic deflation and unemployment would result. The business cycle is no longer an autonomous force but rather an uncontrolled deviation from the path of steady economic advance.[17] Keynes offered the innovative theory that fiscal policy, correctly used, could resolve this volatility and keep a steady full employment economy going.

What this meant was the virtual abandonment of the so-called automatic corrective machinery of the market, replaced by the assumption that a mixed economy of private and public sectors would henceforth work together. Government action both in fiscal and monetary elements would play an especially large balancing role. Keynes modified the national income formula to include whatever spending was necessary for economic health from *government* besides *consumption* and *income.*

Keynesian economics gained control in the United States not in the 1930s, but in the 1950s and '60s. President Kennedy's stimulative tax cut in 1962 is frequently pointed to as an act most in accord with Keynesian thinking. Every student needs to appreciate how far we have moved from the orthodoxies of a self-regulating, private, neoclassical economic system. Keynes himself would be well-pleased with his contribution to this change. In 1934, however, tea with the President was as far as Keynes could go.

TRADE AND COMMERCE

Despite intense conservative efforts to rehabilitate his political reputation, Herbert Hoover has not been judged kindly by historians. A good reason for this negative assessment may well be his administration's association with the Hawley-Smoot Tariff of 1930. The new tariff, denounced in a petition by a thousand economists because it would worsen both the national and global trade interests, raised tariff levels and provoked worldwide retaliation. On average, tariff schedules were increased substantially. One-third of the levies for dutiable items were changed, with 890 being increased, including fifty transfers from the free to the dutiable list. Especially protected by the new act were agricultural commodities, where the tariff rate was increased from 38.10 to 48.92 percent. Although the President was given authority to change the levels of recommendation of the Tariff Commission, Hoover's legacy was a baleful contribution to world trade.

In the Democratic platform of 1932, FDR pledged support for an international economic conference and for world trade by lowering tariffs. The London Economic Conference of 1933 never had much of a chance, since by that time Roosevelt's goal of reflating the dollar came into direct conflict with the French aim of monetary stabilization. In regard to tariffs however,

Roosevelt did redeem his pledge. The Reciprocal Trade Agreements Act of 1934, an amendment to the Hawley-Smoot Act, authorized the President for a period of three years to negotiate trade agreements without congressional approval and to raise and lower tariff rates as much as 50 percent. The Trade Agreements Act, as it was known, had been renewed five times and agreements with twenty-nine countries concluded by 1948.

During the 1930s, United States' trade with the world increased, though it remains difficult to assess how much of the progress was due to the New Deal. The reciprocal trade agreements not only lowered tariffs but broke down the individual quota agreements which the Hawley-Smoot Tariff and the Depression fostered. Also, the provisions of the Reciprocal Trade Act allowed the President to extend the tariff reductions to all countries that accorded the United States "most favored nation" status. Overall, trade increased faster with those countries with whom the U.S. had agreements; the Reciprocal Trade Agreements Act also ushered in a new, more sympathetic approach to the concerns of Latin America. Most of all the New Deal reversed the trend of isolationist trade policy of the twenties which had culminated in Hawley-Smoot.

In perspective then, the New Deal was less a sharp break with the past and more an extension of programs and policies already familiar. It was less of a revolution than a shifting of emphasis and policy. To the man on the street, however, it was a new beginning that ended a horrible nightmare.

NOTES

[1] William E. Leuchtenburg, *Franklin D. Roosevelt and the New Deal* (New York: Harper and Row, 1963), p. 251.

[2] Alfred D. Chandler, Jr., *Scale and Scope: The Dynamics of Industrial Capitalism* (Cambridge, Mass.: Belknap Press, 1990).

[3] Michael A. Bernstein, *The Great Depression* (New York: Cambridge University Press, 1987), p. xiv.

[4] Ibid., p. 208.

[5] John J. Raskob, "Everybody Ought to be Rich," *Ladies Home Journal,* August 1929: 9.

[6] F. L. Allen, *Only Yesterday* (New York: Harper and Row, 1931), pp. 333–334.

[7] I. Studenski and H. Kroos, *Financial History* (New York: McGraw Hill, 1963), p. 353.

[8] *Public Papers and Addresses of FDR* (New York: Random House, 1935), pp. 11–13.

[9] Rainer Schickle, *Agricultural Policy: Farm Programs and National Welfare* (Lincoln: Univ. of Nebraska Press, 1954), p. 190.

[10] *"United States* v. *Butler,"* United States Supreme Court: United States Reports, 297 (1935): 68.

[11] *"Schechter Poultry Corp.* v. *U.S.,"* United States Supreme Court: United States Reports, 295 U.S. 495 (1935): 550.

[12] Christopher L. Tomlins, *The State and Unions: Labor Relations, Law and the Organized Labor Movement in America, 1880-1960* (New York: Cambridge University Press, 1985).

[13] The *New York Times* of February 21, 1985 carried an article on the NLRB which quoted AFL-CIO boss Lane Kirkland as saying that the union movement might be better off if the National Labor Relations Board were to disappear and labor-management relations were to return to "the law of the jungle." In just a half-century we have come full circle, questioning the particular legislation of the New Deal which at the time was hailed as the Magna Carta of organized labor.

[14] "NLRB v. Jones and Laughlin Steel Co.," *United States Supreme Court: United States Reports,* 301 U.S. 1 (1937): 41.

[15] *New York Times,* August 15, 1935, p. 4.

[16] Cary Brown, "Fiscal Policy in the Thirties: A Reappraisal, *American Economic Review,* 46:5 (December 1956).

[17] For an excellent summary, see Gerald M. Meier and Robert E. Baldwin, *Economic Development: Theory, History, Policy* (New York: Wiley, 1957), pp. 101–112.

SUGGESTED READINGS

Berle, Adolf A., and Gardiner C. Means. *The Modern Corporation and Private Property.* New York: Harcourt, Brace and World, 1968.

Bernstein, Michael A. *The Great Depression: Delayed Recovery and Economic Change in America, 1929-1939.* New York: Cambridge University Press, 1987.

Bruchey, Stuart. *The Wealth of the Nation: An Economic History of the United States.* New York: Harper and Row, 1988.

Chandler, Alfred D., Jr. *The Visible Hand: The Managerial Revolution of American Business.* Cambridge, Mass.: Belknap Press, 1977.

————. *Scale and Scope: The Dynamics of Industrial Capitalism.* Cambridge, Mass.: Belknap Press, 1990.

Cochran, Thomas C. *American Business in the Twentieth Century.* Cambridge, Mass.: Harvard University Press, 1972.

Davis, Lance E., et al. *American Economic Growth: An Economist's History of the United States.* New York: Harper and Row, 1972.

Finkelstein, Joseph, and Alfred L. Thimm. *Economists and Society.* New York: Harper and Row, 1973.

Friedman, Milton, and Anna J. Schwartz. *A Monetary History of the United States, 1867-1960.* Princeton, N.J.: Princeton University Press, 1963.

Galbraith, John K. *The Great Crash, 1929.* Boston: Houghton Mifflin, 1954.

Galambos, Louis, and Joseph Pratt. *The Rise of the Corporate Commonwealth: U.S. Business and Public Policy in the Twentieth Century.* New York: Basic Books, 1988.

Harris, Seymour, ed. *American Economic History.* New York: McGraw-Hill, 1961.

Hawley, Ellis W. *The New Deal and the Problem of Monopoly.* Princeton, N.J.: Princeton University Press, 1966.

Leuchtenberg, William E. *Franklin D. Roosevelt and the New Deal, 1932-1940,* New York: Harper and Row, 1963.

Porter, Glenn. *The Rise of Big Business, 1860-1920,* Second Edition. Arlington Heights, Ill.: Harlan Davidson, 1992.

Rothbard, Murray. *America's Great Depression.* Kansas City: Sheed and Ward, 1963.

Schlesinger, Arthur M., Jr. *Age of Roosevelt: The Crisis of the Old Order.* Vol. 1. Boston: Houghton Mifflin, 1957.

Seligman, Joel. *The Transformation of Wall Street: A History of the Securities and Exchange Commission and Modern Corporate Finance.* Boston: Houghton Mifflin, 1982.

Temin, Peter. *Did Monetary Forces Cause the Great Depression?* New York: Norton, 1976.

Tomlins, Christopher L. *The State and the Unions.* New York: Cambridge University Press, 1987.

2 The Economy at War

ORGANIZING AND FINANCING THE WAR EFFORT

Between 1933 and 1939, the New Deal had increased the national debt by $26.3 billion; now as war came near the debt was to soar. The necessity of winning the war pushed aside all questions about the size of the debt. In 1936, the annual federal deficit would peak for the decade at $42.9 billion; in 1945 the annual deficit was about $95.2 billion.

Economic mobilization for war blew away any remaining doubts about the vitality of American capitalism and demonstrated such power that by 1944 American war production was twice as great as the combined war production of the three Axis nations and still consumed less than one-half of the productive capacity of the nation. In five years the United States turned out 247,000 airplanes, 86,338 tanks, 64,500 landing craft, 17.4 million rifles and small arms, quadrupled the merchant fleet, and vastly expanded the Navy—it was indeed the "arsenal of democracy."[1] American capitalism was reborn out of this achievement, and this resurgence of free-enterprise ideology has been the dominant feature of the entire postwar period.

The United States paid for 44 percent of the Second World War out of taxes, much better than the 33 percent figure for World War I, but the total was still less than the 50 percent which had been President Roosevelt's goal. In 1940, the GNP had barely recovered to its 1929 level of approximately $200 billion, and the federal government's share had been $6 billion. Military expenditure had fallen during the Depression and still in 1940 was only 2 percent of GNP. By 1944 GNP had doubled, but military spending had increased almost forty-five times; the net national debt increased fivefold from $45 billion to $229.5 billion, with the federal government collecting $156 billion in taxes. To pay for the war, taxes and borrowing were both raised to new highs. The Treasury promoted seven war-loan campaigns and one for the Victory Loan. Schoolchildren contributed pennies to buy the $25 victory bond, while workers were urged to buy bonds through employee deduction programs (see Table 2.1).

			Surplus/	Gross	Individual

Table 2.1   U.S. Government War Financing in billions of dollars

Year	Receipts	Expenditures	Surplus/ Deficit (-)	Gross Federal Debt	Individual Income Tax Receipts
1940	5.1	9.1	-3.9	43.0	1.0
1941	7.1	13.3	-6.2	49.0	1.4
1942	12.6	34.0	-21.5	72.4	3.3
1943	22.0	79.4	-57.4	136.7	6.6
1944	43.6	95.1	-51.4	201.0	18.3
1945	44.5	98.4	-53.9	258.7	19.0
1946	39.8	60.4	-20.7	269.4	18.7
1947	39.8	39.0	+0.7	258.3	19.3

Source: *Historical Statistics,* 1960, Series Y, 254–257, 265–267.

Between 1940 and 1945, the Congress passed a large number of revenue bills, and each one raised more money for the costs of war by increasing the tax rates and/or broadening the tax base. In June 1940, Congress lowered the amounts for personal income tax exemptions, raised both the personal surtax and corporate income tax rates, and increased excise, gift, estate, and excess profit tax rates. Barely four months later, excess profit and corporate tax rates were raised again. In late 1941, Congress further reduced the personal exemptions, raised the maximum tax rate to 77 percent on personal income, and increased the corporate tax rate to 31 percent. Higher estate taxes, gift taxes, and some new excise taxes were also added. A year later, in October 1942, Congress again raised the minimum income tax rate to 18 percent and the maximum to 88 percent; the corporate income tax rate was raised to 40 percent, and the maximum excess profit rate jumped to 90 percent. Without doubt the most important innovative feature of these revenue bills was the withholding feature of the Revenue Act of 1943. Passed to raise an additional $16 billion, the act adopted a 20 percent withholding tax on personal income. The 1944 tax bill, in two stages, was the last one passed during the war and the only wartime tax measure vetoed as too lenient by the President. This act raised the maximum personal income tax rate to 94 percent and lowered once again the personal income tax exemption for married couples but included substantial depletion allowances for certain industries.

President Roosevelt in 1942 argued that "discrepancies between low personal incomes and very high personal incomes should be lessened;" and, therefore, that "in this time of grave national danger, when all excess income should go to win the war, no American citizen ought to have a net income, after he has paid his taxes, of more than $25,000 a year."[2] Congress rejected Roosevelt's idea. FDR had tried to institute some kind of income limitation by instructing the Treasury to levy a flat 100 percent supertax on "excessive incomes," but Congress eliminated presidential authority to alter taxes. The money squabble reflected the larger issue between the White House and the Congress over who should bear the cost of the war. The broader question of how much the current generation should pay and how much should be paid by future generations was settled on an ad hoc basis—41 percent from tax receipts, the balance from borrowing. One hundred eighty-five billion dollars was added to the national debt, a sum seven times greater than the debt incurred during the Depression decade.

World War II was a costly war. The government borrowed almost $187.5 billion through war loans and victory loans, but 40 percent came from banks, quickly reinforcing the pressures of wartime inflation. Consequently, the war effort became a matter of not only taxation and fiscal policy, but of regulating wages and incomes. The administration was involved reluctantly in the planning and control of the overall economy during the war, especially since state and local governments did not increase their spending significantly during the war years, probably less than 50 percent over the entire period. These funds largely went for modest increases in education, public welfare, health, police and fire protection. By 1946, the share of GNP purchased by state and local governments had fallen to under five percent.

It would have been more prudent to pay for more of the war through additional taxes. Although Roosevelt and the Congress sometimes disagreed on the means, both were deeply concerned with problems of morale if the tax burdens were increased too much. Overall, the tax rates were commendably better than those of World War I and comparable to what other wartime countries were able to achieve. (One cannot blame the habit of debt and deficit spending which has plagued the postwar decades on the war; indeed, the erosion of fiscal discipline came primarily with the affluence of peace.) Moreover, materiel and aid were given to assist beleaguered allies. On March 11, 1941, the President signed the Lend-Lease Act which appropriated $7 billion for help to Britain. Almost $50 billion of aid was transferred to our allies under Lend-Lease; the vast majority of these loans were cancelled at the end of the war.

One thing was sure: the mobilization of the war effort could not be delegated to the market system. Despite the long lead time between the rise of Hitlerism, the breakdown of diplomacy, the outbreak of war in Europe (1939), and the Japanese attack on Pearl Harbor (December 7, 1941), the United States was not at all prepared when war did come—neither in terms of military readiness nor economic mobilization. Strong emotional ties to an isolationalist policy were changed only slowly. Prior to 1941 the absence of a direct threat to American interests prevented widespread acceptance of active overseas involvement. Only the surprise attack on Pearl Harbor spurred the United States to action. The first efforts to manage the war effort resembled those of World War I—inefficient and piecemeal. Only with additional time did the U.S. government develop new forms of planning and control.

The building of the wartime bureaucratic structure began in 1939 when Roosevelt established a War Resources Board headed by Edward Stettinius, Jr. of U.S. Steel to advise the administration on industrial mobilization. This first board had a short life because old New Dealers and organized labor suspected it of being an antiunion representation of Morgan and DuPont interests. Before it expired, however, the War Resources Board had presented a plan for the appointment of an economic czar should the United States find itself at war. FDR had no liking for this proposal and appointed Bernard Baruch, former chairman of Woodrow Wilson's War Industries Board, to draw up an alternate plan; this proposal was also buried. Early in 1940, the President established a Council of National Defense, composed of six cabinet officers and a National Defense Advisory Commission, to help the council. The fall of France in the early summer of 1940 changed the casualness that had pervaded Washington's approach to wartime planning. With a goal of 50,000 planes a year, the Advisory Commission began to shift defense production into high gear; in fact, within months the Advisory Commission had turned over control to the Army-Navy Munitions Board, and the RFC was authorized to finance the building of defense plants.

One month into 1941, the President established the Office of Production Management (OPM) headed by "Bill" Knudsen of Ford Motors and Sidney Hillman of the CIO. The OPM was a kind of government holding company, but the vagueness of its jurisdictional authority weakened its effectiveness. Later, control of consumer prices was vested in an Office of Price Administration and Civilian Supply (April 1941). By fall 1941, a new agency, the Supplies Priorities and Allocation Board, headed by Donald Nelson of Sears Roebuck, was added to this bureaucracy. The SPAB was given a broad mandate to determine and allocate requirements and supplies for the armed forces, the civilian economy, and the British and Russians. Five weeks after Pearl Harbor, Nelson was given overall control of the domestic economy as head of the newly constituted War Production Board (WPB), but Nelson ran a "sloppy" shop and could control neither the large corporations nor the allocation of funds for plant expansion. Not surprisingly, in October 1942, Roosevelt brought in Supreme Court Justice James F. Byrnes and gave him supreme command similar in many ways to the recommendation of the Baruch Plan three years earlier. Byrnes, as so-called "Assistant President," moved up to head the Office of War Mobilization (OWM) in May 1943, and Fred Vinson took over at the Office of Economic Stabilization. To the OWM in October 1944 was added the job of looking at the problems of postwar reconversion, and thus the renamed Office of War Mobilization and Reconversion completed the list of agencies that the demands of war had brought into being.

The construction of this war-management edifice clearly shows the lack of knowledge in estimating and managing the immense changes which were entailed by the conversion of the peacetime economy to an effective war production machine. "Overtaken by events" describes much of the shifting above. But whatever the shortcomings of the government control mechanisms, the American industrial economy, already organized in large oligopolistic units, was superbly equipped to produce a flood of war goods. And so it did. In unbelievable numbers, tanks, planes, and ships, and shoes, blankets, and "C" rations poured out. For more than a decade after 1945, war surplus was a noticeable commodity in every city and town in the United States. We have no good standards by which to judge this wartime bureau-

Table 2.2	Wartime Economic Planning and Control Agencies

(listed by year of establishment)

1939	War Resources Board
1940	Advisory Commission to Council of National Defense
	Office of Emergency Management
	Office of Production Management
	Office of Police Administration
1941	Office of Production Management
	Office of Price Administration
	Supply, Priorities and Allocations Board
1942	War Production Board (combined SPAB & OPM)
	War Labor Board
	War Manpower Commission
	Office of Economic Stabilization
1943	Office of War Mobilization
	War Labor Disputes Act

cracy, nor is wartime a very good time to measure the effectiveness of government controls objectively since the imperatives of winning the conflict overarch other factors. World War II, like all wars, was atypical as a standard to evaluate normal functioning of the overall economy and useless as a yardstick to measure costs.

THE MILITARY MOBILIZATION

Some 12 million men and women were mobilized for the armed services. Most of them were draftees between the ages of 18 and 27—the most productive and valuable population group in a nation of approximately 150 million. FDR, well before Pearl Harbor, had begun to condition the country for universal military service. In September 1940, Congress passed the first peacetime draft, although some of these first inductees had to train with ludicrous wooden rifles and broom handles, so inadequate and scarce was military equipment. World War I surplus was brought out of the closet, but virtually all of this was worthless for the needs of modern wars.

Although by Pearl Harbor the army numbered 1.5 million, the immense job of building the armed services came after the attack. All men between the ages of 20 and 44 were registered for possible labor service, but it was soon discovered that men over 38 were largely unfit for combat and their recruitment was abandoned. To compensate, the minimum age was lowered to 19. All members of the armed services were bound to service for up to six months beyond the duration of the fighting. An incredible 31 million men were registered and nearly 10 million were inducted. A total of 15,145,115 men and women served in the armed services—10,420,000 in the Army,

3,883,520 in the Navy, 599,693 in the Marines, and 241,902 in the Coast Guard.

The needs of these people were staggering. Army bases were greatly expanded and new bases and posts had to be built. Everything was lacking—housing, clothes, food, equipment, buildings of all kinds from hospitals to recreation centers. Training was time-consuming and costly. There were thirteen weeks of basic training, twenty-six weeks additional training after being assigned to a division, and a final thirteen weeks in field training. By no means, however, did every soldier get this full year of training.

The Army Air Force was quickly strengthened to two and one-third million men and given highest priority for manpower and materials. In 1941, the Army Air Force had 292,000 men and 9,000 planes, only 1,100 of them fit for combat. In August 1945, the AAF had 2.3 million men and women and had 72,000 planes in service. Supply Services grew to 1.75 million men,

operated a fleet of 1,537 ships, paid out over $22 billion in pay and allowances, processed more than $75 billion in army contracts, managed 3,700 posts or cantonments in the United States, transported 7.37 million men and 101.75 million tons of cargo, and administered a far-flung medical service.[3]

The Navy grew from 337,349 men plus 66,068 in the Marine Corps and 25,336 in the Coast Guard to 3,408,347, with an additional 484,631 in the Marines and 170,480 in the Coast Guard. The Women's Auxilliary Corps went to 100,000 and the Wacs to 86,000; the Coast Guard SPARS and the Marine Corps Women's Reserve also added to their ranks.

LABOR AND THE WAR

Civilian labor was not conscripted because of union opposition; in fact, despite the emergency of war various categories of workers were given exemptions from military service. The final Selective Service Act also gave a one-year postponement for students enrolled in colleges or universities. Even more important was the deferment of men whose employment in agriculture or industry was deemed essential, e.g., agricultural workers after 1942. Individual draft boards were given wide discretionary powers to grant exemptions. On the whole this system succeeded in mobilizing 12.3 million men, and a generally flexible approach to labor policy plus substantial economic benefits for workers made it reasonably easy to maximize the labor efforts at home both in industry and agriculture.

Full employment, for that was what the war mobilization brought, meant first that a labor force of over 50 million (rising from 46.5 to 53.0) had to be manipulated in a highly effective industrial structure to provide both guns and butter. Abundant jobs and high wages, the latter inflated through overtime earnings, gave incentive to work. The pool of unemployed, underemployed, young people not subject to the draft, married women who usually had not worked in the paid labor market, war wives, older workers, and minorities all came back to swell the work force. In 1939, some 9 million were still unemployed because of the Depression; most of the categories we have just mentioned never had a chance to enter the enfeebled capitalist economy of the thirties. The labor force, despite the drain of manpower caused by military mobilization, increased by 10.5 million; millions of additional workers were drawn into the labor force by wartime conditions. The number of women factory workers doubled between 1939 and 1944; and 5 million women worked outside the home.

New Deal legislation and the vigorous activity of the CIO meant that a large percentage of the labor force was unionized. By the end of the war the largest unions were the AFL, with 7 million members; the CIO which had 6 million; and the UMW which was 500,000 strong. Organized labor was particularly sensitive to what might happen to it as large numbers of men who belonged to unions were drawn into the armed forces while hordes of unindoctrinated "new" workers joined the labor force. Roosevelt used all of his skills to diffuse these concerns. On the Advisory Commission of the Council of National Defense (1940) he had placed Sidney Hillman, respected long-time leader of the Amalgamated Clothing Workers. After Pearl Harbor, FDR obtained an agreement from both labor leaders and management for a no-strike, no-lockouts pledge and pressed the peaceful arbitration of labor disputes through the National War Labor Board (WLB) formed in January 1942. The WLB scrupulously enforced the Wagner Act's commitment to collective bargaining, including the closed shop, and supported the "maintenance of membership plan" under which unions retained their membership and the right to bargain for all workers during the life of a contract. New workers coming into jobs, however, did not have to join a union. By 1945, 15 million workers were unionized.

Given the enormous magnitude of the task, the millions of individuals involved, and the difficulty of ensuring labor freedoms in a wartime democracy, the record is most impressive. Under the leadership of Paul V. McNutt, the War Manpower Commission directed workers to essential war industries and tried to prohibit workers from leaving defense work without the approval of the United States Employment Service. Remarkably little coercion was used. Even after Congress passed in 1943 the War Labor Disputes Act, which gave the President coercive powers to delay or end strikes, such measures were seldom invoked against workers.

Workers' hours and pay increased. Between 1939 and 1944, the average week increased from 37.7 to 45.2 hours in manufacturing, from 32.4 to 39.5 hours in construction, and from 32.3 to 43.9 hours in mining. Although prices increased nearly 25 percent during the war, weekly earnings of workers in manufacturing increased 70 percent. By working overtime, graveyard shifts, weekends, and holidays, workers could double their earnings. In many families there were multiple wage earners. With few consumer goods available, individuals built the savings horde which fueled the long boom of the postwar period.

There were conflicts. Sewell Avery of Montgomery Ward was carried out of his office by federal marshals in 1944 after refusing the government's

Figure 2.1 **Industrial Production, 1939–1945**

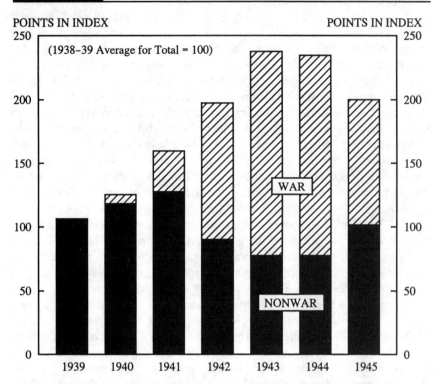

POINTS IN INDEX

POINTS IN INDEX

(1938–39 Average for Total = 100)

WAR

NONWAR

Source: U.S. Bureau of the Budget, *The United States at War* (Washington, D.C.: GPO, 1946), p. 104, cited in H.G. Vatter, *U.S. Economy in World War II*, (New York: Columbia University Press, 1985), p. 16.

order to recognize his workers' union. Much more important was the long drawn-out struggle between the President and the organized mine workers led by the long-time buccaneer of labor, John L. Lewis. No agreement pleased Lewis or could bind him. He viewed the wartime situation as one in which the miners might finally recoup decades of harsh work and low pay. No less, he felt, was due them given the substantial wartime profits of management.

The War Labor Board supported labor's right to a standard of living "compatible with health and decency," but in general its position, except to encourage equal pay for blacks and women and elimination of regional pay differentials, was to maintain the status quo. On July 16, 1942, in response to labor's demands for cost-of-living increases, the WLB issued the Little Steel Formula which granted workers a 15 percent wage increase—an increase clearly influenced by the threat of a work stoppage by 180,000 steelworkers. Still labor continued to feel left behind, envious of the gains made by other groups in industry and farming. Although the WLB stuck to the Little Steel Formula, it did allow vacation pay and higher wages for overtime. The upward creep of wages and prices continued, although the Stabilization Act of October 1942 tried to contain these pressures.

There were strikes and stoppages: 14,731 strikes and 36.3 million work hours lost, but on the whole a very impressive record compared to the total hours worked. Only the conduct of the United Mine Workers (UMW) and their leader John L. Lewis roused Roosevelt's anger. Mine workers had increased their wages almost 50 percent and had called three strikes to get their demands. Roosevelt had taken over the mines briefly, and finally announced that miners would be drafted into the armed services if they "absented themselves without just cause from work in the mines under government operation."[4] Even so Lewis came away with substantial gains. In addition to the nominal wage increases under the Little Steel Formula, miners received compensation for shorter lunch periods and for portal-to-portal time. Because of the intransigence of union bosses like Lewis, Congress retaliated by passing the antilabor Smith-Connally Act on June 26, 1943. This bill, passed over the President's veto, was the legislature's response to the miners and the threat of a December railway strike that forced the government to seize and operate the railroads for three weeks until the wage dispute was settled. The War Labor Disputes Act, Smith-Connally's formal title, was intended to prevent any interruption of war production. The President was given authority to seize any striking war plant; its other provisions—a thirty-day cooling off period before striking and a secret strike-vote ballot—remained ineffective. Roosevelt too, was not comfortable with the bill and rarely used this authority, preferring instead to use the threat of military service against striking workers. The years 1944 and 1945 brought increased, not diminished, numbers of strikes. Portents of the growing antiunion movement of the postwar period had briefly surfaced and would spread across the country. Overall, however, the wartime cooperation of labor was outstanding.

PRICE CONTROLS AND RATIONING

The Second World War produced for civilians shortages of goods needed by the military. The lack of rubber for domestic use led to crash programs to formulate synthetic rubber, for example. There were also shortages of meat, shoes, gasoline, and sugar. If left to the free market, prices would have soared and distribution would have been determined solely by the ability to pay these prices. This seemed unfair when so many Americans were being called on for great sacrifices. To handle these problems the Roosevelt administration instituted price controls and rationing.

In August 1941, the Division of Price Stabilization was made an executive agency and became the Office of Price Administration (OPA). Before Pearl Harbor, OPA's power rested largely on providing information (mostly price schedules and persuasion; it had no powers of coercion). The OPA exerted influence on government purchasing agencies by making available fair price schedules that they were to follow. Finally, in January 1942, the OPA was given statutory power to control prices and rents and to impose penalties for violation.

In 1942, the OPA estimated that an excess $17 billion of purchasing power over and above income, taxes, and goods available posed an "inflationary gap" which could overwhelm the economy if no action were taken to regulate demand. During the First World War, prices had risen 62 percent and the government imposed no price controls. However, World War II promised to be a much longer struggle with even greater pressure on demand. First the government rationed tires, next gasoline on the East Coast, then everywhere; finally fuel oil, sugar, and coffee.

The process of rationing was kept relatively simple. Books of coupons were issued to each individual. For gasoline, consumers were allocated amounts in relation to their needs—businesses got more, and ordinary individuals received only modest weekly allocations of four gallons. Sugar, coffee, meat, shoes, and canned goods were all assigned points and purchased with ration books of stamps and coupons. Although small children frequently outgrew their shoe rations, most others suffered little hardship despite the occasional shortages. However, for all items there was a black market as well as some cheating and even some counterfeiting of stamps and coupons. On the whole, however, the system worked equitably and well. Overall, prices rose only 33 percent over the entire period, a rather remarkable outcome.

By the end of 1942, military needs and Lend-Lease took one-fourth of all foodstuffs, especially canned, bottled, frozen and dried vegetables, fruits, juices, and soups. These items fell to rationing in March 1943. Under the point system, the number of goods that could be purchased was determined by the point value given those items by the OPA and by the number of coupon points the customer had. Almost 95 percent of all food eventually came under OPA rationing. OPA also controlled rents in defense areas. By mid-1943, 456 defense rental areas had been set up under its control. Rents in these areas were frozen at the March 1942 level.

As full employment was achieved and wages rose to new heights, the foundation for a surge in the real standard of living was laid. The average general wage for manufacturing industries increased from 86 cents an hour in 1942 to 96 cents an hour in 1943, to $1.01 in 1944, and to $1.03 in 1945, a rise of about 17.5 percent. For most workers, rationing and price controls, despite shortcomings, prevented these gains from being eaten up by wartime inflation.

AGRICULTURE IN WARTIME

The coming of war in 1939 reduced foreign demand for agricultural products, and surpluses of grains and other products were added to the stockpiles caused by the Depression. Within twenty-four months, however, this situation had been completely reversed. Shipments of food under Lend-Lease accounted for 13 percent of the aid, and the United States became a major food exporter to the rest of the world. The regulation of food production was placed under the Department of Food Production and Distribution, later renamed the War Food Administration. The WFA was given overall control of agricultural policy.

Agricultural production increased about one-third over prewar levels. Farmers prospered. Farm prices doubled, net cash farm income soared from $2 billion to $9.5 billion between 1940 and 1945, farm production increased almost 20 percent, and food crop production even more. Total receipts to farmers from livestock and produce sales plus government subsidies increased from $11.7 billion in 1941 to over $20 billion in 1943. Farmers added $11 billion to their savings. Six million farm owners increased their standard of living and the value of their holdings; farm debt was reduced and farm tenancy fell almost 20 percent. Wartime needs for food kept expanding. Not only did American agriculture feed United States military forces and the home population, it provided for the massive needs of Lend-Lease allies and for the food requirements of all those peoples liberated by the Allied armies. Incredible as it may seem, United States agriculture produced these staggering amounts on the same number of farms, with virtually the same acreage, and with a somewhat diminished work force. After a decade of hardship and deprivation, the sick industry of maladapted agriculture could produce at will for a grateful world. Capitalist agriculture was well-suited to this environment; no period in the entire postwar era was more profitable for farmers.

WEAPONS TECHNOLOGY

The story of the economy during World War II ends with the creation and explosion of the atomic bombs over Hiroshima and Nagasaki. These explosive devices ushered in a new age. The story can be summarized briefly.[5] Dr. Vannevar Bush, president of the Carnegie Institute of Washington, D.C., persuaded FDR in 1940 to establish the National Defense Research Committee with representatives from the War and Navy Departments, universities, and private industry. A year later, this structure became the Office of Scientific Research and Development (OSRD), with Bush as director. The mobilization of scientific personnel achieved enormous results for the war effort and for the postwar society. Out of this directed research came the development of radar, sonar, combat rockets, the proximity fuse, and the atomic bomb. The development of effective radar broke the hold of the German submarine wolfpacks on the sea lanes. Radar in fighter planes produced powerful night interceptors; for bombers, there was an accurate bombsight, and for ships, a new method of fire control. The American forces alone used $3 billion worth of radar.

The race to perfect the atomic bomb was the outstanding achievement of OSRD. Scientists had known that the ability to produce atomic fission could conceivably win the war. Professor Enrico Fermi of Columbia University and Albert Einstein of the Institute for Advanced Study of Princeton

University convinced Roosevelt to start a modest research program of $2 million under the control of OSRD. Scientific research at Columbia, California-Berkeley, Chicago, and other universities proceeded slowly until a controlled chain reaction was achieved in the atomic pile under the football field of the University of Chicago.

With the breakthrough, OSRD turned the project over to General Leslie R. Groves and the Manhattan District of the Army. By incredible effort, work on a bomb was begun in the spring of 1943 at Los Alamos in New Mexico. Under Dr. J. Robert Oppenheimer, the final assembly was begun on July 12, 1945, for the first test four days later. The mushroom cloud, the ball of fire, and the destructive blast inaugurated a new era.

The development of these new weapons marked the birth of a new age in the means and costs of fighting a modern war. The modern defense industry, which Eisenhower later called the military-industrial complex, had its beginnings during these years. For the first time in American history, a permanent and largely secret effort to maintain technological weapon superiority would be written into the federal budget. Virtually every state would benefit from these funds, and very large corporations would lobby vigorously to win these multibillion dollar contracts to develop and produce these new exotic weapon systems.

NOTES

[1] Rexford G. Tugwell, *The Democratic Roosevelt* (Garden City, N.J.: Doubleday and Company, 1957), p. 560; Harold G. Vatter, *The U.S. Economy in World War II* (New York: Columbia University Press, 1985); U.S. Civilian Production Administration, Industrial Mobilization for War, *History of the War Production Board and Predecessor Agencies, 1940–1945,* Vol.I; *Program and Administration* (Washington, D.C.: Government Printing Office, 1947), p. 962.

[2] James MacGregor Burns, *Roosevelt: The Soldier of Freedom* (New York: Harcourt, Brace, Jovanovich, Inc., 1970), p. 257.

[3] Arthur S. Link, *American Epoch,* 3rd ed., Vol. 3 (New York: Alfred A. Knopf, 1967), pp. 517–518.

[4] Ted Morgan, *FDR: A Biography* (New York: Simon and Schuster, 1985), p. 663.

[5] For a detailed account, see Richard Rhodes, *The Making of the Atomic Bomb* (New York: Simon and Schuster, 1986).

SUGGESTED READINGS

Baruch, Bernard, and J. M. Hancock. *Report on War and Post-War Adjustment Policies.* Washington: U.S. Government Printing Office, 1944.

Boyan, Edwin Arthur. *Handbook of War Production.* New York: McGraw Hill Co., 1942.

Brodus, Mitchell. *Depression Decade: From New Era Through New Deal, 1929-1941*. New York: Rinehart, 1947.

Cochran, Thomas C. *The Great Depression and World War II, 1929-1945*. New York: Scott, Foresman and Company, 1968.

Fraser, C. E., and S. F. Teele. *Industry Goes to War*. New York: McGraw Hill Co., 1941.

Harris, Seymour E. *The Economics of American Defense*. New York: W. W. Norton, 1941.

Industrial Mobilization for War: History of the War Production Board and Predecessor Agencies, 1940-45. Vol. 1: *Program and Administration*. Washington, D.C.: Government Printing Office, 1947.

Janeway, Eliot. *The Struggle for Survival: A Chronicle of Economic Mobilization in World War II*. New Haven: Yale University Press, 1951.

Link, Arthur S. *American Epoch*. New York: Alfred A. Knopf, 1967.

Murphy, Henry C. *National Debt in War and Transition*. New York: McGraw Hill, 1950.

Nelson, Donald M. *Arsenal of Democracy: The Story of American War Production*. New York: Harcourt, Brace and Co., 1946.

Novick, David, M. Amhen, and W. C. Trupner. *Wartime Production Controls*. New York: Columbia University Press, 1949.

Polenberg, Richard. *War and Society: The United States, 1941-1945*. Philadelphia: Lippincott, 1972.

Rhodes, Richard. *The Making of the Atomic Bomb*. New York: Simon and Schuster, 1986.

Smith, Elberton R. *The Army and Economic Mobilization*. Washington: Government Printing Office, 1958.

Smith, Ralph E. *The Army and Economic Mobilization*. Washington: Office of the Chief of Military History, Dept. of the Army, 1959.

Toulmin, H. A. *Diary of Democracy: The Senate War Investigating Committee*. New York: R. R. Smith, 1947.

Vatter, Harold G. *The U.S. Economy in World War II*. New York: Columbia University Press, 1985.

Walton, Francis. *Miracle of World War II: How American Industry Made Victory Possible*. New York: Macmillan, 1956.

BOOK II

The American Economy, 1945–1991

3   *Postwar America, 1945–1952*

TRUMAN AND EISENHOWER

A generation of Americans had known virtually only one president, Franklin Roosevelt. His death left a vacuum that under ordinary circumstances would have been difficult to fill. In April 1945 there remained real problems like finishing the war, by no means assured, although America was well on the way to victory. In the Pacific, the war was still fierce, and intelligence agencies warned the American people that a million casualties could be expected in the invasion of the Japanese home islands. To be sure, given the human cost of taking Guadalcanal, Tarawa, and Iwo Jima, these numbers seemed all too possible.

The little man with the fedora who took the presidential oath had little to recommend him that would inspire confidence, much that inspired misgiving. Harry S. Truman, the safe, secure, and tidy Vice President, had a background and career that marked him as modest and mediocre. Before the First World War he worked as a bank clerk and farmer. He served in the artillery in France, and after the war returned to Kansas City, married, and opened a men's clothing store. He was not a success, but when the recession of 1921 ruined him, Truman refused bankruptcy and over the next half-dozen years paid off all his creditors.

Truman won his first political post with the help of the Democratic machine of Kansas City. Defeated for reelection in 1924, he was back in Independence as judge in 1927. For seven years, he built a local reputation as an able and effective administrator and in 1934, backed by the notorious Pendergast machine, he rode the Democratic landslide and became a U.S. senator. Tom Pendergast went to jail in 1939 for income tax evasion, and Truman's career seemed finished. To the surprise of many he fought hard and won reelection in 1940. Only in 1941, as Chairman of a special Senate committee to investigate the defense effort, did he gain any national prominence. Roosevelt picked him for vice-presidential candidate in 1944 to bal-

Chronology

1945
September: Recovery program recommended to Congress
1946
February: Employment Act of 1946 created Council of Economic Advisors
August: Legislative Reorganization Act; Title III required lobbyists to register and report their lobbying expenses
1947
June: Taft-Hartley Act passed over Truman's veto
July: Presidential Succession Act
1948
July: Truman banned discrimination in hiring of federal employees
November: Truman reelected in upset victory; Democrats regained control of Congress
1949
October: Minimum wage raised from $.40 to $.75
1950
February: Beginning of Kefauver investigations of crime in interstate commerce
August: Social Security amendments raised wage base to $3600 per year, increased benefits, extended system to bring in some 9.2 million workers—self-employed, domestic, agricultural, and those in state and local government
December: Celler-Kefauver Act amended Section 7 of Clayton Act to prohibit corporate acquisitions which might substantially lessen competition
1952
April: President Truman seized steel mills to avoid strike by steelworkers
July: Korean GI Bill of Rights granted benefits similar to those given to World War II veterans
November: Election of Dwight D. Eisenhower as President
1953
April: Creation of the Department of Health, Education, and Welfare

1954
January: Eisenhower farm program replaced rigid
mandatory farm price supports with flexible supports
May: *Brown* v. *Board of Education of Topeka* reversed
"separate but equal" doctrine
August: Housing Act of 1954 authorized construction
over a one-year period of 35,000 houses to serve families
displaced by programs of urban renewal; Internal
Revenue Code creates major tax reform
September: Amendments to Social Security Act raised
benefits and extended coverage
1955
June: Second Hoover Commission final report advocated
need to "get government out of business"
1956
June: National Highway Revenue Act allocated funds for
the interstate system
November: Eisenhower reelected for a second term, but
Democrats carried both House and Senate
1957
September: Civil Rights Act
1958
July: NASA established
September: National Defense Education Act greatly
extended federal funds for loans to college students
1959
September: Landrum-Griffith Act (Labor Management
Reporting and Disclosure Act), designed to suppress
gangsterism, racketeering, and blackmail in labor
organizations
1960
May: Civil Rights Act of 1960 strengthened provisions of
1957 act for court enforcement of voting rights
November: Election of John F. Kennedy
1961
January: Eisenhower farewell address warned of the
growth and threat of the military-industrial complex

ance the ticket, and Harry Truman, America's average man, was next in line to the most powerful and important office in the world.

Truman could never achieve FDR's public aura, but over time Truman used his considerable talents, personal integrity, and sheer guts not only to get reelected to the Presidency in 1948 but to build a solid and enduring reputation. In domestic matters he pushed ahead in civil rights, public health, and public welfare systems against increasing opposition from die-hard Southern reactionaries and a growing conservatism. In foreign affairs, he made momentous and far-reaching decisions. First, he approved the use of the atomic bomb against Japan—an agonizing decision, but one supported by Americans. In March 1947, he announced the so-called Truman Doctrine: "I believe that it must be the foreign policy of the United States to support free peoples who are resisting attempted subjugation by armed minorities or by outside pressures." Under the Truman presidency, Secretary of State George Marshall announced on June 5, 1947, at Harvard an idealistic and generous package of aid for Europe's economic recovery. The blockade of Berlin in 1948 was relieved by airlift. NATO, the North Atlantic Treaty Organization, was created as was the the European Common Market. And during the Korean conflict Truman fired General Douglas MacArthur from his position as commander in South Korea. MacArthur's removal perhaps saved the United States from a full-scale war with China, since MacArthur was clearly intent on confronting the Chinese beyond North Korea.

If the country too hastily demobilized and too quickly dismantled the wartime control systems, no other path seemed possible given the mindset of the American people. When Truman announced that he would not run again for reelection, both parties rushed to claim Dwight D. Eisenhower as their candidate.

Normalcy of a kind was virtually guaranteed by the new President, whose civilian attitudes, beliefs, and views were as commonplace as motherhood and apple pie. Eisenhower had led the Allied armies to victory in Europe and had shown leadership abilities as Supreme Commander of the Allied Expeditionary Force in Europe in getting diverse forces to work together reasonably and harmoniously; that was one of his major political skills during his eight years in office. Born in Texas but raised in Kansas, he graduated from West Point in 1915 and began a long tour of routine duties during the interwar years; he even served for five years as an aide to General MacArthur in the Philippines. The Second World War brought him Army leadership posts in Europe and North Africa. Finally he attained the responsibility of supreme commander in Europe. After serving as commander of the American occupation forces in Germany, he resigned in 1948 to become president of Columbia University.

Little indeed was known about the 34th President. He was a political cipher with no distinct ideological affiliation and probably could have been elected on either ticket in 1952. Virtually his entire life had been spent in the military. He liked westerns, bourbon, golf, and poker, but did not like books or intellectual matters. His speech was commonplace, and his addresses studded with platitudes. He was an unremarkable man in office at the perfect time for an unremarkable man, and he did great good. For Eisenhower beyond all else was an honest, decent, open, and traditional American. He fit like a very comfortable pair of old shoes. After twenty-three years of Democratic control, he gave the nation a needed opportunity to integrate the many changes that had taken place. He also gave the Republican Party a new lease on life.

Eisenhower faced few issues and mounted even fewer initiatives in domestic areas. To his credit, however, he brought McCarthy and his vicious anti-Communist vendetta to discredit and disparaged McCarthyism as a threat to political life (for no one could believe that "Ike" was soft on Communism!). The President also demonstrated flexibility in managing fiscal policy. Dear to the Republicans was the balanced budget, but when expenditures exceeded income in 1954, and in the recession of 1957-8, Eisenhower moved toward Keynesian deficit spending as countercyclical federal policy.

Even more to Eisenhower's credit, he did not attempt to roll back the progressive New Deal programs. He expanded welfare and social security programs in 1953 and '54. He maintained federal support of agriculture, and furthered the extension of rural electrification and a federal program to assist farmers and rural dwellers in low-income areas. He continued the liberal trade policy of the New Deal and joined Canada in the St. Lawrence Seaway Development Corporation which, after years of planning, finally connected the Great Lakes via the St. Lawrence River to the North Atlantic. For the first time since colonial discovery, ocean going vessels could navigate our "Inland Seas." The National Defense Act did much needed, if limited, good as did the Civil Rights Act of 1957. To round out the picture, Eisenhower played a major role in building a national highway system. The Federal Highway Act of 1956 sanctioned a 42,500 mile network of modern roads of which 90 percent was paid for by the federal government, 10 percent by the states. Middle-class Americans looked back on the fifties as the most socially stable, most affluent, and the time most clearly resembling the traditional American dream.

FROM WAR TO PEACE: RECONVERSION

Hardly had the second atomic bomb been dropped on Nagasaki when the Japanese sued for peace. On August 14 the Japanese government formally accepted the terms of surrender. The return to peace after the Armistice in 1918 had not been easy, but the reconversion of the United States economy after four years of an extraordinary mobilization of resources and people would bring even more radical changes. It was easy to do away with gas rationing as soon as the fighting ended so that Americans could fill up their gas-guzzlers and return to their love affair with the automobile. But to bring the economy from wartime to peacetime production would take a decade.

There was little order in the demobilization of the armed forces. Some

12 million citizens had been drawn into the armed forces, and few of them had any desire to remain in uniform one hour longer than necessary. Most of them wished to get back to their families, jobs, and careers as quickly as possible in order to make up the years they had lost in the war. No major combatant nation demilitarized more quickly; some said it happened too quickly and blamed in part the hasty demobilization for our lack of vigor in foreign affairs in the immediate postwar years. The War Department had tried to impose some sort of order on this system of demobilization. Points were assigned for length of combat, battle missions, and so on. Men were to be released first who had accumulated eighty-five points; gradually the number of points for release was to be lowered. But the push was on. The U.S. Navy's "magic carpet," i.e., any ship from a transport to a battle carrier, 1,200 vessels in all, returned 4,262,067 Pacific veterans in less than a year after the fighting ended. In 1945, the Army had 8,266,000 troops, but in 1946, it was down to 1,889,200 and by 1949, 658,000—obviously not enough for the defender of the free world to handle its postwar problems.

For all veterans, Congress in 1944 offered the Servicemen's Readjustment Act, better known as the GI Bill of Rights. This legislation provided unemployment benefits for fifty-two weeks and loans for obtaining homes, going into business, or entering farming. But for millions, it was the educational benefits that paid their tuition and gave them a cost-of-living stipend that was crucial. This act made it possible for millions to go to college, making it the most revolutionary legislation for an entire generation. The timing was appropriate, since the legislation gave demobilized veterans the opportunity for higher education, many of whom under other circumstances would not have gone beyond the high school level. The macroeconomic benefits for social welfare and national wealth were immeasurable, for the country's net worth was increased by billions of dollars owing to the contributions of a more competent and highly educated people. The unintended consequences of this single piece of legislation remains one of the happiest stories of the immediate postwar period.

To deal with the other problems of economic transition, Congress in October 1944 established the office of War Mobilization and Reconversion with James F. Byrnes as head. Byrnes was charged with 1) promotion and development of demobilization plans and procedures; 2) settlement of controversies between federal and state agencies in the development of plans and procedures for this transition from war to peace; 3) simplification, consolidation, or elimination of war agencies as the need for these agencies disappeared; 4) determining policies for relaxing emergency war controls; and 5) consultation and cooperation with state and local governments, industry, labor, agriculture, and other groups concerning problems of the transition from war to peace. Most of the 165 emergency war agencies were phased out; by mid-1946, only a dozen remained. The reconversion from war to peace was handled by the long-established permanent bureaucracies of the government. Given the pressures from private interests, and the longing of the country to return to "normalcy," the haste of demobilization was understandable and as well done as could have been expected.

POSTWAR LABOR

Organized labor in the postwar period was powerful and militant. Membership in organized labor unions had increased 80 percent between 1940 and 1947, jumping from 8.5 million to 15.4 million. During the long years of war, labor felt that the increases grudgingly granted it under various government formulae had fallen far short of its just deserts and even far shorter relative to the profits made by other sectors in the economy, especially big business. So long as the war lasted, labor was quiescent. Once peace came, however, all hell broke loose. The end of the war unleashed eighteen of the stormiest months in modern labor history. In 1945, nearly 2 million workers went on strike in numerous industries, and 1946 ushered in greater labor turmoil. Between November 1945 and January 1947, 180,000 auto workers, 200,000 electrical workers, and 750,000 steel workers walked off the job. In all for the year 1946 there were 4,700 strikes involving 4.7 million workers. This wave of strikes brought wage gains of approximately 30 percent to these workers and to others in related mass-production industries, e.g., meat packing, automobiles, and steel; the usual increase was approximately 19½ cents an hour, a figure determined by presidential fact-finding boards. General Motors led the pack by granting a raise of 18½ cents an hour after a strike which lasted 113 days; other industries followed with large increases. What was to become a dangerous precedent emerged during these postwar years. As long as a company could pass on the wage increases in the form of higher prices to consumers, it saw no compelling reason in the short run to fight the union's demands and lose market share to its competitors. The consequences of this thinking would only show up decades later when many of these same mass-production industries found that their inflated costs had made them noncompetitive in world markets.

Meanwhile, major strikes continued to rack the economy. In January 1946, 750,000 steel workers closed down every steel mill in the country. Although this strike ended fairly quickly in February, it dealt a major blow to peacetime industrial reconversion. Organized labor paid a heavy price, estimated at $6.54 million daily loss in wages, but the $6 billion steel industry perhaps lost more. The early victory of the union would be repeated a number of times in the postwar period, culminating in 1959, when the union broke management's power to resist. It is an irony of postwar history that the United Steel Workers achieved the best contract for its members just about the time when big steel began its long industrial descent. M. W. Abel, president of the union, praised this contract as a model for all industry.

During the war, the United Mine Workers had been the least cooperative union and the most obdurate in its dealings with the government. Now in April 1946, 450,000 soft-coal miners closed the mines in a dispute over wages and health and welfare provisions. The coal strike that was to last forty-five days hindered many industries gearing up for peacetime production. For a brief time, railroads suspended their passenger schedules and imposed an embargo on rail freight shipments except for food, fuel, and other essentials. An angry President Truman ordered Secretary of the Interior Julius A. Krug to seize the country's soft-coal mines. Admiral Ben Morell, U.S.N., was to oversee the mines during the government's seizure but there was really no way to get the miners to dig the coal without a degree of coercion that was unacceptable in a democratic society.

While the coal miners' dispute continued, a third major strike began on May 23, 1946, when the railroad brotherhoods called for a work stoppage, paralyzing the transportation system of the country. President Truman, who had seized the railroads on May 17 in accordance with the Smith-Connally Act, had offered a generous settlement which eighteen of the unions accepted. Only the two brotherhoods of Engineers and Trainmen remained adamant. The walkout on May 23 followed. After appealing to the strikers and failing, a feisty Truman asked Congress for the most drastic powers over organized labor that any President had ever wielded. He requested the authority to declare a state of emergency whenever a strike imperiling the national safety occurred in a vital industry regulated by federal law. Workers who remained on strike would lose all employment and seniority benefits and could be drafted into the army. Union leaders could be fined and imprisoned. Two days after his speech, railroad workers returned to work, and four days later an agreement was reached with the coal workers. Because the urgency had vanished, Truman's bill never got out of the Senate. Nevertheless, some observers have pointed out the significant rise in state legislation to curb unions which began that spring; by 1947, twenty-six states had passed comprehensive industrial codes of varying antiunion sentiments, and the federal government indeed would follow these examples.

In 1946, Congress tried to pass the Case bill, which would have placed severe constraints on labor's ability to strike, but Truman vetoed this legislation. A year later, however, Congress passed the Taft-Hartley (Labor-Management Relations Act) over Truman's veto. The Taft-Hartley Act has been one of the most important pieces of labor legislation (and equally one of the most controversial) since the New Deal legislation of the 1930s. For many old-time union leaders, Taft-Hartley was the "slave-labor" act. Though labor has not been able to repeal or rescind it, most unions have learned to live with it. Taft-Hartley was meant to limit the power of the unions in behalf of the public interest, namely, health and safety matters, the protection of individual workers from union coercion, and the placement of government at the center of nationwide labor disputes with effective power to initiate injunctions, cooling-off periods, and special elections. These national emergency provisions of Taft-Hartley were to be used seventeen times by Presidents between 1947 and 1959.

The Wagner Act of 1935 was intended to right the perceived historic inequality of organized union labor vis-à-vis employers and the courts while at the same time curtailing the rise of radical union power. The NLRB followed this philosophy. In contrast the architects of the Taft-Hartley Act saw the nation and the public as hostage to organized union power. Individual workers, they believed, were being deprived of their right to accept or reject union membership; hence a number of restrictive measures were adopted. Labor leaders were required to sign oaths that they were not Communists, and within a year 76,710 union officials had tendered such statements. Unions had to file financial reports, and 17,275 labor unions complied. Taft-Hartley outlawed the closed shop (in which employers were required to hire and retain only union members in good standing) but did not abolish the union shop (in which all employees had to become union members within a specified time). Over 25,000 petitions for union-shop elections were made during the first two years of Taft-Hartley. For the first time since 1935, employers and individual employees could cite unions and employers for unfair labor practices, and hundreds of citations in fact were made.

Because Taft-Hartley became the model for mediating labor-management disputes in the 1950s, the procedures in the law are worth noting. In the case of a strike that might cause a national emergency or threatened national health or safety, the President could ask for a federal injunction to stop the threatened strike. This injunction would allow for a sixty-day "cooling off" period during which the Federal Mediation and Conciliation Service would try to resolve the issue. A fifteen-day period followed during which the union was to vote on the employer's final offer. The NLRB then had five days to certify the voting results. Only then could the injunction be lifted, but if the dispute was still unresolved, the President could ask Congress for appropriate remedies. Furthermore, Taft-Hartley largely prohibited secondary boycotts, jurisdictional strikes, and other so-called "unfair labor practices." Unions were also required to grant sixty-days' notice if they intended to change or terminate a union agreement. The philosophical shift in Taft-Hartley was important. Together with the Lea Act against union "featherbedding" (the practice of requiring more workers be hired than needed to perform a job) and the Hobbs Anti-Racketeering Act, the momentum of union growth was reversed. Almost one-third of the states passed "right-to-work" laws, a euphemism in many cases for union busting. On both the federal and state levels, this ideological shift clearly signified the passing of the New Deal, for no other area of New Deal reform was so harshly treated. It was to be a continuing trend for the next three decades.

POSTWAR AGRICULTURE

The truth is that farm family life is neither all black nor all white. There are, of course, families who live sordid and miserable lives on the land, and on the other hand, many who come as close as the earth affords to meeting the ideal of the romantic's dream of rustic beauty. But, by and large, rural family life is comparable to life everywhere, mixing the bad and good, the joy and sorrow, the littleness and greatness that characterized humankind.[1]

New Deal policies salvaged American agriculture during the 1930s, but it was the war that brought gains in farm income and farm expansion. The prodigious capability of U.S. agriculture was challenged and rewarded by wartime demands. In 1900 one farmer could feed seven people; by 1950 one

Table 3.1	Farming Statistics, 1939–1949	
Year	Farmer's share of consumer's dollar	Gross farm income (millions)*
1939	$0.38	$10,547
1940	0.40	11,008
1941	0.44	13,885
1942	0.48	18,559
1943	0.51	23,024
1944	0.52	24,185
1945	0.54	25,434
1946	0.53	29,238
1947	0.52	34,643
1948	0.51	35,071
1949	0.48	32,167

*Includes cash receipts from farm marketings, government payments, value of home consumption, and rental value of farm homes.

Source: U.S. Department of Agriculture, *Agricultural Statistics,* pp. 619, 627.

agricultural worker produced enough for more than fourteen people. In 1976, one worker supplied enough food for more than fifty-six people.[2] Innovation and productivity went hand-in-hand: in 1925, 10.5 work hours were needed to plant and harvest an acre of wheat, yielding 14.1 bushels. By 1949, 5.7 work hours yielded 16.9 bushels.

The postwar period intensified the use of capital in farming, especially in the dramatic spread of farm tractors and the development of specialized agricultural machinery. Farming was an expensive business and destined to become even more capital-intensive. Between 1935 and 1945 the number of tractors and trucks in use each increased by more than 100,000 per year. Cotton strippers and pickers, grain harvesters, hay balers, field silage harvesters, and milking machines were some of the machines to come into prominence after the war. A new world of farm chemicals, including pesticides, animal antibiotics, and genetically produced F-1 hybrid seed, were all introduced quickly in this period. DDT was used as early as 1943, 2-4-D in 1945. Later, environmentalists and other specialists would point out the dangers of introducing these new chemicals on such a lavish scale into the food chain, but the immediate benefits were evident in the enormous growth in farm production.

High demand continued after the war; as the needs of the military fell quickly, civilian food supplies increased in 1946, although export demands too were heavy. Throughout the war-torn world, shortages persisted and demand for U.S. food and fiber kept prices high. Farm income in 1939 was about $168 per capita but increased three and one-half times by 1950; gross farm income also tripled. Farmers were exhorted by the government to increase their production to help feed the world. The number of farmers, however, continued to decline even though output continued to increase; 2.7 million persons left farming between 1940 and 1947, and more than 60,000 farm laborers were imported annually from Mexico, Canada, and Jamaica to harvest American crops.

The end of the reconversion period was in sight, however. Although more than $3 billion of foodstuffs flowed to Europe in 1948 as part of the Marshall Plan, weakness began to show up in domestic prices. Federal farm price supports, adjusted to postwar realities, were used extensively by farmers. The Commodity Credit Corporation in the last half of 1948 loaned farmers $1.5 billion on crops, and under loan and purchase agreements bought up 27 percent of corn yields as farm prices overall fell sharply 13 percent.

Nineteen forty-nine witnessed a reversal in farming prosperity as the problem of overproduction became dominant once again. With demand abroad dropping, surpluses began to accumulate and prices tumbled. By 1949, the Commodity Credit Corporation had $3.1 billion invested in farm commodities. Secretary of Agriculture Charles Brannan planned a program to stabilize domestic farm income through a "modernized" parity formula that would be more up-to-date, accurate, and flexible, that is, based on current figures rather than the 1910–14 standard and more closely related to supply. The Brannan plan established a "farm income standard," i.e., a guaranteed dollar income for farmers through loans and storage based on the average price supports for nonperishable commodities. Perishable foods would be sold at market prices, and farmers would be paid the difference between the market price and the official support price by the federal government. Congress would have no part of the Brannan plan because of opposition from agricultural interests, though Truman achieved some flexibility in parity in the Agricultural Act of 1949.

Since 1930, it had become an axiom of governmental policy that agriculture in the United States was an industry to be protected from price declines that undercut production costs and inflicted social distress. This policy was in abeyance during World War II because market prices were well above support prices. Beginning in 1949, however, the old problems reemerged, and postwar policies were to a great extent a replay of the New Deal programs. Indeed, Brannan's policy stimulated production and was greatly criticized abroad as a means to dump U.S. farm products on world markets.

BUSINESS IN THE POSTWAR AGE

In 1932, Adolf Berle and Gardiner Means published a book titled *The Modern Corporation and Private Property*. The study, destined to become a classic of its kind, reflected the pessimism of the times. It skillfully traced the growth in the overall importance of large firms and the separation of ownership and control. It said much about the potential political power of the corporation but only little about the impact of large companies on market share and concentrations. Berle and Means's study was a very traditional analysis of the oligopolistic structure of U.S. corporate history that the Second Industrial Revolution (1880–1920) brought into being before the First World War. Part of the Berle and Means's thesis even foreshadowed the themes of John K. Galbraith's *New Industrial State* (1967) in suggesting that the new managerial elite "might well assume broader responsibilities than private profit making and bridge the gap between the narrowness of profit-seeking enterprise and the growing social needs of a complex society." In the main, however, the message of Berle and Means was quasi-Marxist, i.e., capitalism was a monster that would devour not only itself, but also threatened the existence of democratic institutions and the state.

Berle and Means had not been terribly prophetic. What they feared had not occurred, neither during the Depression nor during the war, nor were these things to happen. Competition had not died, concentration had not increased, and government power had not weakened, though corporate size, assets, sales, had all increased and were to grow much much bigger in the ensuing decades. America was still the most favorable country for beginning businesses. Millions of companies functioned outside the oligopolistic umbrella, and competition still flourished despite occasional economic backsliding. These private enterprises ranged from the mom-and-pop businesses to substantial enterprises, but their operation was entirely different from those corporate giants that constituted Fortune's 500. Statistically nine out of ten new restaurants failed, but each year produced a new crop of entrants who had a new marinara sauce or a flakier apple pie or even a new pizza dough. An advanced consumer society such as found in the United States offered enormous opportunities. Contrary to the depressed vision of the 1930s, invention and innovation had not come to the end of the line; in that sense, the postwar world was a new beginning.

Big business had been necessary for wartime mobilization. In order to produce quickly the enormous amount of war material for ourselves and our allies, the government had turned to the large corporations, for only they could provide the resources, skills, and management. Since the demise of the NRA, the Roosevelt administration had not carried on a vigorous antitrust program. The large auto, steel, and aircraft companies could readily convert to wartime production with governmental help. One estimate is that ten corporations handled one-third of all the government's war contracts. The auto companies as a whole produced prodigious numbers of tanks, trucks, bombers.

The federal government through its Lend-Lease operations expanded the productive base of the economy.

Besides the indirect effect of Lend-Lease orders upon the expansion of America's war productive capacity, hundreds of millions in Lend-Lease funds were directly invested before Pearl Harbor in new factories, shipyards, processing plants, storage depots and other facilities in this country, which, taken together made an important addition to our industrial plant. These investments, now totalling nearly $900 million have been made in 34 out of the 48 states in the Union. They range in size from more than $142 million for war plants in Michigan to $14,000 for a dry skim milk plant in North Dakota....Lend-Lease also financed the construction of ammunition docks, heavy-lift piers and floating cranes in American ports which since have loaded munitions for American troops as well as for our allies. It has helped to build a whole system of storage depots from coast to coast and many halfway stations that have contributed to a more orderly flow from factory to shipside of war materials for our own and other United Nations forces.[3]

In key industries such as steel, aircraft, synthetic rubber, petroleum, and aluminum, expansion fostered by government aid and war contracts increased physical facilities and production capacity. To more than a considerable degree, this pattern of growth was to persist in the postwar world. Companies that had expanded and profited during the war moved into the peace with the sense that the most important element in their corporate health was, and would continue to be, government spending. Although the auto companies hurried to reconvert to the production of cars, none of the large wartime companies divested themselves fully of their connections to Washington and to the Pentagon. When President Eisenhower warned of the military-industrial complex in his 1961 farewell address, he spoke the obvious. Just as American business was wonderfully structured to mobilize and produce for total war, so this same highly efficient oligopolistic structure, in which a small number of companies dominated the market in such products as autos, rubber, chemicals, and heavy metals, reconverted quickly and easily to the postwar opportunities. Even before the end of the actual fighting, business executives who had played major roles in Washington began an exodus back to their companies to prepare for reconversion to peace. These companies, which Chandler calls "first players," had invested heavily in manufacturing capability so that they could efficiently produce huge throughputs at low cost. They also elaborated distribution and marketing services which were highly effective, and they had structured management, both line and staff, into highly effective and professional working teams. Dominant in the field before the war, they would emerge as leaders again.

To be sure, reconversion was made easy by the largesse of the federal government. Plants that had been built to expand production in critical areas were sold off, frequently to the companies that had operated them during the war at a fraction of their costs. Tax credits were so liberally granted that companies could deduct massive amounts long after the war ended. The business property of the '50s and '60s arose out of this beneficent environment. Large cash reserves had been built up during the war. Consumer markets boomed at home and abroad because of the pent-up demand caused by the scarcity of consumer goods during the war years. A new surge of confidence not evident since before the Crash infected business managers. The Korean War in the '50s also was a stimulus, but most of all a country and a world starved for American products from TVs to jeans and detergents brought unbounded prosperity. United States foreign aid such as the Marshall Plan translated into credits for goods to be bought in and from the United States. Big ticket items like houses, autos, roads, and reconstruction pushed the economy further along. Although the '50s witnessed two downturns in 1954 and 1957–8, most large companies flourished. It was the period that future generations would look back on affectionately. Although the "first player" foreign companies (the large efficient export sector) would emerge once more in Germany, it would take several decades for their presence to be felt. Japan in the 1950s was still a country rebuilding—the yen was low relative to the dollar, and the Japanese miracle was far on the horizon. It was a poor, defeated country that no U.S. businessman could perceive as a threat. There were both vertical and horizontal mergers domestically, and U.S. companies began increasingly to move offshore. (The great surge in conglomerates and paper expansion, however, largely came after this period.) U.S. business managers were the best, and American goods had a known reputation for quality. Poor performance in the '60s and '70s was to unravel these reputations.[4]

THE INTERNATIONAL ECONOMY: BRETTON WOODS AND THE MARSHALL PLAN

In July 1944, delegates from forty-four countries (but none from the Soviet Union) met at Bretton Woods, New Hampshire, to create a postwar economic monetary and banking system. Keynes, only months before his fatal heart attack, participated, but his proposal for one overarching financial institution to handle both reconstruction and currency exchange was rejected in favor of the American position which insisted on an International Bank for Reconstruction and Development (IBRD or World Bank) and separate International Monetary Fund (IMF). Since the U.S. was to supply the bulk of both institutions' initial funds, its proposal for two separate institutions won out. Keynes's single institution might have been the better choice, since experience has shown that the separation of monetary and development problems in many instances seems arbitrary.

The World Bank's supply of capital was contributed by the sixty-eight member countries in the form of paid-in capital subscriptions. The bank raised funds to make loans for development purposes by selling World Bank bonds to investors at market rates. The World Bank has always been criticized for not making more loans to developing countries. Its loans have been conservative, either those directly to governments or for private ventures guaranteed by governments. Frequently, the World Bank has sent in a team of its own to analyze the economic soundness of the project for which the loan was requested. Most of its loans have been very safe ones, mainly to assist the creation of public works and utilities investments, i.e., electric power, railroads, ports, inland waterways, irrigation, flood control, roads, pipelines, and airports. Although it has earned over the decades the respect of the banking community, the World Bank lacks vitality and passion in dealing with the problems of Third World countries.

The International Monetary Fund was meant to play the dominant role in stabilizing exchange rates—in other words, to replace the prewar gold standard as the international stabilizing mechanism. The IMF was a grant "kitty" from which countries having temporary exchange difficulties could borrow foreign exchange to meet the crisis. The United States paid in $4.13 billion, roughly 40 percent of the total capital. Each member country selected a par value for its money, originally defined in terms of gold, and pledged to keep the exchange rate for its money within 1 percent of its par value. The Fund has stood ready to aid countries whose balance of payments fall into disequilibrium, and the Fund has acted with increasing vigor to serve as policeman where countries have gotten into serious exchange difficulties. Members of the IMF are urged to reduce foreign exchange restrictions and to encourage free (or freer) foreign trade. Like the Bank, the Fund has had its critics but both institutions have a good track record. To insure cooperation, the headquarters for the World Bank and IMF are located in adjacent buildings in Washington.

Perhaps the most dramatic of the postwar measures was the European Recovery Program, commonly called the Marshall Plan. Former general George Marshall, then Secretary of State, took the occasion of Harvard's commencement in 1947 to announce U.S. willingness to aid the economic recovery of Europe if the European nations could act in concert and present a program of needs. At first, until Moscow prohibited their participation, the eastern European countries showed interest in joining, while the western European nations eagerly cooperated. Marshall Plan aid, $5.3 billion for the first year, was approved by Congress, which saw it as a means of countering the Communist threat. The European Recovery Program enabled Western Europe to get back on its feet economically far sooner than would have occurred otherwise; American industry also benefitted from rejuvenated overseas demand. Eventually the Marshall Plan distributed $13 billion in assistance, an outstanding example of American vision. In the countries receiving assistance gross national product rose 25 percent from 1947 through 1950, and industrial and agricultural production exceeded by far the prewar levels.

NOTES

[1]Lowry Nelson, *American Farm Life* (Cambridge: Harvard University Press, 1953), p. 69.

[2]Wendell Berry, *The Unsettling of America: Culture and Agriculture* (San Francisco: The Sierra Club, 1977), p. 33.

[3]Robert Sobel, *The Age of the Giant Corporations* (Westport, Conn.: Greenwood Press, 1972), p. 167.

⁴See Alfred D. Chandler, *Scale and Scope: The Dynamics of Western Managerial Capitalism* (Cambridge: Harvard University Press, 1989).

SUGGESTED READINGS

Berry, Wendell. *The Unsettling of America: Culture and Agriculture.* San Francisco: The Sierra Club, 1977.

Chandler, Alfred D. *Scale and Scope: The Dynamics of Western Managerial Capitalism.* Cambridge: Harvard University Press, 1989.

Galambos, Louis, ed. *The New American State: Bureaucracies and Policies Since World War II.* Baltimore: Johns Hopkins University Press, 1987.

Galbraith, John Kenneth. *The New Industrial State,* 4th ed. Boston: Houghton Mifflin, 1985.

Gimbel, John. *The Origins of the Marshall Plan.* Stanford, Cal.: Stanford University Press, 1976.

Heilbroner, Robert L. *The Economic Transformation of America.* New York: Harcourt, Brace, Jovanovich, Inc., 1977.

Holbo, Paul S., and Robert W. Sellen. *The Eisenhower Era.* Hinsdale, Ill: Dryden Press, 1974.

Nelson, Lowry. *American Farm Life.* Cambridge, Mass: Harvard University Press, 1953.

Peterson, H. Craig. *Business and Government,* 3d ed. New York: Harper and Row, 1989.

Pursell, Carroll W., Jr. *The Military-Industrial Complex.* New York: Harper and Row, 1972.

Rosenberg, Norman L., and Emily S. Rosenberg. *In Our Times,* 2d ed. Englewood Cliffs, NJ: Prentice-Hall, 1982.

Sobel, Robert. *The Age of the Giant Corporations.* Westport, Conn: Greenwood Press, 1972.

Victor, Richard. *Energy Policy in America Since 1945: A Study in Business-Government Relations.* New York: Cambridge University Press, 1984.

Wilcox, Claire. *Public Policies Toward Business.* Homewood, Illinois: Richard D. Irwin, 1975.

4   *Affluence at Mid-Century*

ECONOMIC GROWTH

One of the great surprises at the end of the war was that the U.S. economy did not fall back into a depression similar to that of the thirties; for many Americans the 1950s brought a dramatic rise in affluence. (This widespread middle-class affluence would also create the optimism necessary for the initial acceptance of the Great Society programs of the 1960s.) In 1930, the United States' population was just over 123 million; by the end of World War II the population had grown to 140 million and in 1950 it had increased to 152 million. Per capita annual income had increased from $927 in 1940 to $1,383 in 1950.

Economic performance during the 1950s, however, varied considerably. The rate of growth continued at the high annual rate of 4.7 percent in real terms in the first half of the decade, but then dropped sharply to 2.25 in the last five years after the Korean War. This volatility in economic growth was also evident in employment figures. The lowest unemployment figure (2.5 percent) was recorded in 1953. Joblessness doubled the following year and by the end of the decade settled at just over 4.3 percent. With a civilian labor force of almost 66 million, the potential for creating jobs was substantial. Unemployment persisted throughout this entire period, but two observations should be made: first, the 15-20 percent unemployment of the 1930s was never to return. Although unemployment rates fluctuated widely over the decade, the only major problem continued to be the very high rates of minority unemployment. Second, family income was increasingly based on multiple job-holders. This enabled many families to increase their overall income dramatically so that despite the slow overall growth, consumption and the appearance of affluence were widespread.

The best authority on wealth and income distribution during this affluent decade was Robert Lampman. Lampman found for the 1950s that there had been some reduction in income inequality since the 1920s, though by no means had the New Deal altered the basic shape of the income pyramid. In the United States income and personal wealth were highly concentrated at the top. Lampman pointed out that the individuals in the top 1 percent held 25 percent of the wealth, and his summary elaborates the characteristics of the wealth-holding group:

> Thirty percent of the assets and equity of the personal sector of the economy in 1953 is assignable to the top wealth-holders, i.e. persons with $60,000 or more of estate tax wealth, who were 1.6 percent of the total adult population that year. The top groups owned at least 80 percent of the corporate stock held in the personal sector, virtually all of the state and local government bonds, nearly 90 percent of corporate bonds, and between 10 and 35 percent of each other type of property held in the personal sector in that year. . . .
>
> The top wealth-holder group, defined according to estate-tax requirements has varied in number and percent of the total population over the years. Also, their share of total wealth has varied. It appears, however, that the degree of inequality in wealth-holding increased from 1922 to 1929, fell to below the pre-1929 level in the 1930s, fell still more during the war and to 1949 and increased from 1949 to 1956. However, the degree of inequality was considerably lower in 1956 than in either 1929 or 1922. . . [1]

A leading exception to the general picture of declining inequality was, and remains, the ownership of corporate stock. The ownership of this particular type of asset appears to have become more concentrated over the same period. Figures from the Survey Research Center of the University of Michigan and the Federal Reserve Board confirmed these general parameters:

> . . . the highest 10 percent of income receivers (before federal income taxes) held 35 percent of the total liquid assets in 1950, and the lowest 50 percent of income receivers held 26 percent of all liquid assets. The pattern changed but little through the 1950s. In 1950, 47 percent of the spending units held liquid assets totaling less than $200 in early 1959, 45 percent held less than $200 of liquid assets. Approximately one unit in four had no liquid assets . . . . In terms of net worth (assets minus liabilities), in early 1953 the 11 percent of spending units worth $25,000 or more accounted for 61 percent of the aggregate net worth of $641 billion, whereas half of all such units accounted for only 6 percent of the aggregate.[2]

And poverty remained: in 1947, for example, 36 percent of all spending units had income before taxes of less than $2,000 but received only 12 percent of the total money incomes. "The relative position of the lower strata changed not at all in the 1950s, the 30 percent in the lowest bracket among spending units receiving 9 percent of total money income before taxes in 1950 and 1959. In 1959, 38 percent of all families and unattached individuals had incomes after personal income taxes of less than $4,000."[3] Most important, these data translated into the cost of goods and services in the 1950s meant straitened conditions for many millions of Americans. What emerged in the fifties was the inescapable fact that a hard core of poverty, particularly among the ghetto minorities, failed to respond to normal market mechanisms.

The two most critical indictments of American society's indifference to poverty in this period were John K. Galbraith's *The Affluent Society* (1958) and Michael Harrington's *The Other America* (1962). Galbraith pointed out the growing gap between private wealth and public poverty, and the resultant decline in the overall quality of life, but Harrington struck hard at the persistence of the core of poverty, despite the gains for many. Historians questioned Harrington's statistics on the number of poor; they are by most calculations far too high, but few doubted the sincerity of his emotional demands for social justice.

Poverty was and is often off the beaten track. It always has been. The ordinary tourist never left the main highway, and today he rides interstate turnpikes. He does not go into the valleys of Pennsylvania where the towns look like movie sets of Wales in the thirties. He does not see the company houses in rows, the rutted roads (the poor always have had inferior roads whether they live in city slums, in towns, or on farms), and for many of the poor everything is cramped and dirty. And even if he were to pass through such a place by accident, the tourist would not meet the unemployed men in the bar or the women coming home from a sweatshop.

The new permanent poverty emerged when millions of young people who dropped out of school, who faced raising children as single parents, and who simply could not cope with day-to-day problems, proved immune to the general progress of the society. When that happened, failure was clearly no longer individual and personal, but a product of social and economic forces. The new poverty destroyed economic freedom and seemed to be impervious to hope. This other America does not contain the adventurous seeking of new life and land. It is made up of street people, by old people suddenly confronted with the torments of loneliness and poverty, and by minorities ill-equipped to function in the modern world and facing a wall of prejudice, and by millions who cannot cope either with their own problems or those of the larger environment in which they live and are supposed to function.

The nation's economy, however, as measured by the gross national product, reached $320 billion in 1946, zoomed to $425 billion in 1953 with the Korean War, and by the end of the decade leveled off at $500 billion. These figures translated to a per capita income level of just under $2,000—an increase of almost two-thirds since the end of the Great Depression. Not all of this was real gain. The removal of wartime controls led to a postwar inflation that pushed the consumer price index (CPI) (1947–1949 = 100) from 76.9 in 1945 to 102.8 in 1948. After the outbreak of the Korean War, prices rose to 114.4 in 1953 and by the end of the decade the index was 126.4. This inflationary erosion of income, although serious, was not overwhelming. Americans would look back at the 1950s as a period when inflation was held within tolerable bounds.

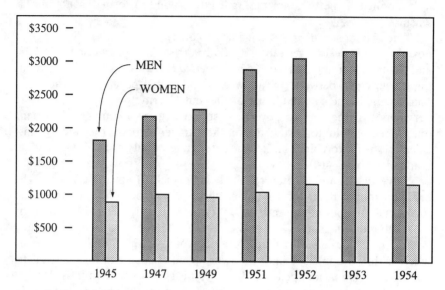

Figure 4.1 Median Income—Gross National Product, 1945–54

Source: Department of Commerce, Bureau of the Census

Table 4.1 United States Per Capita Income and Gross National Product, 1929–1952

	1929	1933	1940	1945	1949	1952
Gross National Product	103,828	55,670	101,443	215,210	258,229	347,956
National Income	87,355	39,584	81,347	182,691	216,259	291,629
Personal Income	85,127	46,629	78,347	171,927	205,867	269,660
Per Capita Disposable Income (dollars)	1,059	782	1,130	1,508	1,424	1,517

Source: *Statistical Abstract of the United States,* 1957.

THE MILITARY-INDUSTRIAL COMPLEX

Perhaps the most dramatic criticism of trends in the American economy during this entire postwar period was delivered by President Eisenhower in his farewell address:

> In the councils of government, we must guard against the acquisition of un-
> warranted influence, whether sought or not sought, by the military-

industrial complex. The potential for the disastrous rise of misplaced power exists and will persist. . . . Only an alert and knowledgeable citizen can compel the proper meshing of the huge industrial and military machinery of defense with our peaceful methods and goals, so that security and liberty may prosper together.[4]

The end of World War II did not bring worldwide peace; the commencement of the Cold War virtually guaranteed the continuation of large military budgets. The outbreak of the Korean War in 1950 and the launching of Sputnik in 1957 confirmed for many the necessity of maintaining a large and state-of-the-art military capability. The passage of the National Defense Education Act in 1958 to increase the number of engineers and scientists was a direct response to the success of Sputnik. Also the publication in 1958 of the prestigious report by the Committee on Economic Development (CED), *The Problem of National Security, Some Economic and Administrative As-*

Table 4.2	**Defense Spending Statistics, 1940–1980**				
	1940	**1950**	**1960**	**1970**	**1980**
Defense Funds for Research and Development (millions)	$469.3*	599.7	5,177.5	7,360.4	14,946.0
Defense Department Outlays (millions)	$9,055.3	39,544.0	92,223.4	78,300.0	136,000.0
Outlays for National Defense as Percentage of Total Federal Outlays	15.7	30.4	49.0	40.2	23.6

*1947 figure
Source: *Historical Statistics,* Series W, *Statistical Abstract*

Table 4.3	**Number of Retired Officers Employed by Major Corporations, 1958**
Boeing Airplane Co.	30
General Dynamics Corp.	54
General Electric Co.	35
General Tire & Rubber Co.	28
International Telephone and Telegraph Corp.	24
The Johns Hopkins University	16
Lockheed Aircraft Corp.	60
North American Aviation, Inc.	27
Radio Corp. of America	39
Raytheon Mfg. Co.	17

Source: *Congressional Record,* June 17, 1959, pg. 11044–11045. Statement by Senator Paul H. Douglas.

pects, which recommended an increase in defense spending as a necessary means to counter the Soviet bloc, was widely noted in Washington. The CED report acknowledged that providing for national security would be expensive. From 1955 to 1957 national security expenditures averaged 11 percent of our gross national product, as compared with a little over 1 percent in the thirties.

> Fear that a high defense burden will weaken the economy has been exaggerated and should not be decisive in the determination of the size of a defense budget representing 10 to 15 percent of the gross national product, or even more. There is no factual basis for the notion that we are within reach of, or exceeding, some "breaking point" beyond which tax-financed expenditures will critically impair economic growth. *We can afford what we have to afford.*[5]

If the CED represented a no-holds-barred attitude toward defense spending, Eisenhower's warning of the unwarranted influence of the military-industrial complex voiced concern about the potential consequences. The Second World War had concentrated the military procurement, production, and delivery systems among several large companies. Acquiring defense contracts had become quite profitable for many corporations, which also saw their work as a public obligation to help in the defense of the country. Permanent links of mutual benefit had been forged between the Pentagon and several Fortune 500 companies. After World War II the armed forces had been quickly sent home, but it was decided that a very large officer corps should remain intact in the event that quick military action was needed. Not surprisingly, this group lobbied for the maintenance and expansion of a large defense capability. Much of the media was sympathetic to the idea of vigorous national security. And many Congressmen and Senators found defense funds a welcome contribution to the economies of their district. It was this hardening of the system of special interests that concerned the outgoing President. The persistent problems raised by the existence of the military-industrial complex were to plague the 1960s and to dominate the 1970s and 1980s, but very little in fact was done except from time to time to raise the issue as a growing threat to the values of a democratic society.

The emergence of this military-industrial complex deserves more careful attention for its impact on the American economy. Professor Seymour Melman argued in *The Permanent War Economy* that "this consensus on the economic benefits of military spending has played a vital role in marshalling the commitment of the American people to a permanent war economy."[6] And he continues:

> By the 1950s a cross-society political consensus had developed around war economy. Businessmen, industrial workers, engineers, government employees, intellectuals all joined in the confident assessment that war economy on a sustained basis was not only viable but economically desirable. From the

standpoint of national leaders, using military spending to ensure prosperity seemed like a politician's dream boat; there is something here for everybody—or so it is made to appear.[7]

This echoes a memorable instance that occurred in 1958 when Virginia congressman Carl Vinson, chairman of the House Armed Services Committee, submitted a military public-works bill of about a billion dollars, saying to his colleagues, "My friends, there is something in this bill for every member." The spending proposals in the bill were enumerated by each state so that every congressman could see the benefits that would accrue to his constituents.

The Korean War provides a good example of this growing dependency on defense spending. In June 1950, the unemployment rate stood at 5.2 percent of the civilian labor force (3.4 million people). With the commitment of American troops by President Truman on June 29 and the rapid expenditures of funds for military needs, the unemployment rate began to fall. By 1951, unemployment stood at 3 percent, and by October 1953 it had fallen to 1.8 percent of the civilian labor force. By then, only 1,162,000 were unemployed, the lowest number in the entire postwar period. The injections of federal funds into the economy were substantial and significant. Cash payments for the military rose $3.3 billion in the second half of 1950. In 1951 the increases were even greater, leaping from $15 billion to $24 billion. In all sectors of the economy, consumers, businesses, and the government rushed to stockpile materials, resulting in overall shortages and price increases. The gross national product rose by almost $29 billion in the second half of

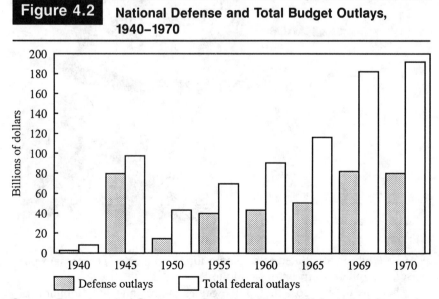

Figure 4.2 **National Defense and Total Budget Outlays, 1940–1970**

Source: Department of Commerce, *Statistical Abstract of the United States,* 1970

Figure 4.3 The Military—Industrial Complex

"It's The Multiple Head Re-Entry Principle"

1950—$10 billion attributed to consumption, $8 billion to government purchases, $11 billion to inventory buildup.[8]

The Korean War cost the United States approximately $22 billion directly and an additional $50 billion in military-related expenditures. During this three-year conflict, the connections between large corporations and military procurement were much in evidence. The Joint Committee on Defense Production in 1954 noted that basic steel production had increased from 100 million tons to 124 million tons; aluminum production doubled; electric power capacity rose from 69 million kilowatts to 103 million kilowatts; petroleum refining capacity rose from 5.4 million barrels of crude to 8 million barrels; the chemical industry increased its capital equipment by $5 billion; and shipments of machine tools quadrupled in the three years after the Korean War.[9]

Significantly, the overlap of military and corporate personnel became a lasting feature of the military-industrial complex. Given the advantages of a private market system, these linkages were inevitable. No one really wanted a nationalized armaments industry because the complex and sophisticated nature of modern war required a dynamism that a state-directed operation could not provide. Still it is surprising that Congress has not acted decisively to monitor and regulate the flow of early-retiring military personnel into the defense companies with whom they had worked during their active careers. For more than three decades retired officers have found second careers as consultants, paid executives, or board members. This easy rite of passage has never been adequately controlled. A simple remedy would be a substantial time-delay requirement such as the Internal Revenue Service demands before its personnel can work in tax-related businesses. Perhaps a limited degree of tolerance for the old-boy network in defense procurement industries exists as long as use of the network does not become excessive.

The emergence of the military-industrial complex underscored a more basic change in the entire nature of government spending. Before the New Deal, the federal budget was only a small portion of the gross national product. The New Deal hesitantly pushed government spending into higher percentages. The Second World War and the postwar period reinforced the trend of federal budgets that were large both in the aggregate and as a percentage of GNP. Almost inadvertently, Americans took to heart in the 1950s and 1960s the Keynesian axiom that government spending is the vital ingredient for maintaining a thriving economy with low unemployment. Lavish defense spending thus became an unquestioned assumption in macroeconomic planning for Eisenhower and his successors.

THE UNITED STATES AND THE INTERNATIONAL ECONOMY

World War II had altered not only the world, but even more so the role of the United States in that world. The range of changes the country faced were unusually large, complex, and nettlesome. Militarily and economically the United States had emerged as the world's greatest power. With the arrival of the Cold War, the United States accepted not only the obligation to protect militarily the western world, but also to bolster foreign economic strength in order to prevent the Soviet Union from subverting established governments. In this regard, global strategy and economic policy went together as the fun-

Figure 4.4 United States Merchandise Exports and Imports, 1928–1960

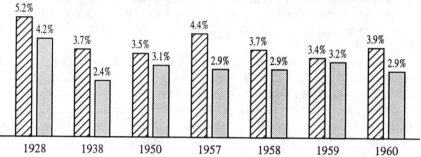

U.S. Exports and Imports as Percent of U.S. Total Product (GNP)

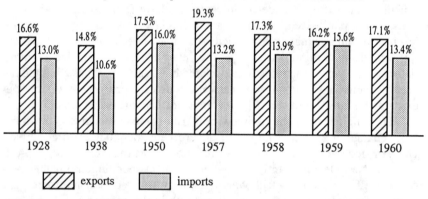

U.S. Exports and Imports as Percent of Total World Trade

exports imports

Note:—U.S. exports include re-exports and exclude military shipments; world exports exclude those of U.S.S.R., Eastern Europe, and mainland China; U.S. imports are general imports.

Source: *Conference on Economic Progress*

damental basis for specific programs. The Marshall Plan was designed to help in the reconstruction of western Europe. In that winter (1946–47) before Marshall's great speech in Cambridge, Massachusetts, Americans were dreadfully afraid that France might go Communist. No one in Washington took comfort any longer in the so-called Morgenthau Plan which was to have stripped Germany of its industrial strength so that, like Carthage, it would never again wage war. Elsewhere in Europe economic conditions were very bad. Fortunately the Marshall Plan would soon provide both the incentive and the resources for a quick recovery.

The formation of the World Bank and the International Monetary Fund in 1944 at Bretton Woods (they became operational at the end of that decade) was part of the emerging influence of the United States in international affairs. As part of U.S. policy, the Export-Import Bank issued credits with

Table 4.4	Estimated Supply of Goods and Dollars by the United States Government to Foreign Countries, 1959

Item	$(millions)
Military transfers of goods and services under grants	1,998
Military expenditures of U.S. government abroad	3,090
Net non-military unilateral transfers to foreign countries	1,839
U.S. government net long-term capital outflow	358
Shipments of U.S. surplus farm products abroad under Public Law 480	927
Total	8,202

Source: Vatter, *The U.S. Economy in the 1950s*, 266–267.

growing frequency. Substantial grants of direct aid also increased, though most funds were earmarked for military purposes, with only small amounts for economic development.

Despite the many positive accomplishments of U.S. economic programs, more could have been done. So great was our concern for the security of democratic government in western Europe that most aid went to these countries. The developing world, or Third World as it came to be called, was largely neglected, and food programs such as P.L. 480 (discussed at greater length later on) were more a boost to American farmers than they were to nations like Burma or Israel, where the "free" agricultural goods from the United States tended to distort the market allocation of resources within these economies. The greatest barrier to more effective and enlightened programs was the long tradition of pushing American goods for export. Not only was this notion popular, but it also appealed to many representatives in Congress. The New Deal program of tariff reduction and reciprocal trade agreements remained the basis of U.S. economic policy, but as soon as any domestic industry faltered or recession threatened, protectionism returned. Given the many special interest groups favoring some kind of protectionism, it is remarkable that the United States was so successful in implementing programs such as the World Bank, the IMF, and the Marshall Plan. Newer organizations and conventions also flourished, notably the General Agreement on Tariffs and Trade (GATT), founded in 1948, and the European Economic Community (EEC) in 1959. The creation of the GATT organization was a very major achievement, since it broadened bilateral agreements into international accords simply by extending these agreements to all countries with most favored nation status. Originally GATT was a brief document that came out of the meetings in 1948 of all the major trading countries in the free world. It had been intended as a temporary agreement which would stand until the preliminary charter of the International Trade Organization (ITO), which had been drawn up in Havana in 1947 during a conference sponsored by the United Nations, was ratified by Congress. That body rejected the ITO, however, because some of its clauses were seen as threats to national sovereignty. However, the most important commercial policy provisions of this charter were carried over into GATT. Since GATT was a trade agreement and not a treaty, it therefore did not have to be ratified by Congress. In 1948, the GATT organization included only nineteen member countries; by 1971, the number had grown to eighty, and today it includes virtually all major countries that participate in international trade.

GATT encouraged free trade on a worldwide basis by reducing tariffs and import-licensing restraints, and by adopting the principle of nondiscrimination between trading partners. GATT also provided means for settling trade disputes. Member nations moreover agreed to abolish quantitative barriers to trade such as quotas. Since the first rounds of meetings in 1948, tariffs and trade barriers indeed have been greatly reduced, a policy much in keeping with the announced goals of the United States. The range of tariff cuts by the United States has been so substantial that for most items tariffs per se are no longer a great issue, though new forms of protectionism such as bilateral agreements and "voluntary" restraints have become very fashionable. The list of industries in the United States that are still protected includes steel, textiles, ships, cars, sugar, dairy products, and military equipment, which altogether account for perhaps as much as one-third of all trade items.

An examination of the trade statistics and balance of payments for the 1950s illustrates the fluctuations of the United States' position in the international economy. Throughout the decade the United States ran surpluses on both the merchandise and current account totals and consistent deficits in the balance of payments as both the government and private companies exported large amounts of capital abroad. This decade was the beginning of large-scale United States multinational investment abroad, especially in western Europe, which was just entering its postwar surge in the acquisition of consumer goods. American companies expanded their facilities, bought European businesses cheaply, or established new facilities, such as the subsidiary of an American soap company which set up a new detergent factory in northern Italy. As the United States accumulated these current deficits, other countries were able to restore their depleted gold reserves and build up their foreign exchange balances. Some of this financial recovery provided the basis for the expanded trade of the next decade. Relative to other currencies, the dollar increased in value and became dominant. Great Britain, bankrupted by the war, had been given a loan by the United States of $3.75 billion in 1950, but attached to the loan was the condition of making the pound convertible with the dollar. Within six weeks, the British pound had plummeted, devalued from $4.03 to $2.80. Only the dollar remained as a stable currency. Nevertheless Marshall Plan dollars not only aided British recovery but the restoration of all Western Europe; the U.S. commitment to accept large amounts of imports quickened the postwar European economic revival. By the same token, the developing world shared only modestly in this resurgence and remained a secondary consideration in American strategy and aid. Observers pointed out that the perceived Soviet threat to western Europe motivated in part American largess. Clearly U.S. public programs were coordinated with its trade policy: in the first part of the decade public outlays were large; in the second half, private outflows rose as government payments diminished.

In addition to these general policies, the government expanded the resources of the Export-Import Bank, which lent over $4.3 billion during this decade. Ex-Im credits could be used to purchase only United States goods; this stipulation was a boon for a small number of large corporations that produced "big-ticket" items. Western Europe received $1.1 billion, and Latin America received $1.5 billion of Ex-Im funds. Of smaller consequence was a number of guaranteed private investment programs for less-developed countries that had been spelled out in President Truman's inaugural address as part of the Point Four program. Not until 1956, however, when the Mutual Security Act made these guarantees more flexible, were there any sizable investments, but in 1958 and 1959 almost $.5 billion in guarantees had been issued and over $1 billion more was pending.

The Korean War also intensified government military payments to Western European allies and to Japan, and the $2.4 billion spent over a seven-year period (1953–1960) further stimulated American payments abroad. This enlarged U.S. role in foreign trade, coupled with a desire to liberalize world exchange, did not come effortlessly. Again and again there was backsliding. In renewing the Trade Agreements Act in 1951, Congress restored the "peril point" provision, i.e., no duty could be reduced if it threatened serious injury to a domestic industry. The addition of such escape clauses was common. If a reduction in rates had caused damage, the previous tariff rates came back. In 1955 and 1958, escape clauses were added to legislation in order to prevent damage to national security. Another measure stipulated that 50 percent of foreign-aid goods had to be shipped in American merchant vessels. Numerous "buy-American" provisos were imbedded in government contract regulations. Still the decade witnessed a substantial decrease in tariffs and a large increase in the volume of foreign trade. Those advocates of "trade not aid" were not merely hoping to protect American exports; they hoped to foster a thriving international economy.

Politically the great achievement of this period was the emergence of the North Atlantic Treaty Organization's (NATO) alliance structure; the counterpart of this in economic strategy was the formation of the Common Market. The European Economic Community (EEC, now known as the EC) was both a common goal of Europeanists such as French Commissioner of Planning Jean Monnet and Foreign Minister Robert Schuman and compatible with United States policy. In 1952, under the Paris Treaty, European planners had put together the European Coal and Steel Community (ECSC). Its success encouraged a more comprehensive system for a unified Europe. After very long negotiations, the Treaty of Rome, which established the EEC, was signed at the beginning of 1958. Both Monnet and Schuman believed that the customs union was only the first step in the forging of some federative organization, a United States of Europe; it may well have been that fear of the loss of political sovereignty was responsible for the formation of the rival European Free Trade Associates (EFTA—member nations were Austria, Finland, Iceland, Britain, Norway, Portugal, Sweden, Switzerland) as a second organization of economic cooperation. Great Britain had been an observer at the EEC talks but did not join. It, however, sponsored creation of the EFTA.

The European Community first consisted of the Inner Six: the Benelux countries (Belgium, Luxembourg, and the Netherlands), France, Italy, and West Germany. In 1973, the entry of Denmark, the United Kingdom, and the Republic of Ireland raised the number to nine; with Greece in 1981 the number became ten, and Portugal and Spain in 1985 have brought the total to twelve. In addition to the dozen full-time members, there are associate affiliations of various kinds. In 1967, after its first decade, the Common Market represented a population of approximately 172 million people with a gross national product of approximately $170 billion and had become an important recipient of American goods and business investment.

The formation of the Common Market suited American interests. NATO guaranteed the allied defense of Europe; H.R. 9900, the Trade Agreement Extension Act of 1958, was a major legislative overhaul of trade policy. The European Community provided a cooperative free-trade structure not only for the internal trade of Western Europe but also for U.S. exports. Within the common EEC zone, all barriers to the free movements of goods, capital, and labor would gradually be eliminated; this ultimate goal may well be attained very soon.

Although it has not made any substantial movement toward political union, the EC has its own monetary system and has become more and more important in trade and currency within Europe and the entire trading world. The organization has fostered the emergence of large integrated European companies which have given Western Europe renewed competitive strength both in U.S. and world markets. Restoring the economic health and vigor of the continent so crucial to the United States, the EC has been an enormous success.[10]

AGRICULTURE

In general, the postwar period was good for American farmers. The end of the 1950s brought windfall gains to agriculture from inflation, much like similar gains in the stock market. In 1960, the same land base had increased fourfold in value since 1940. Yet much of this gain could be realized only by sale of land; rising interest rates, higher taxes, and lower farm earnings were beginning to foreshadow the difficulties of the 1960s and beyond.

The great trends of the 1950s were the reorganization of United States agriculture and the wider recognition of agriculture as a business. To many observers, the axe was about to fall on the small family farmer, who would be swallowed up by corporate agricultural business grants. In retrospect, however, the 1950s was a period in which the secular changes that had been transpiring for decades in American agriculture continued, but at an accel-

Table 4.5 **Number and Size of United States Farms 1920–1975**

	Millions of units	Avg acreage per farm
1920	6.454	149
1925	6.372	145
1930	6.295	157
1935	6.812	155
1940	6.102	175
1945	5.859	195
1950	5.388	216
1955	5.654	158
1960	3.962	297
1965	3.356	340
1970	2.954	373
1975	2.767	391/427
		(USDA definition change)

Source: *Historical Statistics,* Series k4 and k7, and *Statistical Abstract of the United States* 1980, p. 686.

erated pace. The problems of price, production, and government supports were handled in many of the traditional ways. Agribusiness, defined as the integration of food and fiber production and distribution, and corporate agriculture, which includes the incorporation of farms and farm operations, both emerged as trial forms on a small scale. Some agribusiness operations were short-lived. Contract agriculture, in which a farmer produces for a single buyer under an agreement, had a longer history and continued slowly to increase in importance. More significant than these changes, as the statistics demonstrate, had been the exodus of the farm population from the rural areas. The increased social tensions in the 1950s of such northern cities as Detroit and New York City resulted from the influx of refugees from the depleted and unattractive agricultural system of the Deep South; the thousands who moved were very good analysts of opportunity costs and benefits.

A technological revolution in postwar agriculture resulted in productivity gains of almost 6 percent a year for the decade. In other words agricultural productivity nearly doubled in just under twelve years. These changes, exacerbated by worldwide agricultural conditions, were fundamental to the development and evolution of farm policy during this decade.

Mechanized farm equipment became universal and often specialized for particular farming needs. Seeds and animals were increasingly manipulated biologically and genetically to produce more abundant yields and bigger, healthier breeds. Pesticides and herbicides, such as DDT, which was the first hydrocarbon, and 2-4-D, developed out of wartime research, became cheap and were widely used; they increased productivity dramatically. Drugs such as penicillin, developed during the war as an antibiotic, became available for agricultural uses. Turkey growers, for instance, could administer antibiotics to prevent high death rates in immature birds. Specialized crop production became widespread; long practiced in American agriculture, growing exotic items became the only way for many farmers to survive.

The fifties brought enormous changes to the American dinner table. Most agricultural products were increasingly subject to expensive processing as consumers demanded more convenience foods. McDonald's became the single largest purchaser of beef. While potatoes fell in price, oranges rose. To some foreign observers, the American need to start the day with orange juice came close to a religious necessity. Though our forebears ate large quantities of bread, we began to eat far less. These dietary changes had significant impact on agriculture; the greatest policy problems involved the six traditional basic crops—corn, cotton, wheat, tobacco, rice, and peanuts—all of which were affected by the revolution in productivity, declines in domestic consumption, and vulnerability to world market price swings.

In 1959 the *Economic Report of the President* appraised the agricultural price support system. It repeated what was well-known to most economists. The price support mechanisms aided only a minority of farmers, particularly those who produced the major crops. Most farmers, who admittedly produced only a small part of the total crop value, received only little or no support from the elaborately constructed government payment structure.

A new crop of agricultural legislation flourished in the late 1940s and 1950s. In 1948 and 1949, the Agricultural Acts attempted to diminish rigid price support in favor of a plan that would be more flexible in relation to supply; the 1949 Act also introduced a "modernized" parity formula that kept the 1910–1914 base, but also added an up-to-date individual price index (based on the previous ten years). The Truman presidency and the Democratic Congress all favored a policy of high price supports tied to an effort to limit production.

The most innovative approach during this period was the Brannan Plan, discussed earlier in Chapter 3. Although Brannan was able to get support for increasing farm exports, Congress rejected the notion of compensating farmers for the perishable farm goods. Surpluses continued to build up, and in the case of perishable farm goods, loss was extensive.

The Korean War stopped only momentarily the problem of carryover surpluses. Rigid price guarantees set at 90 percent of parity made the Commodity Credit Corporation (CCC) the biggest consumer of wheat in the world; in 1956, it held $8.3 billion of surplus. When farmers voted, they chose to sustain production quotas, 90 percent price supports, and in some cases per farm acreage allotments. Flexible price supports remained largely a token goal. In practice, the old ways held, and output restriction was not achieved. Farmers, at least those with large farms, had come to believe that their prosperity was linked to price supports, to production planning, and to marketing quotas. Agriculture continued its drift away from market forces and towards greater control by the federal government.

Plans to dispose of farming surplus ranged from an expanded food lunch program to P.L. 480, the Agricultural Trade Development and Assistance Act of 1954, which gave large amounts of surplus foods to friendly foreign countries. The latter plan did not succeed in reducing agricultural surpluses significantly. Because the supply could not be reduced drastically and on a continuing basis, surpluses continued to grow. In 1956, the Soil Bank Act provided a schedule of payments to farmers for acreage not planted and a generous long-term payment contract to farmers who transferred crop land to a conservation reserve. The first part of this scheme, the acreage reserve plan, was withdrawn after two years as a failure, but farmers dumped an estimated 28.7 million acres of inferior land into the conservation reserve.

Agriculture was in a precarious state by the end of the 1950s. Not one of its major problems—overproduction, instability of farm income, falling prices, rising costs, loss of foreign markets—was closer to a solution. And the 1960s would bring renewed stress.

FISCAL AND MONETARY POLICY

In many ways the decade of the 1950s was a return to fiscal and budgetary normality. Neither the legislation nor the policies of the Federal Reserve System produced anything more than an unimaginative, conservative public policy. The modest growth record of the fifties clearly reflected these conservative objectives of government policy. On the other hand, inflation was kept within reasonable bounds and unemployment stayed well within the single-digit range.

A steady budget was a principal policy objective, and much lip service was given to slowing its growth rate and decreasing the public debt. Each administration called for the elimination of "waste" in government, but no major budgetary or organizational curtailments were put into place. Government policymakers hoped for a return to a situation where private investment and unregulated market mechanisms determined the overall direction of the economy. Conventional wisdom sanctioned a balanced budget, thus conflicting with the post–New Deal Keynesian philosophy that encouraged a long-term gradual rise in the federal budget as a means to achieve full employment. The Korean War provided economic stimulation during the first part of the decade, but growth slowed considerably for the remaining six years as conservatism reigned. Federal Reserve policy throughout this decade was highly traditional, seeking first to control inflation to the detriment of other goals such as reducing unemployment and encouraging growth.

Business prospered during this decade despite higher overall taxes, particularly the reinstitution of the 52 percent corporate profits tax during the Korean War. The return on invested capital in the decade compared favorably with the return on capital during the 1920s. Yet neither monetary policy, nor the rate of business profits, nor a shortage of capital seems sufficient to explain the modest level of capital investment. During the Korean War government expenditures encouraged a surge in capital investment, but as the effect of these infusions subsided so did business investment; the ex-

Table 4.6 U.S. Federal Fiscal and Monetary Statistics, 1949–1960 (figures in billions of dollars)

Year	Receipts	Expenditures	Surplus or Deficit	Public Deficit
1949	41.6	40.6	1.0	252.6
1950	40.9	43.1	-2.2	256.9
1951	53.4	45.8	7.6	255.3
1952	68.0	68.0	–	259.1
1953	71.5	76.8	-5.3	266.0
1954	69.7	70.9	-1.2	270.8
1955	65.5	68.5	-3.0	274.4
1956	74.5	70.5	4.1	272.8
1957	80.0	76.7	3.2	272.4
1958	79.6	82.6	-2.9	279.7
1959	79.2	92.1	-12.9	287.8
1960	92.5	92.2	.3	290.9

Source: *Historical Statistics of the United States.*

pansions between 1955 and 1957 and in 1958 were each smaller by comparison. The 1950s, especially the final years of the decade, saw few new significant consumer innovations that might have provided the stimulus to investment.

If business prospered, especially those firms affiliated with the military-industrial complex, social welfare suffered. Welfare-type transfer payments dropped a full 1 percent of national income (5.3 percent to 4.3 percent) over the period; moreover these federal grants were increasingly shifted from welfare to aid for highways and airports. An exception to this decline in welfare allocations was the Social Security extensions in 1954, 1956, and 1958 which increased benefits and extended coverage. The attack on poverty had to wait for the initiatives of the 1960s.

The attempt to contain the national debt also came to naught. The stationary limit of $275 billion could not be held, and the debt increased to almost $300 billion by the end of the decade. Interest charges on the debt also rose substantially. In 1960 they totaled $7.2 billion or 14 percent of the federal budget.

Monetary policy in the 1950s was determined by the accord reached between the Federal Reserve Board and the Treasury in March 1951. In general that agreement limited the Fed to control over the discount rate, open market operations, and changes in the reserve ratios. For the Fed these indirect measures of control were in line with its own philosophy. The agreement had allowed it to free itself from the pegged interest rate policy that had severely limited its action. Given its fear of inflation and lacking direct control over prices, the Fed adopted and held to a tight, even slightly restrictive, monetary policy. Almost exclusively the Fed raised or lowered the discount rate in exercising its major control function. Prices in general rose, but probably less than if the Fed had not acted to shrink the quantity of money.

Housing and consumer credit as well as business investments were influenced by Federal Reserve policy, or the lack of it. After 1955, residential housing was negatively affected by Federal Reserve Policy because other investments appeared more attractive than government-underwritten mortgages. Consumer credit, on the other hand, expanded rapidly during almost the entire decade as the Fed sat on the sidelines. The stability of interest rates plus a heated demand for durables by consumers made consumer debt rise from $21.8 billion in 1950 to $56.1 billion by the end of the decade.

Of crucial importance to the health of the economy was the level and rate of business investment in plants and equipment. We have already mentioned the powerful drive in business expansion during the Korean War. A second wave of investments occurred between 1955 and 1957 which included a boom in residential construction, expansion in plants and equipment, and a rise in the demand for military hardware. The third wave of business expansions from 1958 to mid-1960 seemed the weakest and anticipated the low growth rates of the early 1960s. The announced goals of the Fed that came out of the accord with the Treasury in 1951 were repeated by William McChesney Martin in 1960:

> the most constructive contribution monetary policy can make to the vigorous, healthy growth of the economy in the present circumstances is to maintain confidence in the value of money, and thus encourage people to save and invest...[11]

Renewed inflationary pressure flared up sporadically during the 1950s. Still these increases were far less than the explosion of prices after the precipitate removal of controls in 1946. The first jump in prices at the onset of the Korean War were related to military demands, but the second after 1955 was related to the increase in the velocity of money rather than an increase in the money supply; the Fed's conservative policies saw to it that the latter would not be allowed to expand. Specifically the second wave of price hikes was propelled by cost increases in steel, automobiles, and other related industries. Characteristically, oligopolistic industries chose to pass on their increases to the consumer in the form of higher prices. Consequently the mid-1950s saw the beginnings of those mischievous practices that made the consumer the ultimate victim as big business and big labor settled their differences and then stuck the general public with the bill. It was a prelude to the inflation of the next two decades.

BIG BUSINESS IN A DECADE OF PROSPERITY

In 1948, the Federal Trade Commission voiced concerns over a growing business practice and an increasing threat to small business:

> Conglomerate acquisitions are those in which there is little or no discernible relation between the business of the purchasing and the acquired firm. Of

all the types of mergers, the reasons for this particular form of acquisition are the most difficult to ascertain.... The motives underlying conglomerate acquisitions appear to include such diverse incentives as desires to spread risks, to invest large sums of idle liquid capital, to add products which can be handled with existing sales and distribution personnel, to increase the number of products which can be grouped together in the company's advertisements, etc.

But in addition to these factors, there is present in most conglomerate acquisitions a simple drive to obtain greater economic power. With the economic power which it secures through its operations in many diverse fields, the giant conglomerate corporation may attain an almost impregnable economic position.[12]

Three major developments in the history of American business occurred in the 1950s: changes within mature industries such as automobiles and steel; the emergence of the postwar conglomerates; and the regional shift in business locations. The decade on the whole was profitable for business, although by no means a period of boom. Government spending spurred all of these significant changes. Some of these increased outlays were related to the Korean War but a much greater reason for these government outlays was the interest in sustaining the burgeoning military-industrial complex. Most of all, however, the collective wisdom of big business had the notion that the federal government should and would assume responsibility for maintaining a stable economic environment. Business came to believe that the era of violent cyclical fluctuations was a thing of the past.

In the 1950s business grew larger, that is, individual business firms grew bigger. Growth was most rapid in the service sectors, most notably in finance, insurance, real estate, and contract construction. The traditional sectors of agriculture, mining, and heavy industry grew very marginally or declined. The five leading manufacturing industries at the end of the decade were chemicals, aircraft, motor vehicles, steel, and electronics.[13]

Big steel and the automobile industry best represented the industries whose troubles began in the 1950s and were destined to continue over the next three decades. To economists, big steel was a classic example of a mature oligopoly; its exercise of market power determined its decisions on production and price. Instead of streamlined efficiencies, new investments in plants, or increased research and development, steel could improve its return, even after absorbing larger-than-average wage increases and rising cost per unit of output, because of its dominance of the market. Administered prices and, in the case of big steel, price leadership could do all this. Only after persistent criticism by President Truman did big steel begin to enlarge its production capacity (50 percent over the decade) but some of this was eroded by the industry's pattern of operating at less than full capacity. Advanced processes in steel production were adopted only slowly by the industry. Big steel's reckoning came when it found itself ill-equipped to meet the competition of Japanese steel imports, which had been produced since the mid-fifties under more modern technologies at lower costs. By 1985, IBM's sales alone would surpass those of the entire steel industry.[14]

In 1961, the Kennedy administration had a classic confrontation with big steel from which the industry never recovered. What appeared as a temporary decline in the demand for steel in the 1950s became a chronic symptom for a permanently declining industry. In some cases, steel was replaced by new materials, especially plastics. Fewer rails and bridge supports were needed; demand increased for different kinds of steel—lighter steels, stainless steels—and the smaller steel companies could more quickly and easily adapt to these growing markets. In a sense, the 1950s was the golden era of big steel. The future was to be much harsher.

The American automobile industry also lost its glamor in this decade. In the years immediately following the end of the Second World War, the demand for cars soared, and long waiting lists and gray markets developed. But this surge was mostly catch-up from wartime deprivations. By the 1950s the auto industry also was a mature oligopoly, heavily bureaucratized and more attuned to stylistic gimmickry than serious innovation. Overconfident that Americans would buy only American cars, it failed to see the appeal of imported foreign compacts that began to arrive in the form of the dreaded "Beetle" produced by Volkswagen. What distinguished the Beetle from the typical Detroit product was not only its size and shape, but its inherent better quality; this too foreshadowed the future. Within the industry, the weeding out of old names continued: Nash-Kelvinator merged with Hudson to become American Motors, which then produced its most successful car, the Rambler. Studebaker merged with Packard, but this new company would not survive the decade as an effective competitor, nor would Kaiser Motors, a short-lived attempt of the Kaiser family to duplicate its extraordinary success in wartime production and profit making. General Motors and Ford bestrode the auto world like colossi, but Chrysler was already sowing the seeds of its collapse by producing poor quality cars. Despite these signs of decline, the U.S. automobile industry still "was one of the pattern-setters in wage bargaining; and its wage and price policies, plant location decisions, investment programs, and level of employment were of deep import to all persons and all levels of government."[15] But as plants and equipment became older and outmoded, foreign car sales would soar.

Over the next several decades, business journals and newspapers would describe the emergence of a new form of merger and a type of business-empire builder that challenged conventional ways of doing business. The rise of these new folktales and heroes enlightened the literature of money-making in the postwar era. The rise of Litton, Textron, Grace, General Dynamics, Teledyne, LTV, to name but a few, had several common ingredients. All of them were the creation of powerful, charismatic, mercurial business gunslingers who believed that the key to success was exotic and decisive management style. A 'good' or 'great' manager could successfully manage any business; ergo find a business that somehow was a good buy, such as a firm with undervalued assets, and buy it by leveraging these assets. The new addition became part of the overall corporate structure whether or not the new acquisition had any organic or industrial link to what the parent company made or did. For many reasons, United States companies were frequently undervalued, and these new "robber barons" could zero in on a company and swallow it whole. Business observers of the fifties admired these new giants, while those of the 1960s came to distrust them. Recently experts have raised serious questions whether this type of merger or acquisition contributes anything to the strengths of the business system. But this raiding process, begun in the fifties, has generated much speculation and excitement.

The sixties would be the golden age of the conglomerate builders, but the progenitor, Royal Little, who built his empire in the fifties, showed the way. The rise and decline of his Textron conglomerate was a minor saga in the history of the postwar world; there would be more glamorous conglomerates and even bigger failures. What Little did was exploit loopholes in the tax-law structure (in his case balancing tax losses against profits) that could be used for leverage by one company for acquiring another at little or no real cost. Little's experience was in textiles, specifically rayon back in the 1920s, but the postwar period gave him many opportunities to expand. Three times with only moderate success he attempted to build textile manufacturing empires. His discovery of the mother lode and the successful transformation of Textron from textiles to a conglomerate came with his discovery that for success, especially on Wall Street, there need be no connection between the hodge-podge of companies within a conglomerate industry. Indeed, textiles vanished as a part of the overall conglomerate that Royal Little finally put together. Under that big tent, Textron made watchbands (Spiedel), work shoes (Weinbrenner), golf carts (E-Z Go Car), optical products (Shiron), cruise ships (SS *Leilani*), helicopters (Bell), and more than a dozen other products. Little was described glowingly as a postwar "wonder man of American business . . . [and] one of the more innovative entrepreneurs on the scene today." In the nineteenth century, men built railroads without money, and in the 1950s Little taught this lesson anew. Without money but with imagination and cleverness, great conglomerate empires could be assembled.

ORGANIZED LABOR AT MID-CENTURY

Organized labor's history in the 1950s is bounded by two major pieces of legislation: the Taft-Hartley Act (1949), discussed earlier, and the Labor-Management Reporting and Disclosure Act (1959), also known as the Landrum-Griffin Act. In a sense, they track the changing position of organized labor in what clearly was a difficult decade.

Broadly, certain issues stand out. Organized labor used the strike as a weapon to maintain and enhance its position and power, and paid for its intransigence a substantial price in antiunion legislation on both the state and federal levels. Union power as measured by membership peaked in 1956 and eroded substantially over the decade. Nonunionized labor became an increasingly important component of the work force. The union movement failed to produce new aggressive leadership and became more security-minded. It also failed to organize workers in new industries at the very time when the traditional heavy industries were receding in economic importance.

The AFL and CIO merged in 1955, but this reintegration was a defensive strategy, not a move that evidenced new vigor. The union movement was tarnished by accusations of Communist infiltration, as well as internal mismanagement, dishonesty of officials, and corruption. Eleven unions were purged by the CIO in 1957; however admirable the catharsis, organized labor suffered noticeably for this internal upheaval. The corruption within the Teamsters Union became a household topic. But most of all, the empathy and enthusiasm that marked the emergence of free collective bargaining under the New Deal as a major advance in the spread of individual democracy gave way to governmental bureaucratic control and much public hostility. As the public image of capitalists ballooned because of their wartime successes in production and profit, respect for organized labor dropped, and the historical tradition of adversarial relations between capital and organized labor came again to the fore.

Although organized labor had branded the Taft-Hartley Act as the "slave-labor act," the issues that confronted organized labor in the fifties were far more extensive than those posed by this piece of legislation. To be sure, Taft-Hartley restricted union organizations and tightened certain procedures regarding the individual worker's relationship to the union. Nevertheless the great problems came from basic changes in American industry, from the regional shifts in the locations of industry and populations and the increase of nonunion labor. Three-fourths of all union members were in manufacturing, mining, construction, and transportation. Labor employed by government, however, rose to 50 percent by the end of the decade, encompassing 16 percent of total civilian employees. Although many government workers would form public service unions, by no means were all government employees unionized. No one would contend that these unions of white collar workers were anything like the traditional groups such as the United Auto Workers or the United Mine Workers. In the fastest-growing sectors of the new service industries, unionism made only minor inroads. Local and state right-to-work laws, especially popular in agricultural states with little heavy industry or labor union history, reinforced these tendencies.

The shift to California, the Southwest, and parts of the South diffused further the strength of traditional unionism. Even during the Korean War, antilabor Southern senators and congressmen were strong vocal promoters of their regions for the large and lucrative military contracts which came from Washington. Fast food chains like McDonald's did not want union help, and nonunionized construction work undercut by substantial margins the high cost of unionized labor. Organized labor responded feebly to include these workers, but the problems connected with organizing service workers were of a different dimension than anything that had existed historically in union recruitment. The postwar world was rapidly moving away from traditional unionism.

Organized labor responded slowly to other major social changes. Most women workers remained outside union organizations in the fifties, and many craft unions traditionally rejected black membership. In 1959, the highly respected A. Phillip Randolph, president of the Brotherhood of Sleeping Car Porters, became head of the Negro American Labor Council to counteract these discriminatory practices.

Within labor's camps the rifts were great, and only necessity began to bring the AFL and CIO together. The passage of Taft-Hartley was evidence of the winds of change. The reasons which had led to the breakaway of the CIO in 1935 seemed less important in the 1950s. As early as 1953, the AFL and CIO had come to agreement that they would not raid each others' members. Two years later the AFL and CIO merged, or rather a much weakened CIO rejoined the AFL. The CIO was bloodied by the legislation that attacked Communist-dominated trade unions. Eleven unions left or were expelled within two years after passage of Taft-Hartley. When the CIO moved back into the fold, it was less than half the size of the AFL. By 1957, an additional million-and-a-half workers were either in independent or unaffiliated unions, with the nation's largest union, the Teamsters, expelled on charges linked to corruption. The bakery workers and the laundry workers, both large unions, remained outside of the AFL-CIO. Indeed, as organized labor mounted an impressive campaign to clean up its own house in the late 1950s, this effort convinced the public and the Congress that direct oversight of union affairs was necessary, leading to the passage of Landrum-Griffin Act of 1959. The unions, responding to outside criticism, asked for legislation to help them supervise health and pension funds. At the 1957 convention, the AFL-CIO adopted six "codes of ethical conduct," and Walter Reuther's autoworkers union set up a public review board to protect the individual unionist. But the McClellan Committee savaged organized labor, and Congress responded with the Labor Management Reporting and Disclosure Act of 1959 (Landrum-Griffin), which organized labor called its "most severe setback in more than a decade."

The background of this act was the revelation of corruption and improper activities among union leaders, which was given wide publicity by the hearings of the McClellan Committee. According to the provisions of the act, the Secretary of Labor, the NLRB, and the federal courts were brought into the internal operation of the unions even more deeply than they had ever been before. The act specifically laid down basic financial reporting requirements that were obligatory for the unions and further attempted to guarantee internal democracy within the unions. It goes too far to say that labor unions became quasi-public organizations, but the legislation of 1959 marked a further deep intrusion into the actual oversight of union functioning.

Two things might be said in reference to labor's position at the end of the 1950s. In 1959, steel workers struck U.S. Steel in a shutdown that was to last 119 days, but was to bring only short-lived gains because this mature oligopoly was sliding further into decline. The steel workers' contract, which was to be the model for all heavy industry, would not outlast the decade. And one keen observer noted that the organized labor leaders' passion for respectability was a contradiction ideologically and counterproductive to organized labor's interests. Labor's affluence in the 1950s ironically presaged the accelerated erosion of union strength. The steel workers in 1959 won a complete victory. Not only did they achieve a substantial wage increase and better pension and insurance benefits, but they also won on the important issue of maintenance of work rules. The steel industry agreed to set up joint committees for studying work conditions in the industry. The long strike had not been marred by violence, but the provisions of Taft-Hartley had been invoked, and it had taken the Supreme Court's sustaining a Justice Department injunction to get the strikers back to work. Only the threat of a government settlement brought the companies to heel and prevented the resumption of the strike. Labor's victory was a Pyrrhic one. By 1959, there was simply too much capacity in the industry, and foreign competitors, especially the Japanese, were producing steel at a cost 20 percent less than that of the American companies. The obsolescence of American heavy industry, which became a critical problem in the 1970s and 1980s, began in the 1950s.

NOTES

[1] Robert J. Lampman, "Changes in the Share of Wealth Held by Top Wealth Holders, 1922–1956," in *The Review of Economics and Statistics* 41 (Nov. 1959): 391.

[2] Harold G. Vatter, *The U.S. Economy in the 1950's* (New York: W. W. Norton and Company, 1963), pp. 37–38.

[3] Ibid., p. 39.

[4] Quoted in Herbert S. Parmet, *Eisenhower and the American Crusades* (New York: Macmillan, 1972), pp. 571–572.

[5] CED Report, *The Problem of National Security, Some Economic and Administrative Aspects* (New York: Committee for Economic Development, 1958).

[6] Seymour Melman, *The Permanent War Economy* (New York: Simon and Schuster, 1974), p. 16

[7] Ibid., p. 17.

[8] Vatter, *U.S. Economy in the 1950's*, p. 74.

[9] Ibid., p. 82.

[10] In 1962 the Common Market adopted a complex scheme to rationalize European agricultural production. This Common Agricultural Policy (CAP) has been a large setback for U.S. agriculture. The CAP not only has almost wrecked the budget of the EC but has created an undesirable amount of friction with the U.S. The policy has distorted agricultural production within Europe, producing lakes of cheap wine and mountains of butter because of the subsidies to farmers and agreements with the EC's trading partners. And the EC has become a major

exporter of subsidized agricultural products, to the great detriment of American farmers.

[11]*Federal Reserve Bulletin* (February 1960), p. 132, quoted in Vatter, p. 136.

[12]*Federal Trade Commission,* "Report of the Federal Trade Commission on the Merger Movement," p. 59.

[13]Vatter, *U.S. Economy in the 1950's,* p. 152.

[14]*Wall Street Journal,* April 12, 1985.

[15]Vatter, *U.S. Economy in the 1950's,* p. 163.

SUGGESTED READINGS

Chandler, Alfred D., Jr. *Strategy and Structure: Chapters in the History of the American Industrial Enterprise.* Cambridge, Mass.: MIT Press, 1962.

Degler, Carl N. *Affluence and Anxiety: America since Nineteen Forty-five,* 2d ed. Glenview, Illinois: Scott Foresman, 1975.

Goals for Americans. American Assembly, Columbia University, 1960.

Goldman, Eric F. *The Crucial Decade: America 1945–1960.* New York: Vintage Books, 1960.

Melman, Seymour. *The Permanent War Economy.* New York: Simon and Schuster, 1974.

Parmet, Herbert S. *Eisenhower and the American Crusades.* New York: Macmillan, 1972.

Stone, I. F. *The Truman Era, Nineteen Forty-five to Nineteen Fifty-two.* New York: Random House, 1972.

Vatter, Harold G. *The U.S. Economy in the 1950's.* New York: W. W. Norton and Company, 1963.

5 ___ *Kennedy's New Frontier and Johnson's Great Society*

TWO TRAGIC PRESIDENTS— KENNEDY AND JOHNSON

On November 8, 1960, John F. Kennedy was elected President, the youngest president in the nation's history and the first Roman Catholic to sit in the White House. Kennedy has been thought of as quintessentially New England, but he lived in Massachusetts for only brief periods. Both his grandfathers had come to Boston after the Irish potato famine of 1847 and had been active in local politics. JFK himself represented Massachusetts both in the House (1947–1953) and in the Senate (1953–1961). Educated at Choate and Harvard, young Kennedy attended Princeton for a brief period, studied under Harold Laski at the London School of Economics, and served as secretary in his father's office at the London Embassy. Much of his global concern can be traced to this cosmopolitan upbringing.

During World War II, Kennedy became a hero after rescuing crew members from his torpedoed patrol boat. In 1946, he won election from a safe Democratic district in Boston. In both the House and the Senate, JFK positioned himself as a moderate liberal with deep concern for labor, social welfare, and foreign affairs. Massachusetts's interests, however, seemed to come first.

John F. Kennedy was inaugurated the thirty-fifth President on January 20, 1961. In stirring and patriotic phrases, he called the nation, especially the young, to "a grand and global alliance" against tyranny, poverty, disease and war. Americans still quote his challenge: "ask not what your country can do for you—ask what you can do for your country." The first 100 days saw a whirlwind of legislative proposals as the President sought to turn the economy around. The 1000 days of the "New Frontier" saw an activist President increasingly faced with stubborn problems but determinedly pushing ahead. In domestic affairs, he favored civil rights legislation, landing a man on the moon, a nuclear test-ban, medical care for the aged, and protection

Chronology

1961
January: Kennedy's Inaugural Address called for an alliance to combat tyranny, poverty, disease, and war
May: Minimum wage increased ($1.25 per hour) and coverage broadened
June: Housing Act of 1961 to reduce urban blight, improve low-and-moderate income housing
1962
April: Steep price increases
October: Trade Expansion Act broadened President's authority to cut and/or remove tariffs
November: Executive orders prohibiting racial and religious discrimination in housing built with federal aid
1963
August: Higher Education Facilities Act, five-year program using federal funds to construct or improve higher educational facilities
1964
January: President Johnson called for a War on Poverty
July: Civil Rights Act
September: National Wilderness Preservation System established
1965
January: State of the Union address: President called for a vast program to achieve the "Great Society"
April: Elementary and Secondary School Act provides large scale aid to elementary and secondary schools

July: Medicare established to make medical care available for the aged; it is financed through the Social Security System

September: Department of Housing and Urban Development (HUD) established

October: Water Quality Act allowed federal government to exercise broad areas of control, especially in cleanup of oil spills; amendments to Air Quality Act; Higher Education Act provides first federal scholarships to college undergraduates

1966

March: Veterans education benefits provided for all personnel who served 180 days active duty after 1955

October: Creation of Department of Transportation

November: Clear Water Restoration Act; Model Cities bill (Demonstration Cities and Metropolitan Area Re-development Act) encouraged urban rehabilitation and urban planning

1967

October: Unified Federal Budget replaced existing hodge-podge arrangements

1968

April: Open Housing Law passed to prohibit discrimination in the sale or rental of housing

May: Truth-in-Lending Act required disclosure of full information to borrowing consumer

October: Conservation and beautification legislation

of the civil rights of African Americans. Much of his program would find life in the Great Society initiatives.

Kennedy's successor, Lyndon Johnson, was a supreme politician. Born in Texas, he had come to Washington during the New Deal and had served more than twenty years on Capitol Hill in the House (1937–1948) and in the Senate (1948–1961). Before becoming Vice President, he had been the powerful Democratic floor leader and was well-respected as a moderate who was sympathetic to liberal social policies and respectful of Texas conservatism.

Johnson easily adopted Kennedy's programs in civil rights and other New Frontier legislation and skillfully pushed them through Congress. In the presidential election of November 3, 1964, he overwhelmingly defeated the Republican candidate, Barry M. Goldwater, by an electoral vote of 486 to 52. In his 1965 State of the Union message, Johnson outlined his "Great Society" program and sent to Congress special messages on health, immigration, disarmament, tax reduction, conservation, housing, rail transportation, crime, and voting rights. Congress responded by passing the Medicare bill providing hospital and nursing-home care for persons over sixty-five covered by the Social Security Act. Congress also passed immigration and civil rights legislation. Johnson's war on poverty, announced in May 1964 at the University of Michigan, was to dominate domestic programs and policies for the next three years. In foreign affairs, Johnson was enmeshed in the struggle in Vietnam. The rising costs of "Nam" in men and resources eroded his public and political support. Resistance, riots, and student protests swept the country. Inflation and stagnation ground the economy to a standstill. And in April 1968 Martin Luther King, Jr., the outstanding spokesman and charismatic leader of African Americans, was assassinated in Memphis, Tennessee. Crushed by many setbacks, Johnson announced on March 31, 1968 that he would not seek re-election. The war in Vietnam would begin to wind down. Johnson's presidency was ended, not with a bang, but a withdrawal.

PRELUDE TO THE 1960s: THE PRESIDENT'S COMMISSION ON NATIONAL GOALS

On November 16, 1960, the American Assembly of Columbia University reported the findings of its President's Commission on National Goals to the Eisenhower administration. This document, almost four hundred pages in length, represented the wisdom of over one hundred experts in various fields plus fourteen men and women of "acknowledged competence." It was both a quintessential document of its day and something of a backdrop for both the successes and failures of this tumultuous decade. The report's individual recommendations ranged widely from new concerns for industrial well-being to the role of the United States in the world. Specialists raised questions about American programs for the arts and culture, education, farm policy, urban society, and human needs. This national commission articulated the idealistic concerns of an American people coming to maturity in the affluent society of the postwar period. If only a portion of these reforms could have been achieved! But the American strategy of the 1960s was an all-or-nothing wager. In attempting to eradicate all the evils of the era, programs were instituted that often exacerbated the problems they were trying to solve.

Some key concerns from the Commission's Report were:

2. *Equality*

Vestiges of religious prejudice, handicaps to women, and, most important, discrimination on the basis of race must be recognized as morally wrong, economically wasteful, and in many respects dangerous. In this decade we must sharply lower these last stubborn barriers.

6. *The Democratic Economy*

The economic system must be compatible with the political system. The centers of economic power should be as diffused and as balanced as possible. Too great concentrations of economic power in corporations, unions, or other organizations can lead to abuses and loss of the productive results of fair competition. Individuals should have maximum freedom in their choice of jobs, goods and services.

7. *Economic Growth*

The economy should grow at the maximum rate consistent with primary dependence upon free enterprise and the avoidance of marked inflation. Increased investment in the public sector is compatible with this goal.

10. *Living Conditions*

We must remedy slum conditions, reverse the process of decay in the larger cities, and relieve the necessity for low-income and minority groups to concentrate there.

We should also seek solutions for haphazard suburban growth, and provide an equitable sharing of the cost of public services between central cities and suburbs. In many parts of the country, the goal should be a regional pattern which provides for a number of urban centers, each with its own industries, its own educational, cultural and recreational institutions, and a balanced population of various income levels and backgrounds. The needs of a growing population for parks and recreation must be met.

11. *Health and Welfare*

The demand for medical care has enormously increased. To meet it we must have more doctors, nurses, and other medical personnel. There should be more hospitals, clinics and nursing homes. Greater effectiveness in the use of such institutions will reduce overall requirements...[1]

Given the ambition of these goals, how successful were reforms of the 1960s?

KENNEDY'S ECONOMICS

In 1961, a task force report on the economy prepared by the well-known Harvard economist Paul Samuelson described the United States economy as one in a "recession." In his first State of the Union address, January 30, 1961, President Kennedy used this description as a jumping-off point for his proposals to Congress: He described the state of the economy as "disturbing," characterized by seven months of recession, three and one-half years of "slack," seven years of diminished economic growth, nine years of falling farm incomes, and five and one-half million unemployed. Investment and profits had declined. Construction had sagged, and laborers were working fewer hours.[2]

On February 2, 1961, at the beginning of his administration, Kennedy set in motion seven economic measures. Within 161 days, he had injected a new level of energy into the economy. There was new legislation which temporarily extended unemployment benefits for an additional thirteen weeks (it cost $800 million); another bill extended aid to the children of unemployed workers ($200 million) and provided funds to redevelop distressed areas ($400 million) as well as increasing Social Security payments and encouraging earlier retirement. Legislation was approved to raise the minimum wage and broaden its coverage to other occupations ($175 million). Congress passed a bill to provide emergency relief to feed-grain farmers. A final measure provided funds for an estimated 420,000 construction jobs for a comprehensive home-building and slum-clearance program.[3]

In more ways Kennedy sought to stimulate the economy. By executive authority, the President stepped up federal purchases and accelerated building programs for post offices and highways. He lowered interest rates on FHA insured loans and liberalized lending by the Federal Home Loan Banks. For farmers, he broadened the distribution of surplus food and created a pilot food stamp program for the needy. And Sorensen, Kennedy's special counsel, tells us he encouraged the Federal Reserve Board to keep long-term interest rates low. Clearly, this was a young man in a hurry marshalling the powers of his office to push the economy ahead. "The need," Sorensen wrote, "was to get more money into the economy fast."[4] The President acted on his own initiative to direct all federal agencies to accelerate their activities in areas where there was unemployment. The United States Employment Offices were expanded to help workers find jobs. Kennedy, a student of Samuelson, had learned his Keynesian economics well. Despite the additions to the budget deficit, the young President expected not an anemic recovery, but rather a vigorous economy on the move. If Eisenhower had moved ever so cautiously, Kennedy was to forge ahead impetuously.

Not satisfied with these efforts, he concentrated on economic policy the same energies that he would exert successfully in foreign affairs. Under pressure from liberal Congressmen and organized labor, he had threatened in his economic message to Congress of February 2, 1961, that if his actions did not spur economic recovery, he would in seventy-five days submit a massive public works program and a temporary tax cut. By spring, however, these earlier stimulants plus the normal rebound in the business cycle created improvements. Increases in defense spending caused by the Berlin crisis, however, were straining the federal budget. Concern for tax cuts was giving way to possible needs for tax increases. The President's foreign policymakers demanded increased military spending as a means to demonstrate the nation's resolve to the Russians. At first sympathetic to the idea of a tax increase, Kennedy however yielded to his concerns that the economy faced deep, long-term problems which only a high growth rate could resolve.

What were these long-range economic concerns? JFK saw his administration facing economic problems like those FDR had confronted thirty years earlier. Too many workers faced too few jobs; long-range growth to turn this stagnation around required well-planned policies that would go to the heart of these structural problems. Kennedy's advisers argued that even the postwar boom had not been able to provide the twelve million civilian jobs needed. The shortfall of two million positions seemed to presage for them a dismal future unless drastic policies were adopted. In a full-employment economy these two million workers, willing but unable to find work, represented, Kennedy said, "a staggering [loss of] one billion work days, equivalent to shutting down the entire country with no production, no services and no pay for over three weeks." And, of course, this new variety of unemployment particularly affected the unskilled, the African American, and the young, and was highly concentrated in the old industries of coal, textiles, and railroads. The decline of the long-lived Second Industrial Revolution which had started at the end of the nineteenth century was tightening its grip on mid-America. Moreover, almost all work training in our industries took place, in the absence of an apprenticeship system, on the job. Thus the economic malaise was sentencing young people to long-term unemployment because Americans could not create new entry-level jobs. Unlike many European countries, we had almost no publicly supported programs such as the voucher system for training and retraining workers.

Brief as it was, the Kennedy administration deserves high grades for its 7 percent tax credit for investment in new machinery and equipment and for accelerating the depreciation allowances businessmen could deduct for tax purposes, though the effect of these measures was less important than the signals emanating from the market. These policies cost the government approximately $2.5 billion. Even more than this, Kennedy's courage in running deficits without raising taxes not only conformed to the best Keynesian thinking, but also showed a sophistication in economic policy beyond that of any other President in the history of this entire period.

Three particular economic problems were tackled in the remaining years of Kennedy's brief administration: trade imbalance, the steel industry crisis, and tax policy. The Trade Agreements Act (1962) dominated Kennedy's efforts that year. He believed the revision of the Reciprocal Trade Agreements Act of 1934 essential; just tinkering with the legislation, as had been the practice since the end of the war, was no longer adequate if the economic stagnation of the 1960s was to be dealt with. JFK believed that American economic prosperity hinged on solving the increasingly knotty problems with trade imbalances and the lack of competitiveness of American exports. Such difficulties could not be resolved without a major overhaul of basic trade legislation. Since 1959, the European Common Market had prospered mightily and its members had become major competitors of American exporters. Concern that the U.S. was slipping in this competition might, he felt, induce American companies to establish plants within Common Market countries, with a subsequent loss of American jobs at home. The Reciprocal Trade Act was due to expire in the middle of the year (1962), and the President intended to push for a broad measure that would meet the realities of postwar trading in the world.

The Trade Expansion Act (1962) consisted essentially of two parts. First, the act provided for new presidential authority to reduce tariffs; second, it set up ways to deal with increased competition from imports and any problems of domestic readjustments which might arise from the new policies. The President was given four kinds of new tariff-reducing authority:

1. general authority to make reductions in relation to any other country;
2. special authority to reduce or eliminate duties in relation to the European Economic Community;

Figure 5.1   **Federal Budget Receipts and Outlays, 1961 to 1973**

BILLIONS OF DOLLARS

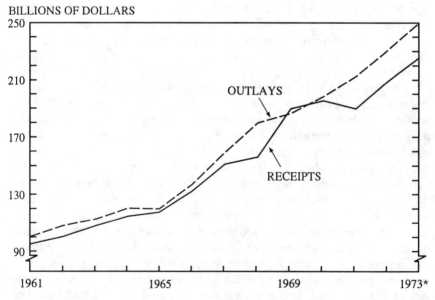

*Estimated

Source: *Statistical Abstract of the United States,* 1973.

3. special authority to reduce or eliminate duties in relation to the less developed nations;

4. special authority to eliminate low duties.[5]

The President was authorized to reduce existing duties by 50 percent. Aimed at countering EEC tariffs, the new American trade initiative gave the President broad powers to reduce duties on industrial products by more than 50 percent or to eliminate them completely in those cases where the United States and the EEC together accounted for 80 percent or more of the world export value of all articles within a specified category. For agricultural products, the 80 percent trade coverage test could be waived if the President determined that reducing or eliminating the tariff entirely would help maintain or expand United States agricultural exports.

In return for these powers to negotiate with the EEC, any tariff concessions granted to the EEC member would be extended to imports from other non-Communist countries. The administration wanted to be sure that these expanded trade advantages would not be frustrated. The elimination of internal tariffs within the EEC should not be the occasion to maintain tariffs against outside non-EEC suppliers—namely, the United States. If there was mutual agreement with the EEC, the President was authorized to further reduce or eliminate duties or other import restrictions on tropical agricultural and forestry commodities not produced in significant quantities in the United States. Finally, nuisance tariffs of five percent or less could be eliminated by the President in reciprocal negotiations. The Trade Expansion Act of 1962 indeed was a major achievement, and the "Kennedy round" of GATT negotiations in 1963 moved the world closer to economic cooperation—but in small steps.

Whatever small gains Kennedy had made in winning the support of the business community unraveled like a ball of string in April 1962. Steel was still the bellwether industry within the economy; it affected the auto, machinery, and construction businesses—indeed virtually every product that used this metal. Steel was an industry, however, clearly living in the past. Already steel was being replaced by plastics and other materials. Even in the auto industry, the demand for steel was dwindling as manufacturers used less metal in cars. Management and labor were both governed by powerful bureaucracies lacking entrepreneurial leadership. Between 1947 and 1958 steel prices more than doubled, and these prices increased three times faster than other industrial prices. Wages for steel workers, however, rose even faster than productivity, but management had been able to pass these costs to the consumer. By 1962 three and one-half years had gone by with labor and management in an uneasy truce. The harsh reality was still not evident that not only was America losing export markets for steel and steel products, but it was also importing massive amounts of lower-cost steel from foreign producers. Kennedy feared that a new round of wage demands and subsequent price increases would ignite inflation and worsen the payments deficit and the loss of gold.

On October 1, 1961, the steel workers received the third and final increase granted them under the agreement negotiated by Vice President Nixon that had ended the six-month steel strike of 1959. Between October 1961 and February 1962, President Kennedy and Secretary of Labor Arthur Goldberg held conversations with both labor leaders and managers in the steel industry. Goldberg's proposals were finally accepted by both sides at the end of March. There would be no wage increases, but fringe benefits were raised by about 10 cents an hour (the union had originally sought 17 cents). Because the agreement seemed to preclude a strike while preventing out-of-bounds increases beyond those related to productivity, this noninflationary settlement heralded the end of a twelve-year cycle of conflict within the industry.

On April 10, 1962, Roger Blough of U.S. Steel asked for an appointment to see the President. At the meeting he handed Kennedy a copy of a press release announcing a $6 a ton increase in the price of steel. Kennedy's anger was unbounded; over the next several days he threw at the steel companies all the power of his office. His relations with big business never recovered. The President took his message to the public:

> The American people will find it hard, as I do, to accept a situation in which *a tiny handful of steel executives whose pursuit of private power and profit exceeds their sense of public responsibility* can show such utter contempt for the interests of 185 million Americans....
>
> If this rise in the cost of steel is imitated by the rest of the industry, instead of rescinded, it would increase the cost of...most...items for every American family,...businessman and farmer. It would seriously handicap our efforts to prevent an inflationary spiral...make it more difficult for American goods to compete in foreign markets, more difficult to withstand competition from foreign imports, and thus more difficult to improve our balance of payments position, and stem the flow of gold...[6]

The administration coerced, cajoled, investigated, and intimidated the steel companies who had followed U.S. Steel and increased their prices. The antitrust section of the Dept. of Justice began an investigation into steel pricing in search of collusion. Secretary of Defense Robert McNamara promised that defense procurement would be shifted to those steel companies which had not raised prices. Inland, Colorado, and Armco were all worked on to remain aloof from the increases. Seventy-two hours after Blough's visit to the President, the press announced: "United States Steel Corporation rescinded today the steel price increase it initiated Tuesday."[7]

What had the President won? Clearly a victory for presidential power; beyond that maybe very little. He had demonstrated that a young and popular President could wield enormous powers over any particular sector of the economy and/or any special interest. But who had ever doubted this? And was it not better that this power be reserved for a larger issue than a $6 a ton increase in the price of steel? Market indicators still signaled that steel was a sick business, and no amount of arm-twisting was going to change this situation. All over the world the capacity of steel production was shrinking. The choices were all bad. In Western Europe, governments stepped in to 'rationalize' steel production and saddled their taxpayers with enormous costs to keep these old plants open. In Austria, it was said, the government could close all the mills, keep the work force on the payroll, and still save money. In the United States, the slow decline in the steel industry continued. Mills closed and the number of steel workers declined, but outside these old manufacturing industries millions of new jobs were created by new service industries and technologies. The government should, however, have done more to ease the hardship of individuals displaced by this industrial transformation by creating some permanent system for the retraining of workers.

On May 28, 1962, the stock market dropped 34.9 points and lost $28 billion, the largest one-day drop in the number of points on the index since the crash of 1929. Was the market overpriced, or did the steel conflict frighten the investment community? Was Kennedy's growth impetus running out of steam? Or, even more scary, was 1929 going to happen again? The ghosts of Hoover and Roosevelt seemed to be walking again the lonely corridors of the White House. JFK, as one would expect, responded energetically. The amount of brain power Kennedy surrounded himself with was enormous—Wilbur Mills of the House Ways and Means Committee, Senator Douglas, an economist by training, Paul Samuelson, Robert Solow, Walter Heller, Douglas Dillon, and John Kenneth Galbraith. The politicians, however, persuaded the President to hold and wait. The President was so greatly concerned about a recession that on June 7 he pledged "a comprehensive tax reform bill. . . [resulting in] an across-the-board reduction in personal and corporate income tax rates which will not be wholly offset by other reforms—in other words, a net tax reduction."[8] When the bill was finally passed, it provided for a $10 billion tax cut. The give-back was a daring piece of legislation. There was no budget surplus—nor was the deficit to be made up through tax increases; there was to be no reduction in spending; there was to be no recession. By the time the tax legislation passed, however, the economy was moving upward again, and the derring-do superfluous.

There was, however, no tax reform. The importance of the tax cut was to demonstrate what fiscal policy could do, if used sharply, to stimulate the economy. In 1963 tax reform was an idea unfortunately whose time had not yet come.

JOHNSON AND THE GREAT SOCIETY

On the plane flying back from Dallas on that terrible day when John F. Kennedy was assassinated, Lyndon Johnson, just sworn in, asked for help in moving the country towards a new democratic initiative. Kennedy's advisors had already begun the initial work to redress the poverty that had stubbornly continued to increase. JFK in all likelihood would have taken action to reduce the suffering of the poor, and Lyndon Johnson readily adopted the cause. Poverty—all poverty—would be eliminated in a great crusade:

We are citizens of the richest and most fortunate nation in the history of the world. One hundred eighty years ago we were a small country struggling for survival on the margin of a hostile land. Today we have established a civilization of free men which spans an entire continent. With the growth of our country has come opportunity for our people—opportunity to educate our children, to use our energies in productive work, to increase our leisure—opportunity for almost every American to hope that through work and talent he could create a better life for himself and his family. The path forward has not been an easy one.

There are millions of Americans—one-fifth of our people—who have not shared in the abundance which has been granted to most of us, and on whom the gates of opportunity have been closed.

The Economic Opportunity Act of 1964 proposed a new antipoverty program at a cost of $970 million—one percent of the national budget. Five goals were announced:

1. To give almost half a million underprivileged young Americans the opportunity to develop skills, continue education, and find useful work.
2. To give every American community the opportunity to develop a comprehensive plan to fight its own poverty—and help them to carry out their plans.
3. To give dedicated Americans the opportunity to enlist as volunteers in the war against poverty.
4. To give many workers and farmers the opportunity to break through particular barriers which bar their escape from poverty.
5. To give the entire nation the opportunity for a concerted attack on poverty through the establishment, under my direction, of the Office of Economic Opportunity, a national headquarters for the war against poverty.[9]

Fourteen task forces had labored on the outlines of these programs since Johnson had first voiced his aspirations to students at the University of Michigan on May 22, 1964. From 1965 to 1967, the dozens of new programs initiated were a testament to the idealism that could be traced back to the early vision of the New Deal. President Johnson himself had been an ardent supporter of Franklin Roosevelt and had himself succeeded to the highest political office. America had given him his chance, and he would do the same for others. If Americans made that extra effort, Johnson believed the final triumph of good over evil would be close at hand. The Kennedy tax cuts of 1962 and 1964 provided the inspiration for the easy, confident approach to the costs of the Great Society programs. Within a matter of months agencies to carry out the President's goals began to blossom. Hostile commentators would eventually count some five hundred government agencies connected to the Great Society programs, while more moderate critics talked only of four hundred thirty-five. The proliferation of government programs occurred with a speed that in comparison made Roosevelt's New Deal appear like an exercise in restraint. But it was not the numbers alone that quickly began to turn off middle-class America. A realistic appraisal of the cost of this war on poverty had never been fully calculated. Individual programs were rushed through Congress or established by the Johnson administration with little regard to their immediate or long-range cost. If poverty was going to be abolished quickly, so the argument went, future costs might not be such a great concern. Whatever the reasoning, the worthiness of the overall program seemed its own justification. Concomitantly, the vigor of the economy and its growth potential would be more than enough to carry the victory. Reacting in dismay, *U.S. News and World Report* in October 1965 projected that the cost of the Great Society would rise from $7 billion in 1965 to $19 billion by the end of the decade and predicted disaster.[10] Conservative Americans began to denounce the more radical programs of the War on Poverty.

In retrospect, one wonders why it took as long as it did for the Congress and the country to draw back from the front lines of the social war. In his January 1967 State of the Union message Johnson was still full of hope. Over the years from 1965 to 1967 he reported enormous gains. Legal barriers to equality had been struck down. Seven million deprived children had received educational benefits and almost one million in 1967 had gone on to college. Millions of Americans, over three and one-half million in the six months preceding his address, had been treated under Medicare, and health care had been brought to older people who previously could not afford it. Nine million new workers were covered by a higher minimum wage, and one million more were schooled in new government training programs. One thousand local communities had set up self-help programs to attack poverty in poor neighborhoods; one million young Americans were given a fresh economic or educational chance through Neighborhood Youth Corps or Head Start. We had begun, Johnson claimed, to rebuild our cities, to rescue our waters from pollution, and "to restore the beauty of our land, our countryside, our cities and our houses." He proudly announced that since 1964 the federal government had returned to state and local governments about $40 billion in grants-in-aid. Johnson predicted that by "1970, we will be spending close to one hundred ten billion dollars."[11] Even a rich society, however, with no other problems would have had difficulty sustaining this level of spending. And Johnson had Vietnam.

Did the Great Society fail as most voters came to believe? The thoughtful answer is still undecided. The conservative indictment against the Great Society is well known: programs were poorly planned and wastefully administered. We "threw money at problems." No attempt was made to estimate future costs or to provide sources for revenue. The War on Poverty overextended the hand of government and pushed the nation too far, too fast. These programs, conservatives claimed, exacerbated racial tensions and social conflict, while inflating the hopes of minority groups, ultimately alienating much of the black community and creating a "welfare mess." Numerous scandals in urban renewal and subsidized housing plagued these programs. Further, the Great Society's efforts to provide medical care contributed to today's ongoing medical care crisis. For the economy as a whole, this experiment into the unknown, they argued, unleashed the genie of inflation. More recently, several new books by conservative authors blame these Great Society efforts for worsening the conditions of the poor. In their judgment, the Great Society not only failed, but was counterproductive. The extreme swing to Reaganite conservatism in the 1980s must in part be attributed to the frustrations and disillusionments of the 1960s. Americans liked to be winners, and the open-ended quality of social welfare, its costs, and its perceived social radicalism frustrated many middle-class Americans.

The programs of the Johnson administration's War on Poverty were concentrated in eleven categories: 1) income support: AFDC (Aid to Families with Dependent Children), SSI (Supplemental Security Income), unemployment compensation, and improved Social Security payments; 2) health care: Medicare and Medicaid; 3) low income housing; 4) education: Head Start and other compensatory programs; 5) manpower services: Job Corps and other work-related programs; 6) civil rights, including legal services for minorities; 7) Community Action Programs; 8) improving the status of blacks; 9) fighting poverty through the Economic Opportunity Act; 10) full employment programs; 11) redistributing income. Total government spending for social services rose by 5 percent of GNP; aid based on need rose by less than 2 percent of GNP.

One of the best evaluations of the Johnson administration's efforts is by Sar Levitan, a distinguished political scientist who has studied the Great Society programs. He argues trenchantly that the Great Society was much more successful than its detractors have cared to admit. The goals of the Great Society, he believed, were realistic ones for the improvement of the nation, though the costs of reaching these targets moved steadily ahead of the planners. These social welfare efforts, long overdue, moved the nation in his view toward a more just and equitable society and were reasonably efficient, especially since in many instances there were no private-sector alternatives to active intervention. The negative feedback and failures have been overstated and exaggerated because they appeared to threaten established ways. In sum, Levitan says that "the benefits were more than the sum of their parts, and more than the impact on immediate participants and beneficiaries." More significantly, he believes "there is no reason to fear that modest steps which are positive and constructive in alleviating age-old problems will in some way unleash uncontrollable forces or will undermine the broader welfare of the body politic."[12]

VIETNAM

The withdrawal from the campaign against poverty will always be linked to the tragedy of the war in Vietnam. The protracted conflict destroyed the popularity of President Lyndon Johnson and drove him from office. Vietnam blunted the aspirations of the War on Poverty, split the country ideologically, and generated runaway inflation. Murray Weidenbaum, in his background paper *The Economic Impact of the Vietnam War,* written for the Center for Strategic Studies at Georgetown University, found four critical elements in United States policy in Vietnam that harmed the economy:

1. Persisting uncertainty as to the nature and extent of the U.S. commitment.
2. A lack of general understanding of the speed with which a military buildup affects the economy.
3. Confusion in interpretation and delay in the release of budget information in 1966.
4. Resultant basic problems in national income policy.[13]

From 1931 to 1939, military expenditures took only 1.3 percent of GNP; in World War II, 48 percent; the Korean War, 12 percent. On the eve of involvement in Vietnam, defense purchases were about 8 percent of GNP. Not only did this figure rise to 9.5 percent of GNP with the escalation of military action, but coming on top of an already highly stimulated economy, the incremental impacts were extremely large and destructive. From 1954 through 1960, fewer than 1,000 American service personnel were in Vietnam. By 1962, the number had risen to 10,000; 1963 brought the number to 16,575, but then the figures simply soared: June 1965, 103,000; June 1966, 322,000; and December 1966, 455,000. The war was supposed to end in 1967.

Costs rose too. By 1968, Secretary of Defense McNamara thought that $2 billion a month for Vietnam was a realistic approximation (the total estimated military budget was $72.3 billion for fiscal 1968). Even as late as the January 1966 budget message, the President was unable to admit that runaway costs had taken over. In fact, Johnson told the Congress:

> We are a rich nation and can afford to make progress at home while meeting obligations abroad—in fact, we can afford no other course if we are to remain strong. For this reason, I have not halted progress in the new and vital Great Society programs in order to finance the costs of our efforts in Southeast Asia.[14]

Despite these assurances, the Great Society and Vietnam were twin pressures that could move the economy in only one direction—towards inflation. The war, business expansion, and overheated demand all meant price increases, but the cost of the war was the most significant factor. Pressures from the war-related costs knocked out the wage and price guidelines of the Council of Economic Advisers. These war expenditures also added to balance of payments difficulties, lack of confidence in the dollar, an outflow of gold, and the threat to the international monetary system as the U.S. economy began to overheat. The prestigious Committee for Economic Development (CED) summed up the crisis: "We paid the unfair and insidious tax of inflation rather than taxing ourselves openly and fairly."[15] By 1969, President Nixon would have to announce a program of temporary mandatory controls on U.S. direct investment abroad. But first the war in Vietnam had to end, and the toxins in the economic system had to be purged. This the Johnson administration could never bring itself to do. A Senate hearing in 1967 produced this memorable dialogue:

> Senator Symington: "... my question is, how long can this nation afford to continue the gigantic financial cost incident to this major grand war in Asia without its economy becoming nonviable?
> Secretary McNamara: " ... I think forever, and I say it for this reason. That there are many things, many prices we pay for the war in South Vietnam, some very heavy prices indeed, but in my opinion one of them is not strain on our economy.[16]

So long as the administration believed the rhetoric about winning the war with no harm to the economy, no change would be forthcoming, though damage, as the CED pointed out, was already extensive. "The real cost to society of allocating production resources to military programs," Weidenbaum wrote, "may be said to be that these resources are unavailable for other purposes."[17]

On January 8, 1969, just days before the new President, Richard Nixon, would be inaugurated, Henry Kissinger met with Le Duc Tho in Paris for the final talks on conditions for peace in Vietnam. By 1968, however, the war had been lost in the minds of the American people, and the concerns for the economy after the withdrawal of U.S. forces began then. The greatest of these concerns was the rampant inflation that the war had unleashed. With the inflation came a host of economic problems both domestic and international. A few hoped that the ending of the war would bring a "peace dividend" which could be used to revive the Great Society programs, which by 1969 had been drastically cut and eroded. This peace dividend, of course, never materialized. Most of the economic problems which faced the nation were exacerbated by the war. Americans who had come of age in this final decade of the "affluent society" thought of wealth only in the limited sense of more material goods—like autos and swimming pools and lawn mowers—and could not comprehend the expense needed for the big ticket items like weapons, health insurance, and a cleaner environment. Faced with scarce resources, Americans were jarred into the need to set priorities. Some wise insights came from the CED's analysis of the growing inflation:

1. The nation needs to take a longer-run view of the inflation problem, and not lean so much in the direction of accepting the risk of a little more inflation in the hope of squeezing a little more employment out of the economy.
2. The record of leaning upon "guidepost" policy to prevent inflation in the presence of strong inflationary pressure of demand has not been good.

Figure 5.2 **The Great Society**

**"ALL POSSIBLE CARE IS TAKEN
TO AVOID CIVILIAN CASUALTIES."**

3. Better information about the most probable size of the defense program than has been available in the past would make it easier for the economic decision-makers, both in Washington and outside, to take into account the economic consequences the program is bound to have.[18]

Much talk was devoted to readjusting the economy after Vietnam, but none took account of a simple but tremendous change that began to occur in the world's economy. For decades, the concern of the United States government was that oil prices should not fall so low as to threaten the political stability of the states in the Mideast. However, by the 1960s the curve of rising energy demands, i.e., demand for oil, was overtaking supply. When these curves intersected, a crisis would result. In 1973, just as American participation in Vietnam finally ended, that day of reckoning occurred and brought with it an unprecedented global energy crisis. For Americans, the war in Vietnam had initiated a decade of economic "stagflation" (inflation and stagnation).

THE UNITED STATES IN THE WORLD ECONOMY

Every President in the 1960s and 1970s faced not only large domestic economic problems, but also turbulent world ones. The greatest reason for the lack of harmony between U.S. domestic and international policies was in the unacknowledged fact that policymakers were trying to reconcile goals which only occasionally were complementary but more and more frequently were either in conflict or irreconcilable. For the first time in their recent history, Americans really did have to recognize their limitations in controlling international economic realities. The relatively simple problems of the immediate postwar years were past.

When JFK took office he had little awareness and even less knowledge of such economic principles as the balance of payments. In his fourteen years in Congress, his major interest, as befitting a representative of Massachusetts, was in restricting the imports of cheap textiles produced in low-wage countries. "At Hyannisport in the late summer of 1960 as his boat was ready to dock," Seymour Harris wrote, "I went over the [campaign] issues in an hour's presentation. Later he had to spend much time on these problems. But I was impressed with the quick comprehension."[19]

The young and activist President sought policies that would reinvigorate a stagnant domestic economy. Kennedy's tax cut in 1962 and (indirectly) Johnson's tax bill of 1964 all aimed at this goal. To be sure, JFK's initiatives in his first six months of office, so greatly admired by his supporters, were highly stimulative to the economy. In the international economy, he moved more slowly, relying on conventional wisdom. The Trade Expansion Act of 1962 was followed by the Kennedy round of tariff-cutting for GATT members, but the negotiations were slow and piecemeal. For the more serious problems of balance of trade, balance of payments, and exchange rates, Kennedy never developed a comprehensive strategy; by his logic lower tariffs would increase trade, and more trade would ease the balance of payments as well as stimulate the U.S. economy. Central to this strategy was the continued high level of American agricultural exports to Europe. Didn't American farmers have a comparative advantage? And besides, the magnificent agricultural surpluses of the 1960s almost demanded an increase in farm exports. But Europe's small farmers would have none of this grand strategy. Well before the institution of the CAP (Common Agricultural Policy) by the Common Market in 1968, France and West Germany had made a broad agreement that for social and political reasons they would protect their peasant-based agricultures. Beset by these and other problems, especially Vietnam, Presidents Kennedy and Johnson made few initiatives in economic policy.

Bretton Woods had laid down the monetary exchange structure of the postwar world. When the pound could not withstand the American pressure for its free convertibility into dollars in the late 1940s, the United States dollar became de facto the major world currency. Maintaining this international dollar, however, was a responsibility that American political leadership had never known. Throughout the 1950s, reasonably small annual balance of payments deficits became commonplace but were shrugged off as harmless. Direct foreign investment by U.S. multinational companies as well as the growing taste for foreign goods both contributed to this recurrent deficit. But the U.S. was the free world's largest economy, so this situation was not unexpected. In the long run, however, dollars accumulated abroad in grand numbers and diminished in value, thus making them weaker compared to other currencies. During the 1960s a world dollar market emerged and began to assign different values to U.S. currency in comparison with its domestic value. By the end of the decade, American goods were increasingly overpriced and uncompetitive. This conflict between the domestic and international value of the dollar led in August 1971 to the first economic crisis of the Nixon administration.

MONETARISM

Modern emphasis on the importance of money as the major regulator of economic growth was born anew in the late '50s through the hard statistical work of Milton Friedman. Unlike Keynes, Friedman was a commoner, born in New York City, the son of a poor immigrant dry-goods merchant who died when Milton was fifteen. Young Friedman studied economics at Rutgers, Chicago, and Columbia, where he came into contact with a host of outstanding American economists: Jacob Viner, Harold Hotelling, J. M. Clark, and Wesley Mitchell. Initially, Friedman worked and contributed to statistical theory, especially at the National Bureau, and in Washington he did detailed analyses of data on incomes and expenditures. A model, hardworking, patient researcher, he brought brilliant new insights into areas which most economists had thought had been thoroughly explained. His questions seemed remarkably simple, and his empirical testing painstakingly thorough. In 1957, he published an explosive work under the quiet title *A Theory of the Consumption Function*. According to Friedman, Keynes was wrong. The stability of the consumption function, which Keynes had accepted as fundamental and on which much public policy hinged, actually varied as individuals adjusted their consumption with respect to changes in their long-term permanent income. Individuals paid little attention to temporary variations. Friedman unearthed a mountain of evidence to support this conclusion.

As early as 1951, Friedman had inaugurated a monetary workshop which was to attract both brilliant students and faculty and occupy his own energies for the next thirty years. Keynesian countercyclical policy meant expanding the public sector through the use of fiscal measures. To a considerable degree, the market mechanism, having failed, would be replaced by the gentle control of bright liberal policy planners. For Friedman however, Keynesian assumptions, especially the consumption function, were wrong, and monetary policy as a macroeconomic policy tool was both more effective and congruent with a free-market-driven economy. In 1948, Friedman had already suggested that the Federal Reserve follow simple rules to reduce the uncertainties of the economic environment by a countercyclical policy of "financing recession-induced increase in the federal budget deficit by money creation and correspondingly by retiring money during a boom-induced surplus".[18]

In 1956, Friedman wrote the first essay in *Studies on the Quantity Theory of Money* in which he presented a theory of demand for money; his article emphasized the stability of money demand. Along with other essays which examined nominal income and inflation in the context of the demand for money, Friedman and his Chicago School recreated a "quantity" theory of money. To answer doubters, Friedman and his colleague Anna Schwarz produced the monumental study *A Monetary History of the United States, 1867–1960* (1963), which traced the history of the money supply and its relationship to gold and exchange rates. Over the course of the next two decades, Friedman and monetarism nudged Keynesian fiscal policy into the backwater of policy debate. Friedman maintained that fiscal policy was impotent in countering cyclical shocks, but many of his larger and specific claims for the benefits of monetary theory as a total panacea for countercyclical policy could not be measured; according to the same economists, "the transmission mechanism and dynamics remain enshrouded in the gloom of a black box."[19] As monetary research increased, however, it did influence policy, especially that of the Federal Reserve. Friedman's students became important researchers, and watching and measuring M1 (the "narrow" money supply) and M2 (the broader money supply) became a permanent and important part of economic policy both here and abroad.

One more issue that Friedman addressed deserves mention. In 1958, the British economist A. W. Phillips published a study on the relationship between unemployment and the rate of change in wages. Phillips showed a close relationship between these two variables, and the Phillips' curve became the banner of liberal politicians who imagined that one could trade off a modest price increase (inflation) that corresponded to a comparable amount of unemployment, a price most people of goodwill ought to be willing to pay. In his presidential address to the American Economic Association (1967), Friedman destroyed this naive assumption. In the long run, there was no such easy trade off. The Phillips curve, he asserted, was a vertical line; any short-run gains reflected only temporary adjustment to inflation and were transitory. In the long run such government efforts to manipulate the economy in this way were counterproductive. Briefly, Friedman holds that:

1. Monetary policy has been neglected as a countercyclical device.

2. Fiscal policy—that is, Keynesian policy—is much less effective than

equivalent monetary measures, which would affect the quantity of money in circulation. Specifically, the reason for the post-World War II prosperity "is not because of the positive virtue of the fine tuning [i.e., countercyclical policy] that has been followed, but because we have avoided the major mistakes of the inter-war period. Those major mistakes were the occasionally severe deflations of the money stock.[20]

3. Monetary and fiscal policies are both unable to smooth minor business cycles (Friedman calls this "fine tuning"). Hence an automatic policy that would increase the quantity of money a certain percentage each year would be very much superior to the ineffective efforts of the Federal Reserve Bank and the Council of Economic Advisors, especially if this automatic policy were accompanied by major efforts to reduce price rigidities through reduction in the monopoly powers of labor unions and big corporations. A steady but small increase in the quantity of money would maintain the effective demand of a slowly growing population at full employment level, without serious inflation.

Experience shows that neither monetarism nor fiscal policy alone holds the answer. The problems associated with achieving long run stability are enormously complex and intermingled with political and philosophical positions. Just as Keynesianism had initial success, so monetarism has had its victories; both have had their defeats. We do better at handling small shocks, but could we suffer another Great Crash? The subdued answer is yes. Would we plunge into a depression as long and severe as the '30s? We really can't tell, though the system is much better structured than it was, and our knowledge and tools enormously better. However, the Savings and Loan crisis of the '90s shows that we still largely forget any lessons history has to teach.

NOTES

[1] *The Report of the President's Commission on National Goals: Goals for Americans* (New York: The American Assembly of Columbia University, 1960), pp. 3-14.

[2] Theodore C. Sorensen, *Kennedy* (New York: Harper and Row, 1965), p. 396.

[3] Ibid., p. 397.

[4] Ibid., p. 397.

[5] Ibid., p. 411.

[6] Ibid., pp. 450-451.

[7] Ibid., p. 458

[8] Ibid., p. 428.

[9] "Special message to the Congress proposing a nationwide war on the sources of poverty, March 16, 1964," *Public Papers of the President of the U.S.: Lyndon Baines Johnson, 1963-64,* Book 1, Item 219, pp. 375-380.

[10]*U.S. News and World Report,* Oct. 18, 1965: 50–52.

[11]*U.S. News and World Report,* Jan. 23, 1967: 104–105.

[12]Sar A. Levitan and R. Taggart, "The Great Society Did Succeed," *Political Science Quarterly* 91 (Winter 1976–77): 601–618.

[13]M. Weidenbaum, *Economic Impact of the Vietnam War* (Washington, D.C.: Center for Strategic Studies [Georgetown University], 1966), p. 12.

[14]"Annual Presidential Message to the Congress, Fiscal Year 1966," in *Public Papers of the President of the United States* (Washington, D.C.: U.S. Government Printing Office, 1967).

[15]Quoted from "Stabilizing Federal Budget for 1967, a Statement by the Program Committee of the CED," in *The National Economy and the Vietnam War—A Statement by the Research and Policy Committee* (New York: Committee for Economic Development, 1968), p. 11.

[16]U.S. Senate Committee on Armed Services and Appropriations, *Supplemental Miliary Procurement and Construction Authorization, January 1967* (Washington, D.C.: GPO, 1967), pp. 96–97.

[17]Weidenbaum, *Economic Impact of the Vietnam War,* p. 52.

[18]CED, *The National Economy and the Vietnam War,* pp. 27–28.

[19]John Eatwell, et al. *The New Palgrave: A Dictionary of Economics* (New York: Macmillan, 1987), p. 424.

[20]Ibid. p. 425.

[21]Seymour E. Harris, *Economics of the Kennedy Years* (New York: Harper and Row, 1964), p. 19.

[22]Milton Friedman, *Monetary vs. Fiscal Policy* (New York: Norton, 1969), p. 79; Milton Friedman and Anna F. Schwarz, *Monetary History of the United States, 1867–1960* (Princeton, N.J., Princeton University Press, 1963); Milton Friedman, *A Program for Monetary Stability* (New York, Fordham University Press, 1959).

SUGGESTED READINGS

Bowles, S., D. M. Gordon, and T. F. Weisskopf. *Beyond the Waste Land: A Democratic Alternative to Economic Decline.* Garden City, N.Y., Anchor Press, 1983.

Halberstam, David. *The Best and the Brightest.* New York: Random House, 1983.

Heath, Jim F. *Decade of Disillusionment: The Kennedy-Johnson Years.* Bloomington, Ind.: Indiana University Press, 1976.

Kotlowitz, Alex. *There Are No Children Here: The Story of Two Boys Growing Up in Urban America.* New York: Doubleday, 1991.

Lampman, Robert J. *Ends and Means of Reducing Income Poverty.* Chicago: Markham Publishing Co., 1971.

Lemann, Nicholas. *Promised Land: The Great Black Migration and How It Changed America.* New York: Random House, 1991.

Levitan, Sar A., and R. Taggart. *The Promise of Greatness.* Cambridge: Harvard University Press, 1976.

Salisbury, Harrison E. *Vietnam Reconsidered: Lessons from a War.* New York: Harper and Row, 1984.

Schlesinger, Arthur M., Jr. *A Thousand Days: John F. Kennedy in the White House.* Boston: Houghton Mifflin, 1965.

Sorensen, Theodore C. *Kennedy.* New York: Harper and Row, 1965.

Stein, Herbert. *The Fiscal Revolution in America.* Chicago: University of Chicago Press, 1969.

Thurow, Lester C. *The Zero-Sum Society: Distribution and the Possibilities for Economic Change.* New York: Basic Books, 1980.

Viorst, Milton. *Fire in the Streets: America in the Nineteen Sixties.* New York: Simon and Schuster, 1981.

Zarefsky, David. *President Johnson's War on Poverty: Rhetoric and History.* Tuscaloosa, Ala.: University of Alabama Press, 1986.

The World's Energy Crisis and the Waning of American Power

NIXON, FORD, AND CARTER

Richard Nixon deserves full credit for his remarkable survival skills. In 1960, he lost the presidential election, and in 1962 he was beaten in California's gubernatorial election. Dogged and determined, hard-working and resourceful, he fought his way back to the leadership of the Republican party and in 1968 defeated Senator Hubert Humphrey, the Democratic candidate for President. He brought to the office wide experience including four years in the House and two years in the Senate plus eight years as Vice President under Eisenhower. A successful lawyer, widely travelled, and intellectually competent, he saw himself as a President who would usher in an era of stability, peace, and order.

In foreign affairs, Nixon took a strong internationalist position on foreign aid and national security. In November 1969, he initiated the Strategic Arms Limitation Talks (SALT) and on the 24th of that month he signed the Treaty on the Non-Proliferation of Nuclear Weapons with the Soviet Union. Nixon could also take credit for the cease-fire agreement in Vietnam in January 1973 and for reestablishing relations with the People's Republic of China. No similar accomplishments were achieved on the home front. Congress was controlled by the Democrats, and President Nixon was in trouble from the start over his nominations to the Supreme Court, over Vietnam, and over the rapidly deteriorating position of the economy—inflation, unemployment, declining industrial production, and falling stock market prices. In August 1971, afraid that America would face a drastic gold drain, he ended the convertibility of the dollar into gold, and shortly thereafter devalued the dollar in international markets. On June 11, 1971, Nixon abandoned his ideological opposition to government economic controls and instituted Phase I—a freeze on prices and wages. Phase I would be followed by Phases II, III, and IV, all of which imposed more and more unworkable bureaucratic controls on the economy. But all of this was ineffective. The Nixon Presidency increasingly was a shambles as the disclosures of the break-in at Watergate surfaced in June 1972. On August 8, 1974, Nixon announced in a television address his resignation, effective the following day. His successor, Gerald Ford, was sworn in; one month later, he granted a full pardon to former President Nixon.

President Ford's first words to the American people were that the country's "long national nightmare" was over. Not so. Ford's presidency, a short one, was as colorless as the President himself, though he had served in the Congress for many years as a representative from Michigan. In foreign policy he followed Nixon's lead on SALT, relations with China, and continued efforts to bring peace to the Middle East. More people remember the tall ships which sailed through New York Harbor on July 4, 1976, to celebrate the Bicentennial than anything achieved during his brief term in office. Ford's three years in office were dominated by the aftermath of Watergate. Of domestic consequence was the passage of ERISA (Employee Retirement Income Security Act) which set minimum federal standards for private pension plans. On the other hand his program of conferences for economists, businessmen, and labor leaders, came to naught, as did his public relations campaign WIN (Whip Inflation Now). Ford's most courageous act was to pledge federal loans of $2.3 billion to avert the bankruptcy of New York City. And the economy continued to deteriorate as Jimmy Carter came into office.

Jimmy Carter, the first President from the Deep South in more than a century, wrested national leadership from the establishment. Intellectually brilliant, emotionally sensitive, technocratically able, Carter the peanut farmer and born-again Christian from Georgia seemed to have a great deal going for him as he took office. Watergate had done great damage to the Republicans, and Carter exuded probity and integrity.

Carter grew up in rural Georgia, studied one year at Georgia Southwestern College in Americus, and one year at the Georgia Institute of Technology. In 1943, he entered Annapolis and graduated three years later with a naval commission. For two years, he served on battleships before he was transferred to the submarine service. In 1951, he applied for admission to the nuclear submarine program under the very controversial Captain Hyman Rickover. To prepare, Carter took courses in nuclear physics and engineering at Union College in Schenectady, New York. From 1963 through 1966, Jimmy served in the Georgia Senate. Although he was defeated for the governorship in 1966, he won election to that office in 1970 and initiated an honest and efficient state administration. Empathetic to blacks, supportive of merit, attentive to detail, Carter began to achieve national notice. On December 12, 1974, he announced his candidacy for the Presidency and fought a hard campaign in thirty of the thirty-one state primaries. Nothing was more impressive than hearing this remarkable man as he fought for the highest office.

In his inaugural address, he promised a "competent and compassionate" government; instead of using a limousine he walked with his wife and family from the Capitol rotunda to the White House. His first official act was to grant pardon to Vietnam war draft resisters. He supported the Equal

Chronology

1970
January: National Environmental Policy Act of 1969 made the protection of the environment a national commitment
April: Water Quality Improvement Act of 1970
July: White House Reorganization Plan created Office of Management and Budget
December: Occupational Safety and Health Act (OSHA) established; Clean Air Act
1971
June: Phase I of Nixon's Economic Policy attempted to freeze prices
1972
October: Supplemental Security Income (SSI) established to grant assistance to the aged, blind, and disabled; Federal Water Pollution Act passed; revenue sharing program to distribute $30 billion of federal tax revenues to state and local governments.
November: Nixon reelected
1973
January: Nixon impounded $12 billion in conflict with Congress's unwillingness to lower social spending outlays. Courts later (1973–1974) ruled the impoundment illegal
February: Devaluation of dollar
August: Agricultural Act ended farm subsidy system and replaced it with a target price system, with federal government to pay difference
October: Yom Kippur War initiated oil crisis
1974
August: Nixon resigned
September: Employee Retirement Income Security Act (ERISA) set minimum federal standards for private pension plans; domestic summit on the worsening economic situation
November: WIN (Whip Inflation Now) campaign announced by President Ford; mass transit aid of $11.9 billion for construction and capital improvements approved by Congress

1975
July: Department of Health, Education and Welfare barred discrimination in admissions, classes, financial aid, employment, and athletics by schools and universities
December: New York City received $2.3 billion in federal loans to avert bankruptcy
1976
November: Jimmy Carter elected President
1977
April: Carter energy program to prevent waste and damage from interruptions in overseas supplies of oil
August: Amendments to 1970 Clean Air Act delayed implementation for two years of auto emission standards
1978
June: Adoption in California referendum of Proposition 13, cutting local property taxes by more than 50 percent; affirmative action upheld by Supreme Court in *Regents of University of California* v. *Bakke*
October: Civil Service Reform created Senior Executive Services of 8000 top federal managers; deregulation of several regulated industries, namely, airlines, trucking, railroads
1979
July: Domestic summit held at Camp David to resolve "crisis of confidence" in the nation related to energy crisis
1980
January: Chrysler bail-out.
November: Presidential election: Reagan won by unexpected landslide

Rights Amendment and took liberal positions on voter registration, environmental protection, the minimum wage, and health legislation. He attempted to stop production of the B-1 bomber, and he supported the admission of Vietnam to United Nations membership.

Carter's first budget requests asked Congress for a broad multibillion dollar program to stimulate an economy plagued by low growth, high rates of unemployment, and soaring inflation. So gifted an individual failed to master any of the major problems the country faced. As OPEC continued to increase petroleum prices, Carter pleaded and moralized, both at home and to the Arabs, but his energy policy was totally ineffective. Although Carter favored the expansion of nuclear energy, the growing concerns over the environment, demonstrations against nuclear facilities such as Seabrook in New Hampshire, and finally the near-disaster at Three Mile Island virtually killed nuclear power as an energy alternative. But most of all, the hostage crisis which began November 4, 1979, when Iranian 'students' seized Americans and held them hostage, paralyzed the President; he seemed helpless. Finally an attempt to free the Americans by force in April 1980 ended as a pitiable disaster as U.S. helicopters crashed in the Iranian desert. Only the Camp David Accord between Israel and Egypt redeemed his reputation. The stage was set for a conservative backlash.

THE INTERNATIONAL ECONOMY

The year 1971 had been pivotal for United States foreign trade as imports exceeded exports for the first time since 1893; the surplus of $2.7 billion in 1970 turned to minus $1 billion in the first nine months of the next year. These developments reflected conditions long in the making that would become more serious. The United States, the major world trading power, was a sluggish giant. Although the dollar value of exports rose to $45.2 billion, imports entered faster as businesses tried to protect themselves from crippling dock strikes by stockpiling materials. West Coast ports were shut down for three months during the summer of 1971, and East Coast ports were under constant closure threats. U.S. exports consisted principally of three things: agricultural products, military equipment, and transport goods such as cars and auto parts (much of them going to Canada to replace inventories after the long strike in Canada against General Motors) and aircraft, particularly wide-bodied commercial jets as well as military planes and helicopters to European allies. Cotton, soy beans, tobacco, wheat, and oils topped the list of an $8.2 billion agricultural export flood.

Imports, however, were fast becoming a problem. Japanese automobiles created a rising tide, capturing almost 17 percent of sales in the American market. Imported footwear, clothing, motorcycles, and televisions—all from countries that paid marginal wages to their workers and thus could sell at a low cost—rose sharply. The balance of payments in the first nine months of 1971 saw a drastic deterioration, from $3.8 billion to $17.5 billion, in the American liquidity position (the measurement of the difference between

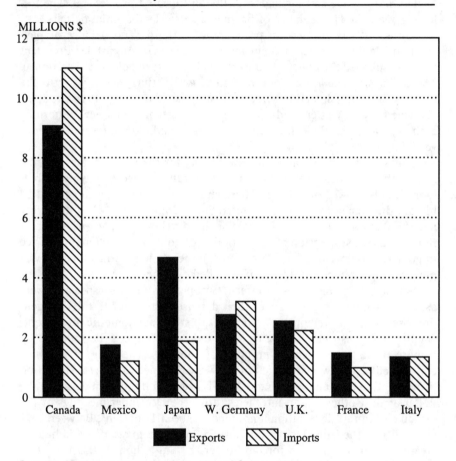

Source: *Statistical Abstract of the United States, 1970*

foreigners' liquid assets and short-term claims versus U.S. short-term claims and liquid reserves), while the balance on the official reserve transactions showed a deficit of $23.4 billion, more than double the previous year. No wonder that the exchange pressures on the dollar, merchandise foreign trade deterioration, outflows of private capital, and currency speculation boded no good for the future.

The deterioration of American prominence in the international economy which began in the sixties was now further complicated by the role of the United States dollar as the major world currency. For example in 1969, as the domestic economy heated up, the United States ran a surplus $2 billion in the first nine months in the official reserve transactions account, despite a striking deficit of $10 billion in the liquidity measurement; United States banks had borrowed $14 billion in foreign markets to meet customers' needs.

Consequently the domestic boom propelled by inflationary pressure carried over into international trade. With money being spent abroad rapidly, the United States trade surplus had virtually disappeared by 1968–69. The following year, the U.S. balance of payments showed substantial deficits.

By mid-1971 the long-run problems of inflation and balance of payments difficulties created a financial near-panic. On August 15, President Nixon suspended the policy of converting all dollars to gold at $35 an ounce. The dollar was cut loose from its connection of thirty-seven years to the treasury price of gold and left free to float. A hasty meeting of the Group of Ten, the leading Western industrial countries, established a new pattern of exchange rates, but the United States could not and did not resume the convertibility of the dollar.

The summer crisis was a rude awakening for the United States and the rest of the world. As the deficit in the overall balance of payments ballooned, gold flowed out of U.S. These large capital outlays, estimated at $2 billion, threatened to reduce the United States gold reserve below the safety net of $10 billion. Nixon acted to reverse this outflow. First, as we have mentioned, was the suspension of convertibility of gold to dollars (later the price of gold was compromised at $38 an ounce); then, a 10 percent surcharge was put on dutiable imports; third, Nixon called on other countries to assist the United States in this crisis. Western European countries especially were asked to assume a larger share of their defense costs. Fourth, the President proposed a "job development" tax credit to stimulate domestic investment; finally Nixon instituted a 90-day wage-and-price freeze to be followed by "Phase II," a more extended program of controls.[1] These directives which constituted his "New Economic Policy" were designed to effect a $13 billion turnaround in the balance of trade. Briefly, the Nixon program devalued the dollar against other major currencies; after the December meetings of the Group of Ten this devaluation amounted to about 11 percent. Between 1961 and mid-1971 the United States had lost $5.25 billion in reserves and had increased dollar liabilities to foreign holders by $13 billion ($21.35 to $34.32 billion). Imports had increased 156 percent but exports had risen only 118 percent.

Nixon's New Economic Policy amounted to a series of makeshift currency changes which completed the dismantling of the Bretton Woods structure and the institution of a hastily improvised nationwide "Planning and Control System."[2] On December 20, Nixon lifted the import surcharge and the discriminatory provisions of the investment tax credit, but the reform of the international monetary system remained still at issue. The Smithsonian Agreement of December 18, 1971, ended the stalemate and initiated the new pattern of exchange rates which the United States had wanted. Nevertheless, the competitive problems that had prompted Nixon's reversal of long-standing monetary philosophy were no closer to being solved in 1972. Despite the crash programs of 1971, United States foreign trade worsened drastically in 1972 as imports exceeded exports by $6.5 billion, more than three times the deficit of 1971. Imports rose 19 percent while exports slowed.

An acquired taste for foreign consumer goods, such as tape recorders, clothing, and electronics, fueled the increase, while the growth in United States exports was confined largely to agricultural products, especially heavy shipments of grain to the Soviet Union.

The international economy was subjected to numerous shocks in 1973. The industrial economies were gripped by rising inflation. The Yom Kippur war was used as an excuse to embargo oil to the West, resulting in a boost of prices for consumers. Most countries were in the short run unable to handle these pressures, and exchange rates and monetary policy seemed out of control. In the United States, Watergate and its ongoing trauma destroyed the ability of the federal government to function. Washington became a city where nothing happened, and where fear and rumor held sway.[3] On the whole, however, both international trade and investment continued for a short time the momentum from the previous year, and some of the extreme difficulties in the United States' balance of payments position began to improve; direct investment by foreign groups in the United States increased considerably as European companies sought out opportunities in the United States market. United States agricultural exports benefitted from crop failures and poor harvests abroad, especially in the Soviet Union. Although the devaluation of the dollar had increased the attractiveness of United States' goods, shipments of overseas oil added $3 billion to the import bill. The difference between higher inflation abroad and lower inflation at home gave American goods only a temporary edge abroad. Domestic productivity continued its slide. The international trading world of the seventies was in chaos as OPEC oil put the industrial world in bondage.

THE ENERGY CRISIS

Early in 1974, OPEC (Organization of Petroleum Exporting Countries) increased crude oil prices 400 percent. This dramatic increase in energy prices and the problems it brought dominated the rest of the decade. For U.S. companies and the American economy as a whole, adjustment to the oil shock was traumatic. All oil-importing countries incurred deficits as hundreds of billions of dollars were transferred largely from Western industrial countries, especially the United States, the largest energy consumer, to OAPEC (Organization of Arab Petroleum Exporting Countries). The international economy faced the monumental task of recycling these oil revenues to the new rich, the oil sheikdoms, from the resource-poor importers. Since the United States was the biggest oil importer, it was sharply affected, though poorer countries were even more vulnerable. Since the price of oil was pegged to the dollar, the dollar's value appreciated. Also, U.S. banks played a major role in recycling oil money. A great deal of Arab money came back to be invested in America. Nevertheless Nixon's economic strategy gave way to damage containment, and the last piece of Nixon's new economic policy,

Phase IV, ended in the shambles of the Watergate crisis. Economic growth slowed because of the oil crisis; and U.S. import costs soared because of the increased cost of oil[4] and the insatiability of American demand. During the first half of 1975, there was widespread speculation against the dollar, and the Federal Reserve intervened continuously to halt swings in the dollar's value. By June, the Arab oil producers owned $1.6 billion in United States government securities; in six months they had added $659 million alone in bank deposits and $449 million in long-term deposits. Money from the Middle East had shifted from short-term deposit liabilities and savings certificates to longer-range and more fundamental investments. Further battering a weary world, the oil cartel raised prices an additional 10 percent on October 1, 1975. U.S. trade soared as the oil-developing countries made spectacular purchases of heavy machinery and industrial goods. For a short time, the trade balance would register a surplus of $11.2 billion. Still, the quantity of American goods exported was 3 percent below 1974, and the country was in deep recession.[5]

By mid-1976, the worst was over and the world economy moved back from recession, but unemployment and stagflation continued to affect the United States. In 1975, four Mideast countries—Saudi Arabia, Kuwait, the United Arab Emirates, and Qatar—had achieved current account surplus of $35 billion; in 1976, the estimated surplus was $41 billion. The major share of their investments with these funds went to the United States, so in one sense the recycling was working to the benefit of Americans.

The second half of the decade showed world trade at nearly $1 trillion, but much of the increase was due to inflation. The volume of world trade was actually slowing and the practice of protectionism increasing. OPEC again raised oil prices 10 percent on January 1, 1977, ruling out any return to pre-1973 conditions. That same year the United States incurred a cumulative deficit of $22.4 billion, a problem that was exacerbated by a dock strike on the East Coast and Gulf of Mexico. A bad situation became even worse on December 17, 1978, when OPEC announced it was raising the price of oil another 14.5 percent in a four-step process for the coming year. The spokesman for the cartel claimed that OPEC's revenues had eroded because of the worldwide inflation and that the importing countries could handle this increase. Sheik Yamani, OPEC's guiding strategist, lectured the West on its bad habits of using energy so wastefully. President Carter to no avail asked OPEC to reconsider its increase because of the damage it would do to the worldwide economy.

As the decade wound down, the national and the global economy were in great disarray. The corruption and extravagance of some of the OAPEC nations were forcing them to pump more crude oil to maintain their conspicuous spending. Far-sighted analysts began to predict the end of the cartel's effectiveness. Conservation of energy in the U.S. was catching on, thus lowering dependency. OPEC shared the weakness of all cartels: the policy of the group was subordinate to the interests of individual nations. Within a short time discord among members would temporarily shatter OPEC's monolithic front.

THE END OF THE CARTER YEARS

The brief respite of 1976–77 gave way to a very serious dollar-gold crisis in 1978 which continued through the final months of the Carter administration. The trade deficit worsened to $34 billion while the rate of inflation climbed sharply to 14 percent, in part because of the government's policy of depreciating the dollar against foreign currencies. On November 1, when the dollar reached historic new lows against all major trading currencies, President Carter moved to support the dollar by lowering the discount rate, by increasing reserve requirements for banks, by ordering the doubling of gold sales by the Treasury, and by sanctioning swap agreements with both the Bank of Japan and the Swiss Central Bank. (A swap is an exchange of currencies in the spot market with the agreement to reverse the transaction in the future.) The decline in the dollar in the late 1970s had both immediate and long-term causes. Speculation against the dollar was one immediate factor, as was the huge amount of dollars ($500 to $800 million outside the United States) all unregulated in the Eurodollar markets. The deterioration of the competitive position of traditional American industries, however, remained the key problem.

The seesaw between the OPEC price hikes and the falling dollar rocked not only the United States economy but the entire trading world.[6] OPEC claimed that the drop in the real value of the dollar was the major reason for its price increases, but the skyrocketing price of oil merely forced the United States trade balance to deteriorate further. Most painful were the homilies delivered to the West by OPEC spokesmen about the need to conserve energy. Yet the United States and the other consumers deserved this treatment. From 1973 on there had been no concerted effort against the cartel. These years of economic trouble saw gold rise from $35 an ounce to more than $800 an ounce as confidence in the dollar fell.[7]

On April 12, 1979, President Carter hailed the international trade agreement reached at the end of a six-year series of trade negotiations known as the Tokyo Round. This conference, in Carter's words, produced perhaps "the most far-reaching and comprehensive" trade legislation in three decades. The Tokyo Round had noticeable effects and marked the height of GATT's authority in the postwar world. Tariffs on hundreds of separate items were to be reduced by one-third over the next eight years. The Tokyo Round opened up foreign government purchases to American bidders; other provisions of this agreement reduced trade restraints. Overall, the Tokyo Round promoted international trade and lessened the impact of the oil shock. The United States hoped that these efforts would aid in paring the trade deficit. Hat in hand, Treasury Secretary G. William Miller travelled to the Middle East to report to the Saudis that Americans would cut their energy consumption. More positive trade results came from the renewed relations between the United States and Red China that had been initiated by President Nixon. Although the volume of exchange with China was still very small in absolute amounts, trade jumped 36 percent in the first nine months of 1979.

The Iranian hostage crisis from November 4, 1979, to January 20, 1981, not only weakened international regard for the United States but also acted to lower the strength of the dollar abroad. In Iran, the revolutionary government generated anti-American riots. Arab oil men exchanged their dollars for West German marks, Swiss francs, and British pounds. As the dollar sank again to new lows, central banks moved to shore up its value, although not without West German bankers in particular counseling the United States on the need for stronger action to cure inflation.

Within a short time, harsh and soaring domestic rates of inflation would provide a kind of cure in the form of a severe recession, which would spread to all other Western economies. The political economy of the Carter administration accentuated all the weaknesses of the U.S. international trading position. Tight money policies persisted in spite of rising unemployment. Beginning in late 1979 United States' and global inflation rates diminished, but at a terrible price. The industrial preeminence of the U.S. disappeared in the chaos of these years.

AGRICULTURE IN THE SEVENTIES

The economic difficulties of American agriculture seem an almost permanent feature in this half-century. The decade of the seventies was no exception. Only when severe catastrophe at home or abroad dramatically lowered supply did domestic agriculture prosper. In the seventies, most of the serious crop failures took place in the Soviet Union. At home, the corn leaf blight (1970) and other disasters tended to have only minimal impact. Increased productivity and precarious prices continued in much the same way as previous decades. The federal government, under various programs, continued to give aid to or subsidize the farm community and helped slow the inexorable attrition of the farming community. In 1970, the number of farms dipped below 3 million, a decline of about 28 percent from the 1960s. Just over 5¼ million persons were employed in farming in 1970; 3,728,000 were family labor and 1,536,000 were hired help, earning a low average wage of $1.46 per hour. Gross farm income rose to $56 billion, but farm mortgage debt climbed to $28.4 billion. However, farms were now somewhat bigger, the income per farm somewhat larger, and their productivity was greater. Mismanagement of their agriculture forced the Russians to become large buyers of American grains and feedstuffs, but even this bonanza did not alter the permanent secular trends in U.S. agriculture.

By now, agriculture was in every way a capitalistic industry. Decades earlier, before World War I, the basic restructuring of agriculture had taken place in the adaptation of crops to land, climate, and markets. Each decade brought more sophistication to these adaptations. Superspecialized crops became common, such as potatoes grown only for french fries and tomatoes grown for tomato paste. Antibiotics to combat animal diseases and hormones to stimulate growth boosted production, which frequently led only to lower prices. Everywhere chemical fertilizers and pesticides, dusted, sprayed, or scattered on land and crops, increased yields. To be a successful farmer was to be part businessman and part chemist. Unfortunately for the farmer, agricultural prices correlated in inverse ratio to the success of agricultural improvements.

In the 1970s public protest groups recognized that farmers were rapidly becoming one of the greatest causes of pollution. New studies showed that runoffs from feed lots and other chemical residues from farms were contaminating the environment. Government regulation of herbicides, pesticides, and agricultural chemicals had been an afterthought; once the seriousness of the problem was obvious, the government intervened, but only in a haphazard manner. Government policy makers seemed more afraid of restricting the profitability of the chemical industries than of the health effects on the consuming public. Likewise, many farmers were proving to be just as short-sighted in their respect for the environment as manufacturers.

In California, a long-standing strike wound down in 1970. Since 1966 Cesar Chavez's United Farm Workers (UFW) had tried to earn recognition from the powerful grape growers but to little avail. Finally, after intense picketing and peaceful protest, growers in the Central Valley recognized the union; others soon followed suit. Nevertheless rivalries continued between the UFW and the Teamsters, which had also tried to organize migrant workers. Grape growers also continued to harbor resentment against Chavez. Seedless red grapes were developed to increase consumption, but California wines, though greatly improved in quality, frequently fell in price because of oversupply—in other words, like the rest of the industry, the future for California farmers and farm workers was never bright for long.

The Agricultural Act of 1970 replaced the Food and Agricultural Act of 1965. It included "set-aside clauses" that reduced acreage for corn and other feed grains, wheat, and cotton, and replaced the "diversion" programs of the previous legislation. After setting aside the required portion of land and meeting conservation requirements, farmers were free to plant crops as they wished. Thus 1971 brought predictably an increase in production, but luckily the Soviet Union agreed to buy 3 million tons of U.S. grain worth about $135 million. These and other foreign purchases boosted exports to a record $7.8 billion and made 1971 a good year. Gross farm income rose to $58.7 billion, net farm income to $15.7 billion, and the federal government paid out $500 million less in farm payments ($3.2 billion). For the next eight years, farm exports generated a temporary boom in the farm industry. Domestic demand remained low, however. Each year from 1972 through 1979 (until the Carter administration, on January 4, 1980, put an embargo on grain sales to the Soviet Union because of its invasion of Afghanistan) saw American farmers outpace all previous levels of production while increasing their indebtedness in order to plant and harvest enormous crops of grain. The Soviet Union accounted for almost half the increase in sales, but Japan and Western Europe were also big, steady purchasers; our feed-grain programs turned these countries into beef eaters. On August 10, 1973, the new Nixon farm bill abolished almost all restrictions on planting, except crops protected by the Southern farm lobby—peanuts, rice, tobacco, and sugar. The legislation established a price structure so that if the market price fell below the target price, the government would make up the difference and farmers would be eligible for price support loans from the government. The Secretary of Agriculture was given the authority to set aside certain acreages from production, but no farmer was to receive more than $20,000 in government payments.

The high quantity of farm exports pushed up domestic food prices. Overall inflation in the United States had been masked for years by the low price of foodstuffs. In 1973, retail food prices jumped an unheard-of 20 percent, and President Nixon peremptorily ordered export controls on soybeans. Crop shortages and increased demand abroad had generated large purchases of American soybeans, and this restriction without consultation of the importing nations was to hurt America's reputation as a reliable vendor for years to come. For this brief period more acreage was planted than ever before, 335 million acres total, more than could be sustained in the long run; yet, only 5 percent of the population was engaged in agriculture! The sheer magnitude of this productive capacity was unbelievable. The U.S. furnished 16.2 million tons of grain to the Soviet Union (part of the reason for the domestic food price hike) and negotiated an agreement to sell the Soviets 6 to 8 million tons annually. So prodigious was this production that gains from farm exports pushed the trade balance into the black by $4 billion in 1976.

Perhaps 1976 can be seen as the peak of this artificial bubble of farm prosperity. Farm land values were rising rapidly, 14 percent alone in 1978, but farm income in 1977 was falling. In December of that year, farmers organized a nationwide strike to protest the low prices of agricultural goods. As 1977 gave way to 1978, farmers drove tractors through the streets of Washington, D.C., demanding 100 percent of parity, but farmers lacked the muscle to force meaningful concessions from the Carter administration. Moreover, overall sympathy for their demands was lacking. Within weeks the protest faded and farmers settled for an additional $744 million in government farm price supports, far less than their original demands.

High rates of inflation, in double digits by the end of the decade—14 percent by 1981—and rising interest rates eroded most of the nominal farm gains by any measurement and brought distress to the entire economy. Agricultural indebtedness was rising far too rapidly. The European Common Agricultural Policy (CAP), instituted in 1962, with its heavy subsidy of inefficient agriculture, had already restricted American export markets unnecessarily; in any case the Carter embargo on grain shipments to the Soviet Union ended the happy times for American grain producers.

Strangely, the Carter administration began to worry that foreigners were buying up American farmland. In October 1978, Congress responded with legislation requiring non-Americans and cooperatives owning land to register with the United States Department of Agriculture (USDA), specifying the amount of land bought, the price paid, and its intended use. Of all the problems that United States agriculture faced, this alleged foreign infiltration was the most ephemeral and insignificant. An intensive Congressional investigation proved beyond doubt that foreigners were not buying up our farmlands, although some were buying vacation property. But the fears persisted.

Agriculture in the 1970s resembled the Flying Dutchman, destined to wander without hope and without a future. Soaring crop yields pointed only to a condemnation of the long-range failures of federal policies. Wisdom clearly suggested that the programs to aid American agriculture contributed to, and exacerbated, the ineffective efforts at adjusting agricultural production to worldwide demands. American farm goods more and more were part of an integrated world agricultural market system. In this global arena, there were opportunities and risks, but critics charged that U.S. agriculture was surely missing most of the opportunities because it was handcuffed by obsolete public policies. Legislation was unimaginative and only cosmetically altered the content of each new farm bill. The practice of price supports which the New Deal had originated in the 1930s remained locked in place. No President felt he had the power to alter fundamentally this system. American agriculture might have had good years, several in a row when prices were better, but the chronic problems—overproduction, low prices, heavy indebtedness, and unstable markets—persisted and prevailed.

LABOR

Organized labor in the 1970s was in disarray. Strikes were commonplace. Labor leadership was nondescript. Organized labor suffered a great loss on May 9, 1970, when Walter Reuther was killed in a plane crash. Beset by inflation and high rates of unemployment, organized labor hunkered down to protect its position through COLAs (Cost of Living Adjustments), and by strengthening overtime, seniority, and health benefits. In most ways, labor in the 1970s continued on the same course as the previous decade. Significantly, the number of laborers who stayed outside the ranks of organized labor was growing, a development that transformed the work place. Contract negotiations for more than five million workers made 1970 a benchmark year. Two major strikes, one at GE, the second in California in the grape industry, finally were settled. Still, labor unrest was widespread. Railroad workers threatened a walkout, but Congress intervened and the strike was postponed until March 1, 1971. Federal air controllers staged a one-day "sickout." Postal workers struck, ultimately involving 200,000 workers, but the dispute was quickly settled. In the fall of 1970, the UAW called a strike at General Motors plants. The resulting new contract gave workers a 13 percent pay raise the first year and an overall 39 percent increase over the next two, a cost of living clause, and improved pension and early retirement benefits. In 1970, although the number of imported Japanese cars was still negligible, the appeal of imported Volkswagen 'Beetles' as we have noted was already spreading.

Organized labor also opposed President Nixon's ninety-day wage-price freeze. George Meany, AFL-CIO president, agreed to participate in the Pay

Board (a committee of five members each from labor, management, and the government) after some arm-twisting from federal officials was applied. At the AFL-CIO convention in Miami, Nixon was not well received by the delegates. Labor leadership was suspicious of movements like the Pay Board, which seemed to circumvent direct bargaining.

At first, the Pay Board, over labor opposition, decided against granting retroactive pay increases; Congress reversed this decision. Conflicts continued. The Pay Board approved a 15 percent pay raise for soft-coal miners, while the President's guidelines set a 5.5 percent limit. Who could blame labor's instinctive disdain for this jerry-built incomes-policy program? Moreover, Nixon's price controls boded ill for labor members. The federal government, lacking a systematic policy, chose to intercede in labor disputes capriciously. Congress intervened in the strike of railway signalmen; the President invoked Taft-Hartley in the longshoremen's strike. In almost every major dispute either there was major federal intrusion or the threat of intervention. To many observers it seemed that the government, rather than the market, had moved into the center of labor-management relations. Was every strike or threatened strike—by railroad men, or teamsters, or miners, or longshoremen—cause for national intervention? they asked. Meanwhile, conditions on the Pay Board continued to deteriorate. After labor was outvoted eight to five in a dispute involving West Coast stevedores, the labor representatives withdrew. Only Frank Fitzsimmons stayed on the Pay Board, which was now a seven-member panel, made up of five public members and one member each from labor and management.

On the whole 1972 and 1973 were still tolerably good years for labor. Real earnings were still on the rise. The average take-home pay for workers improved to $139 per week, and 2.3 million new jobs were created. In 1973, unemployment was reduced to 4.7 percent, and the workers in the electrical industry, teamsters, steel workers, and railway workers all signed contracts without strikes; after only a nine-day walkout against Chrysler, the UAW also signed a contract. A year later, soaring inflation would cut real wages by 5 percent, and worse was to follow as the effects of the oil embargo shook the economy.

In other developments, the UMW was rocked by scandal over the misuse of union pension funds, and its president, Tony Boyle, convicted and sent to jail. The New York State Teachers Association merged with the United Teachers of New York, signalling the growing strength of white-collar unions. Organized labor felt threatened by these changes and had mixed feelings about the passage of the Equal Employment Opportunity Act in 1972, but the AFL-CIO reversed its earlier opposition and endorsed the Equal Rights Amendment. Unions also complained that Occupational Safety and Health Administration (OSHA) standards were not being rigorously enforced. In the 1970s 86 million workers had jobs, but most of these workers did not belong to unions.

During 1974 and 1975, strikes by organized labor would increase sharply, as would unemployment. The Labor Department reported that during the first 9 months of 1974, labor disputes accounted for a record 38 million work-days of idleness. Only among white collar members were union gains impressive. Public employees in 1975 accounted for over five hundred separate strike actions, although most public employee unions were forbidden to strike by law. To lessen the impact of increased unemployment on conventional industries, Congress extended unemployment benefits, voted public works projects, and added public service jobs, but overall the 1970s were not noted for imaginative solutions to the rapidly changing nature of work in American society and the decline of blue-collar unionism. The flexible work standards at the General Motors Lordstown plant, the four-day work week, and the purchase of a handful of run-down companies by their workers under Employee Stock Ownership Plans (ESOPs) were widely noted, but worker boredom, alienation, and dissatisfaction were not seriously discussed. Despite their appearances, the four-day week and ESOPs were more a product of favorable tax legislation than an indication of a coming wave of labor ownership of the means of production.

The last three years of this rollercoaster decade brought no long-term stability to the economic problems of the nation nor a surcease in labor's difficulties. Two years of relative labor peace were followed by 1979, which spawned 3,815 strikes in the first eight months. Unemployment and inflation both hovered around 7 percent but in real terms workers' take-home pay was edging down. Steel companies, one of the large employers of union labor, began to close some of their older plants because of foreign competition, and electronic and apparel manufacturers were hard hit as United States companies transferred operations to lower-cost Asian sites. Raising the federal minimum wage from $2.65 to $2.90 was something of an empty gesture.

Early in 1980, George Meany died, and Lane Kirkland took his place as president of the AFL-CIO. Union membership peaked in 1979 at 21,734,000, but it could not keep pace with a labor force that was growing even faster. Most of the millions of new jobs, especially those for women entering the labor markets in large numbers, were nonunionized and could not easily be integrated with older unions.

Most difficult of all was the strain of union-government relations. On three issues, organized labor came head-on against the Carter administration. In December 1977, 165,000 members of the UMW began the longest coal union strike in United States history. On March 6, 1978, President Carter invoked the Taft-Hartley Act and ordered the miners back to work; they refused. A court backed the miners by affirming that the government had failed to show that the strike would cause "irreparable harm to the national health and safety."[8] For years, organized labor had strongly opposed the Taft-Hartley Act and fought for its repeal. In fact, although Taft-Hartley had been invoked thirty-four times, it had been largely ineffectual. In this case, as in others, Taft-Hartley simply aroused the animosity of workers.

In 1976, labor had supported Jimmy Carter's campaign to win the White House, but over the next twenty-four months the rift between Carter and Meany opened wide. In 1977, the Amalgamated Clothing and Textile

Table 6.1	United States Union Membership, 1979

Teamsters	1,924,000
Auto Workers	1,500,000
Steelworkers	1,286,000
Food and Commercial Workers	1,235,000
State, County & Municipal Employees	1,020,000
Electrical Workers, Brotherhood of	1,012,000
Machinists & Aerospace Workers	920,000
Carpenters	768,000
Service Employees	625,000
Laborers	610,000
Communications Workers	508,000
Teachers	500,000

Source: *United States Bureau of Labor Statistics.*

Workers Union had selected the J. P. Stevens Company as its prime target for unionization. If Stevens could be cracked, the unions' dream of organizing the textile workers in the South's largest industry might be possible. After a year's effort against Stevens, the union found itself losing; no more Stevens plants were unionized than when the action started. The union claimed that Stevens used poorly defined federal laws, especially the National Labor Relations Act (NLRA), to flout the union's efforts. Organized labor sponsored a series of amendments to the NLRA, known as "the labor law reform bill," which passed the House but failed against a conservative filibuster in the Senate. The bill died, and Meany believed that Carter had not supported the bill strongly enough. Relations between the president of the country and the president of organized labor was characterized as that of "two spitting cats."

The final issue that was never resolved was labor's role in economic policy. After the collapse of Nixon's wage-price program, Ford and Carter turned to voluntary efforts. Toward the end of 1978, the Carter administration announced a program of "voluntary" wage-price guidelines, the aim of which was to keep increases in wages and fringe benefits to 7 percent and to hold price increases to the range of 6 to 6.5 percent. The program included an insurance provision to give workers a tax rebate if living costs exceeded 7 percent. From the start, the program was unworkable. Labor especially was afraid that such arrangements might intrude on traditional collective bargaining. In 1979, the AFL-CIO agreed to participate in a new wage and price restraint program. The agreement was hailed as unprecedented, a new position for labor in the determination of economic and social policies. One hundred and fifty years of adversarial relations could not, however, be changed so easily, and this voluntary agreement passed into the same oblivion as the previous arrangements. Similarly, the election of Douglas Frazer, the head of the UAW, to Chrysler's board of directors as a trade-off for concessions by workers ushered in no new world of labor-management peace.

Unions had come far indeed since the New Deal, but as the 1970s ended, organized labor was losing ground and on the defensive. The next presidential election would bring unions face to face with a chief executive whose philosophy all but rejected their right to exist.

NOTES

[1]Robert F. Lanzillotti, Mary T. Hamilton, and Baline R. Roberts, *Phase II in Review: The Price Commission Experience* (Washington, D.C.: The Brookings Institute, 1975), pp. 1–8.

[2]Otis L. Graham, *Toward a Planned Society: From Roosevelt to Nixon* (New York: Oxford University Press), 1976, pp. 213–238.

[3]*The Americana Annual* (New York: Americana Corporation, 1974), p. 299.

[4]"The Oil Crisis in Perspective," *Daedalus: Journal of the American Academy of Arts and Sciences* 4 (Fall 1975): 1–293.

[5]Sidney Sonenblum, *The Energy Connection: Between Energy and the Economy* (Cambridge, Mass.: Ballinger Publishing Co., 1978), pp. 35–38.

[6]George A. Nikolaieff, ed., *Stabilizing America's Economy* (New York: H. W. Watson Co., 1972), pp. 232–234.

[7]Barry Commoner, *The Poverty of Power: Energy and the Economic Crisis* (New York: Knopf, 1976), pp. 1–4.

[8]*New York Times,* April 12, 1979.

SUGGESTED READINGS

Commoner, Barry. *The Poverty of Power: Energy and the Economic Crisis.* New York: Knopf, 1976.

Daedalus: Journal of the American Academy of Arts and Sciences, "The Oil Crisis: In Perspective," 4 (Fall 1975), 1–293.

Graham, Otis L. *Toward a Planned Society: From Roosevelt to Nixon.* New York: Oxford University Press, 1976.

Harrington, Michael. *The Twilight of Capitalism.* New York: Simon and Schuster, 1976.

Heller, Walter W. *New Dimensions of Political Economy.* Cambridge, Mass.: Harvard University Press, 1966.

Lanzillotti, R. F., Mary T. Hamilton, and Baline R. Roberts. *Phase II in Review: The Price Commission Experience.* Washington: The Brookings Institute, 1975.

Lebergott, Stanley. *The American Economy: Income, Wealth, and Work.* Princeton, NJ: Princeton University Press, 1976.

Nikolaieff, George A., ed. *Stabilizing America's Economy.* New York: H. W. Wilson Co., 1972.

Sampson, Anthony. *The Seven Sisters: The Great Oil Companies and the World They Shaped.* New York: Bantam Books, 1975.

Sonenblum, Sidney. *The Energy Connections: Between Energy and the Economy.* Cambridge, Mass.: Ballinger, 1978.

Steiner, George A. *Government's Role in Economic Life.* New York: McGraw-Hill, 1953.

Tugendhat, Christopher. *The Multinationals.* Harmondsworth, Middlesex, England: Penguin Books, Ltd., 1978.

Weidenbaum, Murray. *Business, Government and the Public.* Englewood Cliffs, NJ: Prentice-Hall, 1977.

7   *The Reagan Revolution*

Historians are not yet ready to pass judgment on Ronald Reagan, the fortieth president of the United States. Reagan articulated that his administration's programs would mark a new direction in United States history for decades to come. He was right, though not perhaps in the way he intended: many of the problems that face the country, most notably the swelling of the budget deficit, resulted from Reagan's policies. Other decisions, such as the appointment of conservatives to the federal judiciary, will continue to affect legal issues for a long time.

Ronald Wilson Reagan was born on February 6, 1911, in Tampico, Illinois. He attended school in Dixon, Illinois, and went to Eureka College. Reagan's political views were midwestern, isolationist, and strongly pro-Roosevelt, a gesture of gratitude to the President who had given his father work at the depth of the Depression. In 1932 he graduated from Eureka with a B.A. in economics and sociology. In the fall of 1932, he began broadcasting football games. His dream, even as a sportscaster, was to become a Hollywood actor. In 1937, he was signed by Warner Brothers to play the lead, a crusading radio announcer, in *Love Is On the Air*. Most of his films were nondescript, but his role as George Gipp in *Knute Rockne—All American* (1940) was a serious one, and gave him a nickname, the 'Gipper,' which he would use as President.

Reagan gradually began to move to the right politically. For a decade (1952–62), he served as spokesman for the General Electric Company, giving speeches with such titles as "Our Enduring Freedoms," and "Encroaching Controls." By 1962, he had come full circle and was ready to enter politics as a Republican. Four years later he won the gubernatorial election in California. Despite his conservative pronouncements, his actions in California marked him more as a pragmatist than a hard-liner. However, he did act to "clean up" student radicalism at Berkeley, to cut expenditures in social services, and to reduce the welfare roles.

In 1980, Reagan easily dominated the Republican primaries and won the nomination at the party's national convention. Pledging his support for

Chronology

1981
February: Debt ceiling raised to $985 million
August: Economic Recovery Tax Act of 1981
December: Interfund borrowing authorized for Social Security Trust funds
1982
August: Omnibus Reconciliation Act cut spending by $133 billion, tightened pension rules and eligibility for food stamps, home loans, and farm subsidies
September: Tax Equity and Fiscal Responsibility Act of 1982 provided $98.3 billion in new revenue and $17.5 billion spending cut
October: Savings and Loan Reform Bill changes regulations; Job Training Act (replaces CETA); federal unemployment benefits extended from 12 to 16 weeks; Export Trading Companies bill passes easing antitrust barriers for small firms trading abroad
1983
March: Phase I jobs bill passes
April: Social Security Act Amendments of 1983 raised retirement age, delayed COLAs, raised taxes
July: Paul Volcker confirmed for reappointment as head of the Federal Reserve
September: Fiscal year 1983 deficit announced as $195.4 billion
November: Revenue sharing extended three years; IMF contribution increased $8 billion; payments to dairy farmers to cut production; low income housing reauthorization
1984
July: Debt ceiling raised to $1.573 trillion; $63 billion dollar deficit-cutting legislation passed
October: Social Security disability revisions; omnibus trade bill passed
1985
September: Fiscal year 1985 deficit balloons to $211.9 billion
November: Debt ceiling temporarily raised to $1.904 trillion

December: Balanced Budget and Emergency Deficit
Control Act of 1985 (Gramm-Rudman-Hollings bill)
1986
April: Consolidated Omnibus Budget Reconciliation Act
of 1985
June: First trillion dollar budget passed
October: Expanded job training bill passed; Tax Reform
Act of 1986; mandatory retirement due to age barred
1987
February: Clean Water Act appropriated $20 billion for
water pollution problems; Stuart B. McKinney Homeless
Assistance Act
April: Surface Transportation and Uniform Relocation
Act allocated $88 billion for highways and mass transit
aid
August: Alan Greenspan appointed head of Federal
Reserve; U.S.-Canada free trade agreement passed;
Competitive Equality Banking Act of 1987; First FSLIC
bailout provides $10.8 billion
October: Stock market crash; economic summit called by
President
December: Budget Reconciliation Act of 1987; Employee
Retirement Income Security Act (ERISA) revised
1988
April: $83 billion allocated in school aid (elementary,
secondary, and adult education)
August: omnibus trade bill signed; it defined overall
trade policy, clarified remedies for unfair practices
October: Welfare reform bill signed; it stipulated some
work requirements, strengthened child support
enforcement, extended child care supports, other minor
provisions
November: George Bush elected President

voluntary prayer in public schools, tuition credits for private schooling, opposition to school busing, abortion, and the Equal Rights Amendments, and calling on all who supported family, work, neighborhood, peace, and freedom, Ronald Reagan seemed like a new Moses to every conservative and some disillusioned Democrats. He won the election in a landslide.

A flat economy and double-digit inflation greeted the new President. His policy was to turn this economic malaise around by reducing government expenditures and by sponsoring the largest tax cut in history, some $335 billion over three years. In its enthusiasm to support Reagan, Congress jumped on the tax-cutting bandwagon. The gap between federal income and spending was to be made up by a stimulated economy freed from excess taxes and regulations. In practice, massive increases in defense spending and the greed of special interests negated Reagan's intentions. Deficits soared, borrowing increased, and the national debt surpassed the $2 trillion mark. Nevertheless inflation was cut, stock prices climbed, millions of new jobs were created, albeit largely lower-paid ones. A semblance of prosperity was enhanced by reassuring statements from the White House. Reagan exuded charm, grace, and good manners. When John Hinckley, Jr. wounded him severely, he quipped to the doctors in the operating room, "Please tell me you're Republicans." No President received higher ratings in public opinion polls.

Almost from the start, Reagan had to beat a retreat. Reaganomics could not contain the soaring deficits, and new taxes were voted. Reagan fought with Congress over funds. He became embroiled in the worst scandal of his presidency in 1987 when Oliver North and John Poindexter, close advisers, were shown to have sold arms to the Iranians and shunted the profits to the Contras. The trade imbalance continued to worsen, and millions of Americans worried about continued Japanese takeover. In October 1987 the stock market crashed as the Dow-Jones index lost 500 points. Most of all, however, poor Americans felt harassed by an unfeeling administration and appeared to be poorer despite the assurance that they were better off. Social services were cut, made worse by a sense of hardness and moral judgment that came with the drawbacks. The belief that the federal government had to play a much smaller role was naïve, doomed to failure.

What did Ronald Reagan leave that might last? Surely, a personal success story that would influence every politician for decades to come—that good looks, charm, and appeals to simple truths and patriotic values were more important than trying to educate the electorate to understand more fully the complex problems which faced the nation. Current problems could be pushed into the future with political impunity since future generations would bear the costs. However, Reagan took much credit for the resurgence of supply-side capitalism, especially the creation of new jobs and capital gains. The total collapse of centrally planned economies in Eastern Europe was contrasted with the clear effectiveness of a private enterprise system. And the melting of the U.S.S.R.'s hard line to "glasnost" and "perestroika" was also attributed to Reagan's policies of firmness and strength. Will the

Reagan view of a conservative America replace the long Progressive and New Deal traditions in social welfare, in public policy, and in human relations? Few now believe that this can be.

FORTUNE'S PROPHECIES FOR THE 1980s

In October 1979, *Fortune* began a series of telling articles on the prospects for the next ten years. "The Decade Ahead: Not So Bad If We Do Things Right" led off the series. The article predicted, on the basis of economic data furnished by Townsend-Greenspan, the New York economic consulting firm headed by Federal Reserve chairman Alan Greenspan, that economic growth of 3.4 percent a year was the best Americans might expect. This anticipated figure was somewhat lower than the 4.1 percent of the sixties but considerably better than the 2.8 percent of the seventies. The lead article stated: "After the economic shocks and disappointments of the seventies, it's heartening to think that the eighties could bring substantial recovery in real growth. But to get it, one will have to slow down the pace of inflation."[1]

The greatest concerns expressed were that oil prices might again take off, eroding substantially the will to reduce inflation. Others feared that government regulations to guarantee clear air, water, and safety would impose higher costs. Extending social welfare programs would also escalate expenses. Although these regulations and programs improved the quality of life, they invariably also burdened the private sector with increased costs. In the 1980s Americans would have to devote a larger share of GNP to capital investment and defense, declared *Fortune;* during the seventies defense spending had dropped from 7.15 percent GNP in 1970 to 4.5 percent in 1979. By now it was recognized that increased capital investment was essential if the United States was to remain competitive.

Since it was anticipated that population increase would slow to less than 10 percent for the decade, this rate of growth, 3.4 percent, would yield a dividend for the decade of 28 percent growth in real terms, and perhaps even a bit more if productivity climbed at a faster rate. Since the work force in the 1980s would grow more slowly and be more experienced, this advantage could strengthen the economy. If, however, productivity fell, these positives would be of little value. The eighties would have to reverse the trend of falling productivity that had become endemic since the mid-sixties. Since the falling growth rate also contributed to inflation, productivity would have to be sufficient to keep inflation low and to bolster economic health; controlling federal spending to reduce the national debt was also a must if significant revival were to occur. Inflation would abate only if the government could determine a mix of fiscal and monetary policy that would signal a long-term commitment to real noninflationary growth. If this occurred, interest rates would fall and capital investment would increase. Greenspan suggested that a range of 11 to 12 percent annually for investment in the eighties—up from 10 percent in the seventies—was crucial. Adopting measures to strengthen the supply-side economy, Greenspan felt, was the best way to restore genuine noninflationary growth.

Perhaps the most accurate predictions concerned the demography of the '80s. American society would become maturer, older, and yet more productive. With this shift would come improvements, *Fortune* predicted, such as less violence and less crime. From 1946 to 1962, the baby boom added 45 million people to the United States. Their presence in the overall demographic pattern was very evident; the aging of that generation had brought great pressure on social and economic institutions. In the 1980s the age cohort 15 to 24 would drop sharply as a percentage of the population. The cohort 25 to 45 would be the largest; those over 60 would also be a large and costly group to care for, but its proportion of the total population (11 or 12 percent) would not climb significantly. In the work force women who were younger and more educated would be replacing older men less educated. Nineteen million women had joined the labor market between 1960 and 1978, creating one of the major social and economic revolutions of the century, a revolution that appeared to be permanent. Today more than 50 percent of all women work, with enormous consequences and implications ranging from childbearing and-rearing to comparable worth as a goal for salary equalization. (*Fortune* did not anticipate the extent of this transformation!)

Fortune predicted that minority problems would, however, continue and poverty would persist. Young blacks would compete with unskilled white women coming into the labor force. Disadvantaged blacks would be the worst off, since curtailed government programs and the higher levels of education needed for these emerging labor markets would work against their breaking out of the ghetto. Illegal aliens would be both an asset and a liability. One *Fortune* estimate placed the figure of illegal aliens at between 2 and 15 million; in many parts of the country, especially the West and Southwest, and in many industries, such as low-cost textiles, apparel, and agriculture, these workers found steady but low-paying employment despite continuing legislative efforts to curb their entry into the U.S.

Demographic studies would reveal also the changing character of households. There would be more divorce and cohabitation, declining marriage rates, fewer children, and delayed child-bearing. A host of related industries would spring up around these trends, from fast-food shops and microwave ovens to innovations in child care and education. Traditional attitudes would be sacrificed for fast-paced lifestyles as individuals rationed their time. Marketing strategists would be kept on their toes to meet these new needs and demands. In short, the portent of demographic trends seemed to promise good things for the economy, but not without costly tradeoffs.

Productivity, many said, would get back to the annual 2.1 percent average growth of the period 1966–1973 but not to the 3.2 percent levels attained in the 1950s and '60s. Improved investment in capital goods and a somewhat older, more experienced labor force would reverse the disastrous 0.8 percent rise per year of the seventies. Real output per worker hour, the standard definition of productivity, had to be adjusted for the realities of the postindustrial society. It became recognized that providing workers with a life that balanced exertion with leisure boosted morale and productivity. Nevertheless, many longed for a return to the historical high rate of increased and upgraded productivity that had been one of the most important ways of lifting the standard of living for each generation of Americans.

Some economists like Lester Thurow saw the decline in productivity closely linked to the shift to service industries. The low productivity of McDonald's-type service jobs, however, were not representative of American industry. Communications and financial services, in contrast, were high productivity fields. Overall, however, *Fortune* believed that the transition from industrial employment to service fields would bring much individual hardship. "The most important source of productivity growth is advances in knowledge,"[2] *Fortune* concluded. How rapidly the knowledge-driven industries of the Third Industrial Revolution spread throughout the society, I believe, may well hold the long-range answer to our well-being.

Fortune singled out five major new concerns—environment, health, education, defense, and energy—that would demand expenditures of over $2 trillion by 1989. These new claims betokened a departure from traditional government expenditures such as the infrastructure that dominated its economic activity in the nineteenth century. Unlike the highways and railroads of yesterday, these contemporary concerns would take a larger percentage out of GNP. Each of these five demands could be met with a wide range of policy alternatives, but even lean and tight budgets for these areas projected heavy costs. *Fortune* also worried about exploding energy costs wrecking the economy.

The eighties promised a substantial rise in the real standard of living. "By 1990," *Fortune* said, "two families out of five might qualify as upper income."[3] Real disposable income would rise 3.75 percent a year, and even the median family income before taxes would increase about 20 percent by 1990. Upper-income families, those with over $25,000 in income in 1977 dollars, would grow by 10.4 million to 25.6 million for the nation. Many subgroups, however, would not fare well. Minority groups, single women raising families, and illegal aliens would not come close to the money tree. To be young and rich was the media's image of the idealized baby boomer. The earlier generation of baby boomers would benefit less in the 1980s than the "yuppies" who would help sustain the American myth of happiness based on money and material goods.

How many families would be "superclass"? Two income-earning professionals was the first ingredient, and in the 1980s there would be many of these. Highly paid professionals would often have spouses that earned an equivalent or even higher salary—two lawyers, two business executives, one lawyer and one executive, a businessman and a government bureaucrat. Combined incomes could reach $200,000. Their large disposable incomes made for expensive tastes such as gourmet foods and designer clothes. This group would receive a great deal of attention from the media far beyond their actual proportion of the population. Black families, to be sure, would form only a tiny percentage of the super-rich, though the number of black families earning $50,000 or more would double in the '80s. Two-parent black families as well as black professionals would continue to narrow slowly the income differential between blacks and whites, but the crisis in black families, especially female single-parent families, would continue to worsen. The epidemic of pregnancies among unwed teenagers would be the single greatest pressure creating permanent female poverty, both black and white.

The postindustrial consumer markets would burgeon in the eighties. These markets to a large degree would cater to the affluent society. *Fortune* envisioned appliances that would listen and reply (a feature already available in automobiles), designer bedsheets "festooned with peonies, on a background of wild plum," and weekend trips to Paris or London. But most disposable income would go for more traditional expenses—housing, cars, furniture, clothes, health care, education. Education at private colleges in fact would rise to $70,000 or more for a first degree (BA, BS), and $500 a day for a hospital stay would be ordinary. On the flip side, a gem diamond— one carat, flawless—which cost $60,000 in 1980 would fall to $8,000 by 1985; gold jewelry would also be cheap, falling to less than half its 1970 price.

Manufacturers would have to realize, *Fortune* continued, that consumer durables would have to meet higher standards of quality and require less care because these features were offered by foreign competition. The two-income family would not stay around waiting for a repairman to show up "sometime in the afternoon." The inflation of the seventies had produced a caution for investing money wisely and contributed to more expensive and more varied housing—condominiums, time-sharing arrangements for vacation lodging, second homes—as excellent tax shelters. Consumer electronics, from televisions to videocassette recorders, would be a growth industry. Americans at home with their VCRs could watch everything from Shakespeare to hard porn by renting videocassettes at minimal cost. Americans would also effect a revolution in diet: "more [lean] meat, poultry, fish, green vegetables, and fresh fruit; fewer potatoes and dry beans."[4] The search for the "fountain of youth" would generate a multibillion dollar industry in health spas and health equipment. At the same time the number of fast-food outlets would proliferate. Americans would dress better, gamble more, smoke less, seek out the exotic corners of the globe for new travel experiences, fear the death of the world through nuclear disaster, and become familiar with a virulent new disease, AIDS. In all, the *Fortune* series gave some remarkably accurate glimpses of life in the '80s.

THE REAGAN PRESIDENCY

The goal of President Reagan was to "put the nation on a fundamentally different course—a course leading to less inflation, more growth, and a brighter future for all of our citizens."[5] In addition to revitalizing the economy, Reagan promised to close the alleged military "window of vulnerability" and to institute a New Federalism—a return of significant discretionary power to state and local governments and much greater control to individuals over their own economic fortunes. Although the essence of the program was a philosophical conservatism, the key programs were embedded in a crude monetarism: namely the "black-box" of supply-side economics where uncalculated and unknown things happened once private enterprise and private initiative were freed from government restraints. Growth was to be assisted by a set of huge tax cuts over a three-year period, beginning with the Economic Recovery Tax Act of 1981. This combination was supposed not only to rejuvenate the economy, but usher in a great moral renewal of individualism, local responsibility, and efficient government. Although a social safety net would remain for those "who really needed and deserved help," the rest would be thrown back on their own resources—individuals and groups alike. The assumption was that the economy would soar to heights previously prevented only by the ever-encroaching dead hand of government. A half-century of constraints, interference, debilitation, excessive regulation, and liberal-egalitarian coddling, when sloughed off, would bring a promising rebirth.

Every president has a moral vision, and Mr. Reagan's vision was no less grand and noble than his predecessors'. And great moral visions are simple visions; otherwise they would not engage the strong emotional backing of ordinary people. Thus the election of 1980 was a revolution—or as much of a revolution as we have been able to mount since 1933. But by mid-decade, concern that the Reagan experiment would recast social and economic policies gave way, it seemed to many people, to a fear not only that the revolution had failed, but that the republic had to be saved from the revolutionaries themselves. Signs of rot had begun to appear. Robert Stockman, ex-head of the Office of Management and Budget, confessed that there was uncontrolled greed among Reagan's supporters. Volker's monetarism in 1981, it appeared, did no more than push down the soaring inheritance of inflation by generating a massive recession. Tax cuts failed to revitalize the economy. Innately conservative businessmen paid more attention to the market than to the political exhortations of the Republicans for more investment. Intransigent special interest groups—farmers, businessmen and labor—exacerbated the adversarial nature of politics in American life and prevented a bipartisan solution to economic distress. The hurt of the poor, the unemployed, and the many who could not cope in our complex and competitive society remained. Reaganomics has left a disarray that can be resolved only slowly. The disclosure of corruption in the department of Housing and Urban Development and the pathetic breakdown of the Savings and Loan industry was further evidence of the moral emptiness of Reagan's administration.

In his first administration, Reagan attempted to obliterate the Progressive legacy of the New Deal that had been carried on by Kennedy and Lyndon Johnson. Suppressing the soaring cost of social programs was only one part of the plan. Three other issues dominated the first Reagan term: tax policy, fairness, and federalism. The Economic Recovery Tax Act (ERTA) of 1981 granted a 25 percent across-the-board reduction in personal income tax rates and contained a provision to index personal taxes in 1985. ERTA was the largest tax cut in United States history. By the end of 1984, taxpayers would have received a $300 billion tax reprieve, and if it had simply been extended to 1987, the revenue lost to the federal government would have been over $1 trillion. However, more than offsetting these figures were the supposed benefits to the economy, which would be revitalized by large-scale capital investment, increased productivity, and real growth.

Although the revenue lost was large and the risk substantial, the tax act was by no means an entirely irresponsible fiscal act. Many Americans had come through the decade of the 1970s bruised by inflation and stagnation. Oil prices had lofted energy costs, inflation had gotten out of control, and tax-bracket creep had siphoned off a larger portion of take-home pay. Economists might tell Americans that the 1970s were pretty good in real terms; millions of people felt otherwise. Compared to the 1960s, the economy was worse; looking ahead, the end of the 1980s seemed ominously threatening. Already, voters in many states had forced state governments to limit their spending. Logically, many citizens felt the federal government should be similarly constrained. Both political parties recognized this growing concern. In some cases the Congress even hurried to go beyond Reagan's initial cuts. Had everything gone according to plan, some long-run dramatic changes might have occurred. It was incredibly naïve, though, to believe that everything would fall into the proper place, given the inexperience of Reagan's financial advisors.

Governments have to live with unintended consequences. It is impossible to anticipate all the economic fluctuations which will occur, and that is largely why government economic planning has such a poor track record. For Reagan, almost nothing fell into place while his military budgets soared. The magical happening that had to take place within the supply-sider's "black box" didn't occur. The recession deepened, growth halted, investment eased, and business leaders hunkered down to wait out the storm before they would think of new investments. Instead of revitalizing the economy, ERTA merely gave back revenue to the higher-income groups. As federal deficits soared, the Reaganites retreated. By early summer 1982, a new tax bill tried to retrieve $100 billion for the federal coffers; by early 1983, new social security changes and "user" taxes—5 cents per gallon on gasoline—looked like the first of a series of changes to cut back on booming federal deficits. The Reagan administration never effected the indexing of personal income taxes, and the unbalanced budget seemed destined to become a long-term and painful fixture of the federal budget process. As Palmer and Sawhill predicted in 1983:

> Eliminating deficits will necessitate a combination of tax increases, cutbacks in planned defense outlays and considerable spending restraint in domestic programs. However, tax increases and reductions will require that

President Reagan retreat from his original policy objectives, while substantial domestic spending restraint will require that Congress overcome strong political opposition to cuts in Social Security and Medicare.[6]

The dilemmas over these choices seemed formidable and fraught with negative national and international consequences.

The problem of "fairness" cannot be resolved by economists. Reagan's policies affected every social program. The "cuts"—some were only reductions in the planned increases—varied in severity from draconian to nominal and were not made across the board. Some expenditures, especially defense, rose tremendously and some services held their own, but most social welfare programs for the poor did not keep up. Determining what should be sacrificed, however, seemed to be based more on ideological or political philosophy than on any objective calculation.

Conservatives count the seven years from 1982 to 1989 as the "greatest, consistent burst of economic activity ever seen in the U.S." Martin Anderson, a senior fellow of the Hoover Institute, has cited five areas in this "Great Expansion": creation of jobs, creation of wealth, steady economic growth, lower income tax rates, and lower interest rates and inflation. Here are his numbers:

> During this period, 18.7 million new jobs were created, more than half of them paid over $20,000 a year. Total employment grew to 119.5 million, and the rate of unemployment fell to just over 5 percent, the lowest level in 15 years;
>
> Some $30 trillion dollars worth of goods and services were produced, a world record. Net asset values, including stocks, bonds and real estate rose more than $5 trillion, about 50 percent;
>
> Eighty six months of economic growth established a new peacetime record, five months longer than the wartime record of World War II, and 23 months short of the wartime record set during the Vietnam War in the 1960s.
>
> Personal income tax rates were cut from 70 percent to 28 percent. Interest rates and the rate of inflation also fell following the severe measures taken by the Federal Reserve in 1981;
>
> The Standard and Poor index of stock market value almost tripled, while in the entire period 1970–1982, it rose only 35 percent.[7]

Supporters of Reaganomics also claimed that spending on public housing, welfare, Social Security, Medicare, and health all increased by billions of dollars, though a closer examination showed that these gross numbers did not keep up with need in real terms.

The working poor and near-poor families and the two million families who received Aid to Families with Dependent Children (AFDC) and had incomes up to 75 percent above the poverty level had been hurt the most. If the President had been true to his word about the "trickle down" benefits, these people would not have suffered. But there was no consensus in the administration or in the country on the needs of the poor, and surely none on the costs of caring for the poor. The "social safety net" had become a meaningless euphemism in American society. Since the heyday of the Great Society's War on Poverty in the late 1960s, the proliferation of agencies to help the poor, the mountainous regulatory paperwork, and rocketing costs had alienated large numbers of voters. About $220 billion has been spent annually on social programs, almost 275 times the expenditures of 1935, 20 times 1955, and not quite double 1975 figures. The enormous commitment and cost of solving poverty has confused a great many Americans, though poll after poll has shown a willingness to pay increased taxes to aid the poor. Federal spending on medical care rose twelvefold between 1965 and 1980, Medicare from $7.5 to $36.7 billion, and Medicaid from $3.0 to $14.6 billion. Federal medical costs approached $100 billion by the end of the 1980s. It was feared that the fiscal projection of all the social welfare programs plus payment on the debt plus the defense budget, if unchecked, would soon eclipse federal revenues. In desperation, Congress passed mandatory cuts, the most significant of which was the Gramm-Rudman-Hollings Act of 1985.

Reagan's federalism, like the federalism of all Presidents back to Hoover, died quietly. The short-run strategy was to institute a block-grant system that would consolidate the many federal grants into a very small number of bulk credits for the states to distribute. More complex and permanent governmental functions would be divided between the states and the federal government. State and local governments would have significantly more authority than they had in the previous two decades. Washington made swap arrangements with the states taking, for example, full responsibility for the costs of Medicaid if the states would assume full responsibility for Aid to Families with Dependent Children.[8] Although the merits of Reagan's "dual federalism" stimulated much debate, the prognosis for any such program was bleak. The states were unwilling, and unable, to take on new burdens. Domestic policy in the United States was the product of implicit partnerships between different levels of government and would continue to remain so. By 1990, the United States was no closer to any readjustment of the financial and fiscal responsibilities of government which have become so chaotic in the postwar world.

In fact, the most serious problem was not the trade deficit, nor the budget imbalance, although these were important, but the ferocious ideological attack on the social welfare structure that resulted in a stand-off between Reagan and the Congress. The gridlock over deficit reduction which developed in the summer of 1985 resulted from the determination of the administration to hold the line on spending and lock all future administrations, Republican or Democrat, into a financial straightjacket that would necessitate a continual pleading for social spending. If taxes could not be raised because of the threat of veto, and defense spending could not be cut because of the power of the military-industrial complex, then only spending on social welfare or other bare-bones domestic programs remained to be cut back. The tax simplification proposals only added inflexibility to this dilemma. If state taxes were to be no longer deductible from federal income tax, further pressures would be put on state budgets to reduce the impact of state levies by reducing services, and thus even greater pressure would be exerted on reducing social spending.

In the half-century since the New Deal, we have not seen so formidable an attack on the federal government's role as the responsible agent for maintaining social justice. Despite an American predilection that favors individual over community needs, this Reagan policy was not a desirable or fruitful contribution. Although millions of Americans grew rich during Reagan's presidency, they have also come to accept a simplistic notion that government, especially the federal government, can serve no useful good. This grotesque view of the social contract is not only a libel of past history, but a baleful prospect for a future America. The goal of every generation must include the effort to make government work better for all the people in our society. Critics charged that the Reagan administration left a legacy of public indebtedness, of fiscal disarray, and of individual corruption not known since the Harding administration. Worst of all, no administration in this century did more to distort responsibility and weaken the response of the well-to-do to help those less fortunate and less competent. Behind the "teflon" presidency was a cruel and indifferent emptiness.

DEREGULATION

One area in which even its critics believe that the Reagan presidency will achieve lasting recognition is in its deregulation of major American businesses, namely airlines, telecommunications, trucking, banking, and natural gas. With few exceptions, these deregulatory programs have been largely successful for consumers and have significantly improved the performance of the industries involved. Undoubtedly, these results will encourage in the short run continued and increased deregulation.

Most explanations of regulatory theory have emphasized the self-interest aspects of continued regulation. Vested groups, such as bureaucrats and company executives who are regulated, in fact come to depend on the maintenance of regulation as a preferred way of eliminating and keeping out rivals. Despite the appearance of order and stability, regulatory regimes are inherently unstable. Economic, technical, and legal changes generate pressure for new measures to meet the new situation; what frequently results is a partial or piecemeal deregulation that accelerates and results in a "deregulatory snowball." Faced with mounting predicaments, regulatory agencies have great difficulties in adjusting to the new demands of both old and new participants. Competitive threats from abroad seem especially to cause near panic within the regulatory bureaucracy. The disadvantaged clamor for full deregulation to meet the new onslaught. Foreign competitors can for a time exploit the market advantages of being outside the regulatory umbrella, though in the long run, politicians will try to put an end to this imbalance. Caught between a rock and a hard place, there are only two ways for the bureaucracy to go: extend the system of regulations to cover as many new players and as many new situations as possible, or allow the market mechanism, with its quick, even justice to handle the problem. For the last ten to fifteen years, the U.S. government has moved largely in the latter direction. The courts too are part of the process. MCI's 1977 entry into the long distance telephone service market, for example, was protected from the extension of regulatory measures by court decisions.

The financial industry provides perhaps the best example of these forces in motion. The banking sector is currently undergoing rapid technological and organizational change because of computerization that is limiting costs, altering its capital to labor ratio, and forcing it to provide new services and products. At the same time a variety of new financial institutions have arisen that are able to offer many services previously provided only by banks. After decades of what can only be regarded as a de facto monopoly, banks are now finding themselves faced with fierce competition from other institutions that are not subject to the same government rules and decrees. This "disintermediation" is partially responsible for the savings and loan crisis.

Modern banking practices in the United States date back to the Depression. At that time, both the Congress and President Roosevelt felt that the industry's problems were due to poor management and overcompetition between banks, abuses from which the public had to be protected. The Glass-Steagall Act (also known as the Banking Act) of 1933 restricted banks in their lending practices, the types of accounts that they could offer, and most important, split commercial from investment banking, thereby prohibiting these institutions from underwriting, distributing, or dealing in stocks and securities. Other laws were soon to follow. This system of rules and regulations at both the state and federal level was designed to promote both stability and profitability while preventing further economic decline or collapse. The regulatory system was administered and overseen by the Federal Reserve Board, the Controller of the Currency, the newly created Federal Deposit Insurance Corporation (FDIC), and by parallel and often overlapping state agencies. Using the authority of the antitrust laws, the Justice Department regulated and sometimes forbade the expansion and merger of banks. The end result of this system was the creation of a diverse and decentralized American banking industry with more than 10,000 banks.[9]

Thus regulated, the industry prospered from the end of World War II until the late 1970s when the restructuring of capital around the world opened U.S. banking to global competition and threatened the banks' role as the controller of capital and credit. The rise of other financial entities that adopted bank-like functions while remaining free of government restrictions created new tensions. Retailers, brokerage firms, insurance companies, and investment firms began successfully to compete with banks by offering money market accounts, interest-bearing checking accounts, IRAs, and other services. This new competitive environment proved to be a dangerous one for traditional financial agencies, who soon found that their attempts to adapt these new financial investment practices were hampered by governmental regulation. Throughout the 1980s, in an attempt to come to terms with the situation, state and federal regulators began to peel off these restrictions. Congress also attempted to rewrite existing banking legislation, but special interest groups managed to block major changes.[10] In order to market more easily government debt, other regulations were relaxed.

The deregulatory wave began with the passage of the Depository Institutions Deregulatory and Monetary Control Act (DIDMCA) in 1980 which phased out interest rate ceilings by 1986, weakened state usury laws, and allowed banks, savings and loans, and credit unions to offer interest-bearing NOW accounts. In addition, S&Ls were granted greater flexibility to make mortgage loans, offer consumer loans, hold commercial paper, and offer credit cards. The provisions of this act, therefore, opened the door for competition between banks and rival financial institutions.[11]

Congress took no further action in 1980 because it feared that the S&Ls would not survive full price-deregulation. Demands continued, however, for extensive action and further deregulation. The recession of 1982, which lowered interest rates, finally convinced the Congress to go further, and it passed late in 1982 the Garn-St. Germain Depository Institutions Act. Savings and loan institutions were now granted new powers to offer both corporate and overdraft checking accounts. Fully deregulated price competition between brokerage money market accounts and banks was also enacted by allowing the latter to offer accounts with checking privileges that paid market interest rates.[12]

In the wake of this act's passage a wave of bank failures swept the industry. The year 1981 had seen only ten. By 1984 the number had risen to 79 and by the following year 997 banks and 434 S&Ls found themselves on the regulators' list of troubled institutions.[13] Although the Garn-St. Germain Act bears some responsibility for these failures, it cannot be held completely responsible for this chaos since much of the competition from rival financial institutions was already in place.[14] The regulatory framework surrounding the U.S. banking system promoted the interests of small locally based institutions over those of large regional ones. The McFadden Act of 1927 had essentially banned interstate banking and restricted competition within and between geographic markets. Banks that ventured across state borders were made subject to the laws of each state, which hampered profitability and discouraged banks from ambitious growth. The national deregulation of the early 1980s had done nothing to remove these restrictions. Most states have, however, acted in the last few years to reduce these restrictions with the result that thirty-six states have passed some type of interstate banking legislation, often in the form of regional compacts which allow reciprocal entry into neighboring states.[15] In Massachusetts, which already has such a compact covering all of New England, the state legislature's Joint Banking Committee cleared a bill in February 1989 which would open the state to full interstate banking by June 1, 1990. Although this bill required the approval of the entire legislature, it clearly illustrates the growing trend towards full interstate banking and will become effective in 1993.[16]

The flourishing practice of securitizing loans has also hampered bank profitability. Prohibited by the Glass-Steagall Act from entering into this highly lucrative market, in which traditional loans and mortgages are re-packaged into securities to be bought and sold, banks are placed at a distinct disadvantage to financial institutions for which no such restrictions apply. In addition to the opposition of the securities firms themselves, legislators and regulators found themselves confronted with the demand to shield investors, depositors, and the FDIC guarantees from the added risks of these novel activities. Thus they were reluctant to deregulate this area of the financial industry.[17] However, the issue was partially resolved by a Federal Reserve Board ruling in April 1987 that allowed several large banks to affiliate with firms that handled both large volumes of federal, state, and local government bonds or other securities permitted by Glass-Steagall and that conducted a small amount of business with formerly off-limits securities. Banks could, therefore, underwrite and trade government bonds not backed by taxes and could begin to deal in commercial paper. Challenged, this ruling was first upheld in the Second U.S. Circuit Court of Appeals and subsequently confirmed by the Supreme Court in June 1988. A majority of the justices held that the Glass-Steagall prohibition on banks dealing in securities did not forbid these new activities.[18] Currently the Federal Reserve Board allows bank affiliates to underwrite mortgage-backed securities, municipal reserve bonds, commercial paper, and securities backed by various debts provided that they do not produce more than 5 percent of the affiliates' gross revenue. The Glass-Steagall prohibition is, therefore, bypassed because these affiliates cannot be said to be primarily engaged in securities trading.[19]

Deregulatory proceedings have not, however, been confined to banking. Other industries, including television, telecommunications, railroads, and airlines have also been deregulated. Emboldened by the new economic climate of the 1980s, the telecommunications industry experienced its first taste of deregulation since the formation of the Federal Communications Commission (FCC). Established under the Communications Act of 1934, the FCC regulated telecommunications while allowing telephone services to continue operating as a monopoly. The telephone service offered under this arrangement was generally of high quality, was cheap because of economies of scale and FCC rate regulation, and continued to improve gradually with the introduction of new technology. Total monopoly control by AT&T, however, was never intended.[20]

As early as 1958 the FCC had authorized private microwave networks to operate and by 1969 MCI was offering to small businesses point to point telecommunications services between Chicago and St. Louis. Other applications soon followed. In 1971 the FCC decided to allow specialized communication services to compete directly with the phone companies. In an effort to foster and promote this competition, regulations were streamlined and some carriers were made exempt, allowing companies like MCI and Sprint to operate without government oversight while they expanded the scope of their services. The end results were decreased prices and the development of a variety of long distance services from which customers could choose according to their needs. Despite these developments, local service has largely continued on a monopoly basis since there has yet to emerge any competitors; phone companies enjoy their exclusive hold on this sector of the industry.[21] In addition to the deregulation of telephone service, similar moves have been taken in regard to telecommunications devices. With the introduction of independently produced phone equipment and accessories in the 1980s, competition began in earnest and eventually culminated in the court's decision to break up the Bell System. Consumers are now able to choose their own equipment in addition to their desired type of phone service; subsequent price wars have acted significantly to reduce costs. Services can now be purchased in pieces; one provider for long distance, another for data transmission, and yet another for local calls. As more and more providers enter the field and competition increases, the phone companies find themselves freed of restrictive tariffs and regulations, thus allowing them even greater competitive leeway[22] and freedom to enter new business and global ventures.

The situation surrounding the television industry, which, unlike telecommunications, has never been rate-regulated, is quite different. In this context the battle for deregulation has centered on seemingly noneconomic issues such as programming requirements, station ownership, and the Fairness Doctrine. Until the 1980s "free television," in which customers were not charged directly for programs, dominated the home entertainment market and was extremely lucrative. This situation was soon to change as rising program costs, increasing debt-service payments, and competition for the sale of commercial time between the growing number of stations began to cut into profits. Cable television began to vie for customers' attention at an unprecedented rate. Only 22 percent of American households had cable in 1980. Eight years later it had risen to 52.5 percent and, by virtue of its deep penetration into the viewer market, cable television was able to compete aggressively and successfully with local stations for sales of national and local commercial time.[23]

In 1981 the Federal Communications Commission (popularly known during the Reagan era as the Fowler Commission) began deregulatory initiatives which encouraged, aided, and accelerated new entry into broadcast markets and enhanced the competitiveness of noncable television. The FCC had formerly required applicants for station construction permits to prove that they had sufficient funds to build and operate a station. New station growth was restricted by this requirement as FCC financial standards were often very stringent. The Fowler Commission saw fit to abolish this rule in 1981.[24]

The regulations governing ownership were then addressed. FCC rules and policies forbade the trafficking of broadcast licenses in the belief that stations should be owned and operated in the public interest rather than for speculative reasons. This so-called "three year rule" presumed that licensees failing to operate a station for three years before selling it were guilty of license trafficking; in 1982 the Commission abolished this rather arbitrary rule. Since 1954, in order to limit the possibility that broadcast monopolies would arise, the FCC had limited ownership to a maximum of seven stations in each service: seven AM, seven FM, and seven television stations. Since 1984, the Fowler Commission has raised these limits to twelve in each category.[25]

Most important for the industry, however, was the lifting of programming requirements and increasing the amounts of commercial time available for sale. The FCC had required a certain percentage of broadcasts to be composed of educational and news programs. Furthermore, the Fairness Doctrine had required stations to present opposing points of view on issues of public importance. Commercial time was limited by the FCC to 16 minutes per hour for television, 18 minutes per hour for radio. In 1984 the Fowler Commission abolished both these limits as well as the Fairness Doctrine and loosened programming requirements.[26]

The march of deregulation also affected transportation. Government control of railroads began in 1887 with the creation of the Interstate Commerce Commission (ICC) and was directed at controlling excess profits, stabilizing rates, and preventing carriers from discriminating against shippers. By 1920 changing legislation had come to embody four enlarged objectives: the control and prevention of monopoly practices by the railroads, the protection of shippers from discriminatory practices, the provision by railroads of different types of unremunerative services and, finally, the insurance of adequate profits for the railroads.[27]

By the 1970s it became increasingly apparent that the market rules under which the industry was operating were no longer effective. In October 1980 the Staggers Rail Act was passed. This act was based on the assumption that most transportation in the United States was already competitive and that greater reliance on market forces was therefore necessary for a healthy rail industry. Railroads were freed by the Staggers Act from a variety of obligations to provide unprofitable services or potentially lucrative ones at unprofitable rates. The rail industry enjoyed greater latitude to restructure its rates and services and to discontinue some services by abandoning unprofitable lines. Strict regulation was only to be retained in areas where shippers faced a rail monopoly. Consequently the railroads were able to cut costs and to increase their competitiveness in the transportation market by negotiating lower shipping prices for their customers.[28]

In October 1978 President Jimmy Carter signed the Airline Deregulation Act that lessened to a considerable degree the restrictions in this industry. Although deregulated, airlines were by no means left unregulated. The ADA curtailed the powers of the Civil Aeronautics Board, which was to cease its operations by January 1, 1985. The issues of safety and authority over international travel, however, continued to be regulated by the FAA or were transferred to the Department of Transportation. Regulatory control over mergers provided for by the antitrust laws was transferred to the Department of Justice. Prior to the passage of the ADA the Civil Aeronautics Board had granted individual carriers franchises to operate certain routes and had regulated the fares that airlines could charge. Some experts claimed that these regulations prevented the implementation of cost control measures and protected weak and inefficient airlines from the rigors of competition. The most significant accomplishment of the ADA was its ruling that any carrier who possessed the appropriate planes and personnel could freely enter or exit any domestic route and that, as of January 1, 1985, fares were to be set at the exclusive discretion of the airlines themselves. Thereafter price wars between competitors began, and a large number of new carriers entered the market. Most of these newcomers were small commuter airlines able to serve regional markets and small airports more efficiently than their larger competitors. Although there have been some bankruptcies and forced mergers to save beleaguered airlines, deregulation has, for the most part, benefitted the industry by opening it up to the competition of the market place.[29]

Government regulation is designed to protect those governed and their customers by controlling prices, products, and services offered, as well as distribution and market entry. However, protection works best when the regulated industry is stable. Technological, economic, legal, and social evolution all act to upset this balance and institute profound changes that require reaction and adaptation. Without deregulation, industries are prevented from changing appropriately with the times and become unable to compete in an economic environment in which unregulated rivals, foreign or domestic, are free to operate. Banking, telecommunication, and transportation deregulation, once implemented, resulted in generally greater prosperity, although not all flourished in the increasingly competitive market system.

We will over time swing back toward imposing new regulations for many of the same reasons which have led to the current surge of deregulation, but much credit must be given to the Reagan presidency for enhancing the political and ideological environment so that these changes could be made. It would, however, be a tragedy to transfer these successes into an axiomatic and simplistic notion that government regulation has no role to play. There remain many areas where the market does not work well, or works to produce conditions which are unacceptable in human and social terms.

NOTES

[1]"The Decade Ahead: Not So Bad if We Do Things Right," *Fortune*, October 8, 1979: 83.

[2]"Better Prospects for our Ailing Productivity," *Fortune*, December 3, 1979: 73.

[3]"The Upbeat Outlook for Family Incomes," *Fortune*, February 25, 1980: 122.

[4]"Two Income Families Will Reshape the Consumer Markets," *Fortune*, March 10, 1980: 119.

[5]John L. Palmer, and Isabel V. Sawhill, eds., *The Reagan Experiment* (Washington, D.C.: Urban Institute Press, 1982), p. 1.

[6]Ibid., p. 7.

[7]Martin Anderson, "The Reagan Boom—Greatest Ever," *New York Times,* Jan. 17, 1990, p. A 25.

[8]Palmer and Sawhill, *The Reagan Experiment*, pp. 10-13.

[9]B. P. Holly, "Regulation, Competition, and Technology: The Restructuring of the US Commercial Banking System," *Environment and Planning A* 19 (May 1987): 633-52.

[10]Robert E. Taylor, "Banks Win in Fight Over Regulation: While Congress Squabbles Agencies like the Fed. Ease Rules," *The Wall Street Journal,* October 25, 1988, p. A8.

[11]Thomas H. Hammond and Jack H. Knott, "The Deregulatory Snowball: Explaining Deregulation in the Financial Industry," *Journal of Politics* 50 (February 1988): 3-30.

[12]Ibid.

[13]Ibid.

[14]Kenneth J. Meier and Jeff Worsham, "Deregulation, Competition, and Economic Changes: Assessing the Responsibility for Bank Failures," *Policy Studies Journal* 16 (Spring 1988): 427-39.

[15]Joann Paulson, "Recent Changes in the US Financial Markets Relevant to Midwestern Communities," *Policy Studies Journal* 16 (Autumn 1987): 93-115.

[16]"Massachusetts Panel Clears an Interstate Banking Bill," *The Wall Street Journal,* February 1, 1989, p. C13.

[17]John R. Cranford, "Bank Deregulation: A Debate over Firewalls," *Congressional Quarterly Weekly Report* 46 (April 16, 1988): 1014-15.

[18]John R. Cranford and Elizabeth Wehr, "Banking Regulation," *Congressional Quarterly Weekly Report* 46 (June 18, 1988): 1670.

[19]Taylor, "Banks Win in Fight," p. A8.

[20]Eva Powers, "Public Interest Implications of Telecommunications Deregulation," *Policy Studies Journal* 16 (Autumn 1987): 146-59.

[21]Ibid.

[22]Ibid.

[23]Victor E. Ferrall, "The Impact of Television Deregulation on Private and Public Interests," *Journal of Communication* 39 (Winter 1989): 8-38.

[24]Ibid.

[25]Ibid.

[26]Ibid.

[27]L. Orlo Sorenson, "Impacts of Rail Deregulation on Rural Communities," *Policy Studies Journal* 15 (June 1987): 760–78.

[28]James M. MacDonald, "Railroad Deregulation, Innovation and Competition: Effects of the Staggers Act on Grain Transportation," *Journal of Law and Economics* 32 (April 1989): 63–95.

[29]Kenneth W. Thornicroft, "Airline Deregulation and the Airline Labor Market," *Journal of Labor Research* 10 (Spring 1989): 163–81.

SUGGESTED READINGS

Cranford, John R. "Bank Deregulation: a Debate over Firewalls." *Congressional Quarterly Weekly Report,* 46 (April 16, 1988): 1014–1016.

Cranford, John R., and Elizabeth Wehr, "Banking Regulation," *Congressional Quarterly Weekly Report,* 46 (June 18, 1988): 1670.

Ferrall, Victor E., "The Impact of Television Deregulation on Private and Public Interests," *Journal of Communication* 39 (Winter 1989): 8–38.

Hammond, Thomas H., and Jack H. Knott, "The Deregulatory Snowball: Explaining Deregulation in the Financial Industry," *Journal of Politics* 50 (February 1988): 3–30.

Holly, B. P. "Regulation, Competition, and Technology: The Restructuring of the US Commercial Banking System." *Environment and Planning A* 19 (May 1987): 633–52.

Kiling, Robert W. "Trucking Deregulation: Evaluation of a New Power Structure." *Journal of Economic Issues* 22 (December 1988): 1201–11.

MacDonald, James H. "Railroad Deregulation, Innovation and Competition: Effects of the Staggers Act on Grain Transportation." *Journal of Law and Economics* 32 (April 1989): 63–95.

Magaziner, Ira C., and Robert B. Reich. *Minding America's Business: The Decline and Rise of the American Economy.* New York: Vintage Books, 1983.

Meier, Kenneth J., and Jeff Worsham. "Deregulation, Competition, and Economic Changes: Assessing the Responsibility for Bank Failures." *Policy Studies Journal* 16 (Spring 1988): 427–39.

Palmer, John L., and Isabel V. Sawhill, eds. *The Reagan Experiment.* Washington, D.C.: The Urban Institute Press, 1982.

Paulson, Joann. "Recent Changes in the US Financial Markets Relevant to Midwestern Communities." *Policy Studies Journal* 16 (Autumn 1987): 93–115.

Pepper, Thomas, Merit E. Janow, and Jimmy W. Wheeler. *The Competition: Dealing with Japan.* New York: Praeger, 1985.

Powers, Eva. "Public Interest Implications of Telecommunications Deregulation." *Policy Studies Journal* 16 (Autumn 1987): 146–59.

Reich, Robert B., and John D. Donahue. *New Deals: The Chrysler Revival and the American System.* New York, Viking-Penguin Inc., 1985.

Sorenson, L. Orlo. "Impacts of Rail Deregulation on Rural Communities." *Policy Studies Journal* 15 (June 1987): 760–78.

Taylor, Robert E. "Banks Win in Fight Over Regulation: While Congress Squabbles Agencies Like the Fed Ease Rules." *The Wall Street Journal,* October 25, 1988, p. A8.

Thornicroft, Kenneth W. "Airline Deregulation and the Airline Labor Market." *Journal of Labor Research.* 10 (Spring 1989): 163–81.

BOOK III

The Rebuilding of America: Some Critical Social and Economic Issues

8 | The Business System

THE LEGACY OF ANTITRUST REGULATION

Nothing distinguishes the U.S. economic system more than the adversarial relations between labor and management and between business and government, even though government backing of business continues to be a dominant part of the overall economic environment. The federal government's backing of business interests is woven into the fabric of our history, but so too is the long history of antitrust legislation and federal regulation. The antimonopoly statute that fixed this adversarial course was, of course, the Sherman Act of 1890. It was said that John Sherman himself did not understand the bill; certainly no one who voted the measure in 1890 could anticipate the Supreme Court's fluctuating interpretation of the statute over the next decades. In passing this law Congress was responding to public antipathy toward monopolies, to the inadequacy of protective state laws, and to investigations started two years earlier by committees of the House of Representatives and of the New York state senate. Most of those who voted for the Anti-Trust Act believed that it gave force to the common law prohibitions against monopoly; the law mattered little anyway to pro-business conservatives, who were more interested in the passage of the strongly protectionist McKinley Tariff. Section 1 and Section 2 of the Sherman Act seemed to clearly define the nature of a trust:

> Sec. 1. Every contract, combination in the form of trust or otherwise, or conspiracy, in restraint of trade or commerce among the several States, or with foreign nations, is hereby declared to be illegal....

> Sec. 2. Every person who shall monopolize or attempt to monopolize or combine or conspire with any other person or persons to monopolize any part of the trade or commerce among the several States, or with foreign nations, shall be deemed guilty of a misdemeanor....

But the emasculation and manipulation of the Sherman Act by the Supreme Court led during the Progressive era to the first legislative surge to establish a coherent antimonopoly policy. The most important measures taken were the Clayton Antitrust Act and the Federal Trade Commission Act, both passed in 1914. Along with the Sherman Act, these measures were intended to make certain that companies which committed wrongs would be severely punished. The Clayton Act attempted to close the loopholes in the Sherman Act and prohibited certain business practices which would in effect lead to monopoly; those practices included interlocking directorates, price discrimination, and the acquisition of rival companies which might lead to a substantial lessening of competition. The newly established Federal Trade Commission (FTC) was to prevent unfair competition. What were the outcomes of this sustained effort to control these massive corporations? On balance the record is enormously uneven and very flawed. American antitrust law was unusually punitive against individuals or corporations that tried to create monopolies, especially when we consider the experience of western European nations at the same time. In particular, the government of Germany encouraged the formation of cartels and actively supported their operation. Even in the United States the practice of monopoly control was gravitating naturally toward oligopoly.

Even with the legislative reenforcement of the Clayton Act and FTC, antitrust policy continued to be only a small nuisance to corporations and an unattractive public policy issue for politicians. No President or attorney general devoted much effort to antitrust prosecutions. Two important Supreme Court decisions, one involving U.S. Steel and another concerning the acquisition of a company by stock purchase (*Federal Trade Commission* v. *Western Meat Co.*), gained a brief notoriety in the 1920s, though eventually the Court reversed its position in both cases. In the 1920 case against U.S. Steel, the Court had tried to introduce a rule of reason into the problem of corporate size. The court disagreed with the government's case, which had been based on the government's reading of the Sherman Anti-Trust Act. A majority of the justices rejected the notion that strength in any producer or seller is a menace to the public interest and illegal because there is potential in it for mischief. "The Corporation is undoubtedly of impressive size . . . but we must adhere to the law, and the law does not make mere size an offense, or the existence of unexerted power an offense."[1] In 1926, the Court held that the Clayton Act clauses against the purchase of a competitor applied only to stock purchase and not to the purchase of the assets of a company by another company.[2] Both decisions reflected the ideological conservatism of the Court, its sympathy for big business, and its naivete about corporate strength and business in twentieth-century America.

In the 1920s, the Congress passed the Webb-Pomerene Act, which allowed corporations to form export cartels that would be exempt from prosecution by the Justice Department under the antitrust acts. Business, however, was so unsure how it could manage international cartel arrangements and not be subject to prosecution for collusion in the domestic market that it simply opted not to participate. This same uncertainty permeated the entire New Deal period. By the mid-1930s, most corporations saw President Roosevelt as hostile to their interests. The attempt at reviving the economy through domestic cartels under the aegis of the National Industrial Recovery Act was a disastrous failure. When the NIRA was declared unconstitutional, not only was the holiday from antitrust regulation over, but the Roosevelt administration inaugurated the most vigorous antitrust campaign in our recent history. That in itself did not stop the Congress in 1937 from passing the Miller-Tydings Amendment, which exempted fair-trade contracts from the Sherman Act.

Over time, new aspects of economic theory, especially the acceptance of the idea of "imperfect competition," a broad range of business practices that lie between price competition and monopoly, affected not only business but also the decisions of the Supreme Court.[3] Antitrust violation came to include the structure of the industry in addition to size and predatory behavior. Before and during the Second World War the antitrust statutes were virtually in abeyance despite the growing fears expressed by economists of oligopolies and market power. However, in 1939, the Supreme Court, in the Interstate Circuit case[4] (*Interstate Circuit* v. *United States*) involving chain movie houses in Texas that all charged the same admission, had ruled that evidence of collusion was not the only

> prerequisite to an unlawful conspiracy. It was enough that, knowing that concerted action was contemplated and invited, the distributors gave the adherence to the scheme and participated in it. . . . Acceptance by competitors without previous agreement is sufficient to establish an unlawful conspiracy under the Sherman Act.[5]

In 1946 the Court returned to this theme of tacit collusion among oligopolists in the Second Tobacco Case.[6] For years the three leading tobacco companies, American Tobacco, Reynolds, and Ligget and Meyers avoided direct competition. Moreover, the companies purchased field shares of the supply at the same daily price. They also had identical price lists and coordinated changes in these prices. However, "there was not a whit of evidence that a common plan had ever been contemplated or proposed. The government's evidence was admittedly wholly circumstantial." The Court nevertheless found the defendants guilty:

> No formal agreement is necessary to constitute an unlawful conspiracy. . . . The essential combination or conspiracy in violation of the Sherman Act may be found in a course of dealings or other circumstances as well as an exchange of words."[7]

But the most important decision involving the Sherman Act and the complex problem of market share was that which Judge Learned Hand delivered in the important Alcoa case of 1945. Alcoa had first been brought to trial in 1938 for its exclusive control over virgin aluminum production under the original Hall and Bradley patents (1903). The government contended that Alcoa had violated Section 2 of the Sherman Act by vertical price manipulation between the price charged for crude aluminum and the prices offered customers for finished goods. The district court found the company not guilty; the government appealed and in a landmark decision, Judge Hand ruled against the company, restored the power of Section 2, and set the stage for a renewed attack on oligopolies that had massive market power. The court found that Alcoa manufactured more than 90 percent of the virgin aluminum ingot in the United States; this alone was "enough to constitute a monopoly" whether or not the company had ever used this power. Although good behavior was a defense recognized by the courts in other cases (such as the U.S. Steel case), in Alcoa's case market dominance could not be ignored. The distinction between potential and exercised power, "is ... purely formal; it would be valid only so long as the monopoly began to operate; for, when it did—that is, as soon as it began to sell at all—it must sell at some price, and the only price at which it could sell is a price which it itself fixed. Thereafter the power and its exercise must coalesce." Alcoa was found guilty of accumulating market power even though it had not used it.

> It was not inevitable that it should always anticipate increases in the demand for ingots and be prepared to supply them. Nothing compelled it to keep doubling and redoubling its capacity before others entered the field. It insists that it has never excluded competitors; but we can think of no more effective exclusion than progressively to embrace each new opportunity as it appeared, and to face every newcomer with new capacity already geared into a great organization, having the advantage of experience, trade connections, and the elite of personnel.... No monopolist monopolizes unconscious of what he is doing. So here "Alcoa" meant to keep, and did keep, the complete and exclusive hold upon the ingot market with which it started. That was to "monopolize" that market, however innocently it otherwise proceeded.[8]

Similarly, the Federal Trade Commission was given new life by the passage of the Wheeler-Lea Act (1938) and the Celler-Kefauver Amendment (1950). These measures were a response by Congress to adjust antitrust regulations so as to bring them closer to changing business realities. In 1931, the Supreme Court, in a strange interpretation of the FTC's powers, had ruled that the FTC could act only if the alleged practices had an adverse impact on a firm's competitors, even though the case in question involved a patent drug company that had advertised its product as a safe and effective way of eliminating "excess flesh off the human body." The FTC had issued a cease and desist order because the product was harmful, but the conservative justices had ruled that the FTC had exceeded its power. Therefore, the Wheeler-Lea Act amended Section 5 of the Federal Trade Commission Act to read: "Unfair methods of competition in or affecting commerce, are hereby declared unlawful."[9]

Since 1914, when the Clayton Act had been passed to bolster the Sherman Act of 1890, there had been growing calls to strengthen Section 7, which was meant to forbid combinations or mergers that might create a monopoly or restrain commerce. The difficulty lay with the prevention of mergers. Senator Estes Kefauver was a leader in the fight to strengthen Section 7; in 1950 he succeeded. The original language of Section 7 referred only to the acquisition of the stock of a company, not its assets, to secure a merger. The Celler-Kefauver Amendment closed this very big loophole that companies had used for almost four decades to get around the intent of the antitrust laws. It took a scare report by the FTC that "the giant corporations will ultimately take over the country" if the government did not act, and the pending merger between two giants of the steel industry, Columbia and Consolidated, to push Congress to pass the new legislation. The Celler-Kefauver Amendment amended Section 7 of the Clayton Act:

> That no corporation engaged in commerce shall acquire, directly or indirectly, the whole or any part of the stock or other share capital, and no corporation subject to the jurisdiction of the Federal Trade Commission shall acquire the whole or any part of the assets of another corporation engaged also in commerce, where in any line of commerce in any section of the country, the effect of such acquisition may be substantively to lessen competition, or to tend to create a monopoly.[10]

The American business system, however, continued to erode the effects of antitrust legislation, and the postwar decades brought forth a rash of new conglomerate mergers. In the postwar period as global competition increased, the adversarial assumptions on which the entire antitrust structure rested would be questioned. Though big business wielded enormous influence, it was not omnipotent because the economic system was too heterogeneous, too individualistic, and too contentious to establish a "Corporate Commonwealth."[11] Nor did it seem able to diminish the adversarial labor-business-government triangle that left the American economy more vulnerable to dynamic overseas competitors. In the 1990s, antitrust legislation needs to be reevaluated in light of this competitive global economy; many formal legal constraints seem increasingly anachronistic and disadvantageous to American business.

DEREGULATION AND THE FUTURE OF BANKING

The deregulation of U.S. banking, aggressively furthered by the Reagan administration, not only reversed banking philosophy in this country since the New Deal but also ushered in a period of great uncertainty for the future. No one would deny that the time was ripe for a reexamination of the banking structure in place since the 1930s. Banking has become one of the leading "industries" in the international economy. No longer are we sure what a "bank" is (despite Congressional definition) just as we are no longer certain what "money" is.

Gerald Corrigan, president of the Federal Reserve Bank of New York and long-time member of the Federal Reserve System, described this banking revolution at the ABA International Monetary Conference in Philadelphia in 1984. If current proposals before Congress were to be enacted, Corrigan said, they would give banks new power: bank holding companies operating through their nonbank subsidiaries could engage in certain securities, insurance, and real estate activities; barriers to interstate banking, with a few exceptions, would be eliminated; the process of deposit deregulation would be completed by removing prohibitions on interest payments on demand deposits and required reserves held at the Federal Reserve. If all this were done, and over time some of it was highly likely, Corrigan predicted that the banking system would be entirely transformed. It would then be faced with four monumental policy questions. Corrigan asked the bankers:

> what will happen to the number, size, and functional characteristics of our banking and financial organization? What consequence, if any, will these changes and the changed financial structure have for the conduct and effectiveness of monetary policy? Will the risk characteristics of banking and of the banking system increase or decrease in the environment of the future? What do all of the above imply about the need to adopt public policies regarding banks and banking markets to the prospective environment?[12]

Prior to Corrigan's speech, then Vice President George Bush had headed a twelve-member high-level Task Group on Regulation of Financial Services. On January 31, 1984, the committee released part of its report; some of these recommendations are embodied in legislative proposals that have been before the Congress. Most likely much that is in the Bush report will find its way into policy. Two major themes dominated the Bush report: the first was the necessity of further deregulation of banking; the second, reached after compromise with FED chairman Paul Volcker, is the continued dominant role of the Federal Reserve in policymaking. In fact, during the discussions Volcker circulated a white paper supporting the Fed's continued regulatory power. Any circumscribing of that power, he argued, would severely undermine the Fed's ability to control monetary policy and manage financial crises. Volcker's victory was embodied in the powerful position given the Fed in the Bush proposals; it may be a very long time before the Fed is again challenged.

The Bush Committee also recommended the creation of a new federal banking agency to replace the current Office of the Comptroller of the Currency and eliminate most of the regulatory duties of the FDIC (Federal Deposit Insurance Corporation). Remaining intact would be the Federal Reserve Board's control over the fifty largest and most powerful bank holding companies. The proposed new agency would be attached to the Treasury Department and would become the regulator of all federally chartered commercial banks and all but the largest 50 bank holding companies left under the Fed's control. The Federal Banking Agency, subject to a two-thirds veto by the Federal Reserve Board of Governors, could decide which nonbanking activities would be allowed to become bank holding companies. Lucrative new ventures in insurance, real estate, and securities were the plums dangling before the eyes of all bankers, so Fed control here was vital. The Fed would regulate all state-chartered banks, either directly or by delegating some authority to state regulators under federal supervision. The restructured FDIC would be limited to, but gain additional powers over, deposit insurance. According to the Bush Committee proposal, the Federal Reserve would remain in supreme command in the banking system, but the new agency would still have substantial power to deregulate banking further.

The questions Corrigan raised now seem even more pertinent to the future of banking. Some growth in size, integration, and consolidation in banking is virtually assured, and some expansion of interstate banking is certain. However, there will still be a very large number of banks, although not the 14,800 banks that now exist. The diversity of financial opportunities will encourage banks to grow bigger and offer more services. Other banks will specialize. The United States is not likely to become a country of a half-dozen big banks with thousands of branches, like Britain. The gathering-in process will produce many changes, after which perhaps some, but not all, of the confusion in banking will diminish. To be sure, traditional functions and nomenclatures—"savings banks," "commercial banks"—will be even more blurred, but there will remain much variety in the U.S. banking system. If deregulation continues along the lines of the Bush Committee proposal, banks will compete ferociously for deposits and increased profits. Just as competition will increase the kinds of new product expansion, so it will also spread geographically as advances in technology shrink distance and time barriers. Specialists predict also that nonbank firms will acquire banks as holding companies, which will enable them to perform and profit from many activities which had been the exclusive domain of banks. The loss of confidence in S & Ls and financial institutions in the 1980s and Black Monday's stock market crash in 1987 make these emerging changes even more likely. On February 5, 1991, the Bush administration formally presented its plan for sweeping changes in the nation's banking system. Most of the changes advance the proposals of the Bush Committee and agree with Gerald Corrigan's assessment. It will be many months before final legislation is passed, but given the entrenched position of banking interests, the likelihood of profound changes is minimal.

A particular danger from deregulation is that the speculative activities of local and regional banks might leave them in so weakened a condition that they infect through the process of loan syndication the entire system. The difficulties of the Continental Illinois Bank in 1984 illustrated how vulnerable the banking network is. Banking may be riskier in the future but not necessarily irresponsible. If carefully removed, the outmoded regulations of the 1930s will no longer hamper banks that want to expand into new functions. At the same time, security and safety for the consumer must be assured. This delicate balance will not be easily achieved as witnessed by the collapse of many savings and loans in 1988–1989. In the farm belt, S & L portfolios were overconcentrated in farm loans; in Texas, commercial banks invested in energy loans; and the investments of large metropolitan banks were concentrated in "evergreen" loans to Third World countries.

Nevertheless, banks continued to be restricted in the 1980s from many operations by long-standing New Deal legislation. In every way the restrictions were costly. Since banks were precluded from many new opportunities, nonbanks skimmed these profitable areas away. Especially irksome and costly were the constraints on interstate banking. In international banking too, the U.S. has lagged. One estimate pointed out that if U.S. banks could lower their operating expenses per dollar of assets to the Canadian level, they would increase their profitability by more than $20 billion, more than the after-tax profit banks realized in 1983. As banks fretted under these constraints, they saw the Dreyfus Corporation draw off $1.3 million profit from Gold MasterCard users.

After years of analysis Sears decided that entry into the credit card market was the most profitable alternative for its marketing future. Its Discover cards marked a new beginning in nonbank lending activities. Sears claimed that 60 million individuals had a Sears credit card, and that 50 percent of American families shopped at Sears. This enormous base in retailing, they argued, would virtually ensure Discover's success. The Discover card holder is able to set up an IRA without a fee, get access to instant cash from automatic teller machines (ATMs) in designated locations, receive discounts at Sears plus other free items from selected companies. Cooperating merchants pay a smaller surcharge to Sears than to other credit card companies. How did Sears manage this feat under existing banking legislation? In 1981, Sears purchased Dean Witter Reynolds, Inc. for $607 million. Sears already had acquired Allstate Insurance and Coldwell Banker in real estate. Sears then bought the Greenwood Trust Co. and used this tiny opening to enter the credit card market dominated by banks that offered Visa and MasterCard. Once the Supreme Court refused to strike down limited-service banks, Sears was able to move. And it will continue to encourage the use of Discover cards in ATMs to transfer funds from savings and certificate accounts, mutual funds, individual retirement accounts (IRAs), etc., as well as to pay Allstate premiums. Sears may not be exaggerating much when it says, "we're going to change the way people think about plastic." American Express and Citicorp have similar broad benefits for users of their cards but are not directly tied to a single vendor like the Discover card.

Closely connected to these developments in interstate banking is the future role of U.S. banks in the international finance system. Just beginning is the entry of foreign banks into the U.S. and the expansion of U.S. banks abroad. The internationalization of banking in the U.S. will continue and intensify as the new powers and market opportunities of U.S. banks are made available to foreign banks. As this internationalization of banking occurs, changes in U.S. regulations will be transmitted abroad instantaneously. Americans will have to become much more sensitive to the effects on global banking rendered by decisions that heretofore concerned only domestic institutions.

At present only the few largest U.S. banks have played a significant role in lending to developing countries, though their deep commitment has resulted in heavy losses to such countries as Mexico, Brazil, and Argentina. (Other smaller banks have pieces of these loans through the process of syndication, where a large bank will sponsor a loan and then sell parts of the loan to smaller institutions.) The threat of default even by a small country such as Peru sends panic through the system. The confidence in the security of international loans has become shaky, so much so that the U.S. in the spring of 1985 finally admitted that foreign bank debt was a world problem. At that time then Secretary of the Treasury James Baker proposed a new solution. His plan attempted to persuade private bankers to increase their lending to these indebted borrowers, but because the Treasury proposals required the setting aside of more bank capital as security against risky and imprudent loans, Baker's position actually enhanced a preference for lending only to safe borrowers, not to the barely solvent developing world. It is certain, however, that the U.S. government and U.S. banks are increasingly aware that they must continue to be a source of development capital for the rest of the world and a manager for international debt financing.

The fluctuating price of oil since Iraq's invasion of Kuwait and subsequent Gulf War, the economic liberalization of Eastern Europe, and the collapse of the Soviet Union's economy add new complexities for achieving sustained noninflationary growth throughout the world. Business activity in international capital markets is being carried to new heights by the liberalization of European and Japanese domestic financial markets. International bankers (U.S. bankers included) now foresee a global market in which all types of security, equity as well as debt, can be traded around the clock, free of national regulations and time-zone constraints. Not since before World War I, when the world was still on the gold standard, did anything approximate what is now coming into being. So long as interest rates remain low, the opportunities for international securities will remain high. Throughout the world, the decline of the dollar has also made for other opportunities not known since 1981 and before. All financial markets will in all likelihood catch this international fever. The pursuit of wealth and power has a long and undistinguished history, but the realization of the potential harm that could be wreaked on this emerging world system will encourage prudent behavior on the part of U.S. bankers. By the end of the century, many of these international cooperative ventures will be the accepted normal condition. The cooperation of the G-5 countries (U.S., Japan, West Germany, Great Britain, France) to lower the value of the U.S. dollar vis-à-vis other currencies is an example of sheltering world currencies from volatile interest rates. The dollar had been so overvalued in the mid-1980s that U.S. goods became overpriced in international markets.

Compared to the dynamism in private markets, the old international lending institutions created by the Bretton Woods Agreement (1944) seem to be entering a period of maturity. The action in the currency exchange markets, in the securities markets, and bonds and stocks far outpaces the programs of the International Monetary Fund (IMF) and the World Bank

(IBRD). However, the International Development Agency, an agency of the World Bank set up to grant "soft" loans (loans repayable in the receiving country's currency) to developing countries, is coming back to life. The present and future cooperation between private banks and national central banks does not necessarily indicate the revival of the internationalism of the immediate post–World War II years. Without doubt the enthusiasm for the return of market-dominated controls will diminish from today's heights. Although at present the U.S. has opted for a new emphasis on private markets, the World Bank and International Monetary Fund will continue as important players in international banking and finance.

After World War II, Keynesian theory dominated U.S. and international economic policy. More recently, monetarism largely supplanted it. The near future, however, looks as if it will be dominated by neither. A new pragmatism which is neither Keynesian nor monetarist is being developed by economists like Ronald McKinnon of Stanford and James Tobin at Yale. McKinnon has perhaps gone the furthest, and his work fits well in the international environment. McKinnon's monetarism incorporates capital mobility and 24-hour global money markets. McKinnon places the cause of over- and undervalued currency in flawed secular monetary policy. When the Federal Reserve or the central banks of other countries set monetary targets, their range is determined by domestic considerations. Frequently, however, international demand for that particular currency bids up its value and negates the intended effects for domestic policy. To counteract this practice, McKinnon believes "the Federal Reserve system should discontinue its policy of passively sterilizing the domestic monetary impact of foreign official interventions."[13] Central banks should supply enough of their currencies to keep exchange rates stable. For McKinnon, a closer cooperation among the Federal Reserve, the Bank of Japan, and the West German Bundesbank could enable them to control the world money supply and be able to adjust their own policies to the movements in the exchange markets. McKinnon's work is largely academic and not without its critics, but changes in the international economy may bring about this cooperation and coordination more rapidly than many today feel possible.

The last major change in the currency markets was the switch from fixed to floating exchange rates in the early 1970s. This system of floating rates, however, is being supplanted by direct action by the big five economic powers to prevent more serious economic problems, such as the passage of protectionist measures by the U.S. Congress. If schemes like the Baker Plan can begin to restructure "evergreen" debt on a worldwide basis, other plans must be developed for international monetary reform. The United States is beginning to understand that much of the world has caught up with it industrially and that soaring trade and budget deficits are unacceptable, both for economic and political reasons, to it and the rest of the world. Still the largest economic power in the free world, the U.S. has to acknowledge that it is in its best interests to accept the Japanese thesis that the international economy is a three-legged stool consisting of the U.S., Japan, and Western Europe. Japan and Europe also stand to share in the benefits of a greatly expanding international trading system if the three parties can work together.

This book has emphasized the positive aspects of this emerging international securities and trading world, but it should be kept in mind that the regressive tendencies of nationalism could reassert themselves. The United States could yield to protectionist forces and try to go it alone; Japan could continue its export offensive without regard for the impact on other countries; Western Europe could hunker down to a lower standard of real income with permanent high rates of unemployment; and a long-term shortage of oil could be precipitated by a Saddam Hussein who would hold the industrialized countries for ransom.

On a lighter side, banking is going to be more fun for most consumers, and banks will be even more of a necessity for all of us. Inevitably we will be caught up in the new technologies. ATMs and cash dispensers are now commonplace. The real impact of automation, however, has been in the internal operations of banks. Even now electronic data processing and fax machines make it possible for large corporate customers to establish direct links between their own accounting departments and those of banks, and to make direct transfers to customers and other banks via telecommunication links.

Sears disappointed the consumer in not making the Discover a "smart card" with a financial history in its chip, but this will arrive well before the end of the century, as will some form of a personal payments system. Already Singapore anticipates that soon it will jump from a cash society to a cashless one without the intermediate step of check processing. Other countries already have surpassed the United States by allowing customers to buy goods and pay bills of all kinds through direct links to their bank accounts. Since banks currently lose money on many of these small individual transactions, they too have a powerful incentive to participate in the lucrative opportunities now available. The spread of interstate banking will further this process; the internationalization of banking will complete the circuit. Banking has withstood many revolutions in our history, but it may change even more in the next fifteen years than it has in the past fifty.

THE BUDGET DEFICIT
AND ECONOMIC OPPORTUNITY

Budget and trade deficits have forced Americans into a dependency on world financial lenders which they have never known in their history. Not only will the Japanese, as the world's wealthiest lender, continue to extend their influence, but the maintenance of a favorable exchange value for the U.S. dollar is subject to the goodwill and friendly policies of the G-5 and G-7 industrial countries. These financial allies share with the United States the responsibility for maintaining some kind of stability in world exchange problems, but until U.S. policy changes demonstrably to lower the federal budget deficit it is more a part of the problem than one of the problem solvers. President Bush had been obdurate in his resistance to higher taxes until the passage of the 1990 tax bill. However, many believe that the President and Congress finally have found a way to cut the budget deficit substantially over the next five years. The eye-popping numbers call for immediate redress: the national debt at over $3 trillion, the trade deficit at $150 billion, and the budget deficit over $360 billion. Foreign bankers, money markets, and investors play a continuous roulette game with these numbers. The debt-carrying charge of $200 billion annually plus interest to foreign lenders is a substantial mortgage on our future. The current fall in the value of the dollar, in part because of this deficit, makes the United States a bargain basement for foreign buyers of real assets, companies, and real estate. A sudden cutoff of this foreign support would greatly increase our payment problem. In particular, the troublesome gridlock between Congress and the executive branch on budgetmaking must end so that a program of revenue increases and spending cuts can permanently bring down these hyperinflated numbers. As former Federal Reserve Board Chairman Volcker has said, a recession would complicate greatly our present abilities to handle both domestic and international financial problems. Just as the savings and loan failures, with their estimated $100 to $300 billion bailout, testify to the disasters of the freewheeling approach of the recent past, so too do the debt, budget, and trade deficit figures cry out for immediate remedial attention. The longer these cancers continue, the greater the danger that they will do permanent damage to our domestic and international economic future.

ENTREPRENEURS AND THE BUSINESS SYSTEM

When Joseph Schumpeter wrote in *Capitalism, Socialism and Democracy* (1942) about the contribution of the entrepreneur in a market system, he defined the entrepreneur in very narrow terms as an individual who makes a major contribution in one of five specific areas. The entrepreneur 1) initiates a new good, 2) originates a new method of production, 3) captures a new market, 4) frames a new pattern of transportation, or 5) contributes a new kind of leadership. Although Schumpeter never envisaged the extension of entrepreneurial action into the context of planned and team research, he was convinced that the social and intellectual conditions necessary to produce and reward entrepreneurs would be eroded by the rise and spread of socialism. He thought that socialism would emasculate the very core of the market system. Schumpeter viewed even the slightest attempts at social legislation and monetary regulation as a threat. We are indeed fortunate that Schumpeter's dire predictions that the market system would not survive seem less realistic today than when he made them in the 1940s, but the United States' real success in cultivating a vigorous market system does not eliminate the need to inspect continually the health, opportunity, and general conditions which make entrepreneurs able to venture and succeed in American society.

One of the very exciting aspects of the present is the extraordinary growth in the number and variety of entrepreneurial activities which are being spawned by this incredible period of change. For young and old, individuals and companies, there are so many possibilities that no previous historical period offered. It is in the surrounding business environment that the greatest concerns lie. The lifeblood of business is the availability and cost of capital. The amount of capital available has always been linked to the amount of savings in any society. Although there is no acute shortage of capital, we have, to a great degree, substituted foreign sources of capital for domestic ones. Some observers, like Peter Drucker, have proposed that the differential cost of capital is the most important reason for the success of Japanese businessmen. Companies in Japan have produced a continuous flow of capital at very small cost. In the United States, by comparison, the relatively high cost of capital has prevented American companies from competing in world markets. Increasingly also the United States has become dependent on foreign sources of capital to pay for our public debt. Government thus competes with business and individuals for this relatively scarce source of lendable funds. Government borrowing drives up interest rates and forces business to pay more for its capital needs.

If our government could borrow less, reduce the national debt, and create a constructive bipartisan process for balancing the budget, much economic gain would result. But the Republican party has been pledged to a no-increase-in-tax policy, while the Democratic party feels that crucial social programs have been financially starved by a fiscal policy which benefits the well-to-do. The best we had been able to do prior to the deficit-reducing legislation of 1990 is the Gramm-Rudman bill, which forces automatic debt reduction by making spending cuts across-the-board. Just as troubling is the fact that Social Security taxes, which are heavily regressive, are used to finance the debt. Even more deceptive is the huge cost of bailing out the failed S & L's, of which some $100 billion is hidden by financial sleight-of-hand, not even recorded as part of the overall budget deficit. If the federal government sets no standard for a prudent spending policy, how can the country expect individuals to act other than to maximize their short-term gratifications? In an impulse-ridden society, we need the most persuasive policies to move individuals to forego present consumption in order to ensure a better future. Television, mass advertising, and popular culture push a policy of "buy now, pay later" to whet appetites for the 80 million items that the economy produces. The government also has not encouraged individuals to save. Inflation and stagflation had ravaged personal savings during the 1970s and 1980s. High personal taxes (at least before the Reagan administration) had cut take-home pay to the bone. While the Reagan administration in 1981 allowed full deductions for individual retirement accounts (IRAs), the Congress in 1986 restricted them as a program which aided the rich. A few years later, there is much talk about reinstating the full-scale exemptions, perhaps with some minor changes. Social Security taxes have risen enormously over the past decade and bear heavily on most workers, taking away from other forms of savings.

Would Americans save more, given the right incentive? Many observers think so. Certainly other countries, such as Germany and Japan, have benefitted greatly from their programs that encourage higher personal savings. Americans policy makers, however, seem to be blocked in endless discussions of equity, rich versus poor, etc., while overall savings continue to fall. Americans now have one of the lowest savings rates of any industrialized country. Over the longer period our society would only gain immeasurably from a larger and cheaper pool of capital. Without very large amounts of cheap capital, we will surely not be able to compete successfully in the global economy of the Third Industrial Revolution.

The very low savings rate is paralleled by a fall in relative productivity compared to workers in other countries. Slumping productivity needs to be confronted on three levels. First, the educational system must be reformed to improve the competence of all workers and all Americans. The recognition by Americans that education is the key to national survival, not just economic well being, is absolutely essential. As the major supplier of massive training and educational programs to upgrade skills, the federal government needs to encourage and finance the necessary ongoing programs. Second, corporate management needs to sharpen its sophistication and lengthen its horizons to keep up with global demands in the 1990s. Though the days of rigid, authoritarian control in companies have given way to a more flexible and egalitarian style, managers in the United States must apply the knowledge of consensus and concurrent management in manufacturing to tackle the causes of falling productivity. Third, a cleanup of widespread and unproductive business dealings must be effected to restore the respect of American business. "Golden parachutes," junk bonds, leveraged buyouts, reckless takeovers, and financial corruption are all symptoms of a business philosophy that supplants the national interest with greed for short-term profits. Although this kind of dealing applies to only a small percentage of the ten to fourteen million enterprises in the United States, the resulting publicity has created mistrust and resentment of big business in general. Obviously a healthier climate between business and the general public will do much to raise the incentives for better productivity.

NOTES

[1] *U.S.* v. *U.S. Steel Corporation* [251 U.S. 417 at 451].

[2] *Federal Trade Commission* v. *Western Meat Co.* [(96) 272 U.S. 554].

[3] Joan Robinson, *The Economics of Imperfect Competition* (London: Macmillan, 1933).

[4] *Interstate Circuit* v. *United States* [306 U.S. 208].

[5] Claire Wilcox, *Public Policies Toward Business* (Homewood, Illinois: Richard D. Irwin, 1975), p. 170.

[6] Second Tobacco Case [228 U.S. 781 at 810].

[7]Wilcox, *Public Policies Toward Business,* p. 171.

[8]*United States* v. *Aluminum Co. of America* [148 F. 2nd. 416 (2d Cir 1945)].

[9]H. Craig Petersen, *Business and Government,* 3d ed. (New York: Harper and Row, 1989), p. 75.

[10]Ibid., p.77.

[11]Louis Galambos and Joseph Pratt, *The Rise of the Corporate Commonwealth: U.S. Business and Public Police in the Twentieth Century* (New York: Basic Books, 1988).

[12]Unpublished remarks by E. Gerald Corrigan, President, Federal Reserve Bank of Minneapolis, "New Frontiers in Banking—1984 and On: Regulation and Deregulation," speech before the American Bankers Association, International Monetary Conference, Philadelphia, June 5, 1984.

[13]R. I. McKinnon, "Currency Substitution and Instability in the World Dollar Standard," *American Economic Review* 72 (June 1982): 320-33.

SUGGESTED READINGS

Bryer, Stephen. *Regulation and Its Reform.* Cambridge: Harvard University Press, 1982.

Derthick, Martha, and Paul Quirk. *The Politics of Deregulation.* Washington: Brookings Institution, 1985.

Galbraith, John Kenneth. *The New Industrial State,* 4th ed. Boston: Houghton Mifflin, 1985.

Heilbroner, Robert L. *The Economic Transformation of America.* New York: Harcourt Brace Jovanovich, Inc., 1977.

Petersen, H. Craig. *Business and Government.* 3d ed. New York: Harper and Row, 1989.

Reich, Robert, and John D. Donahue. *New Deals: the Chrysler Revival and the American System.* New York: Times Books, 1985.

Schultze, Charles. *The Public Use of Private Interest.* Washington: The Brookings Institution, 1971.

Seligman, Joel. *The Transformation of Wall Street.* Boston: Houghton Mifflin Co., 1982.

Smith, George David. *The Anatomy of a Business Strategy: Bell, Western Electric and the Origins of the American Telephone Industry.* Baltimore: Johns Hopkins' University Press, 1985.

Sobel, Robert. *The Age of the Giant Corporations.* Westport, Conn.: Greenwood Press, 1972.

Stein, Herbert. *The Fiscal Revolution in America.* Chicago: University of Chicago Press, 1969.

Tedlow, Richard, and John Richard, Jr., eds. *Managing Big Business.* Boston: Harvard Business School Press, 1986.

Teece, David J., ed. *The Competitive Challenge: Strategies for Industrial Innovation and Renewal.* Cambridge: Ballinger Publishing Co., 1987.

Vogel, David. *National Style of Regulation*. Ithaca, NY: Cornell University Press, 1986.

Wilcox, Claire. *Public Policies Toward Business*. Homewood, Illinois: Richard D. Irwin, 1975.

9

The Physical Environment: Roads, Bridges, Water, Acid Rain

THE PROBLEM OF INFRASTRUCTURE

New building projects are glamorous, shiny-bright, and stir the imagination; repairs and rebuilding, however, lack sex appeal. When a dam breaks or a bridge collapses, or when a city rations water, or even worse when people are killed in some catastrophe that could have been prevented, we become aware for the moment that we should have paid more attention to these things in disrepair. The basic allure that is so important for political responses, however, is very slight for infrastructural matters; other problems will grab away the media coverage. Yet all the data suggest that much of the work done since World War II on the basic man-made physical environment is inadequate. There is a need for fundamental repair and reconstruction. Moreover, much work that was never done must be attended to immediately. By the end of the century, Americans will face very serious problems with virtually every area of the infrastructure.

The infrastructure is the physical foundation of our society—roads, dams, bridges, sewers, reservoirs, water systems. Every time you hit a pothole or cross a shaky bridge, you realize immediately that something is wrong with the infrastructure. But unlike the hero of *Les Misérables*, most of us do not go wandering through the sewers, nor are we terribly interested in their condition or upkeep until and unless something goes wrong. Besides, the numbers and complexities of these physical artifacts are so large and so universal that outside of our own local areas we lose interest quickly. Still, four million miles of roads and streets in various degrees of trouble cannot be dismissed lightly as long as the automobile remains the major vehicle of our transportation system. Estimates put a half-million bridges, 60,000 urban and community water and sewer systems, and 2,300 airports at risk. (Admittedly these figures probably point to potential problems rather than real ones, since the figures tend to emphasize replacement rather than repair and are based on optimum standards rather than those of reasonable use.) We can and do use these facilities for many, many years after they begin to need to be replaced. A bad road is still a road that often can be used for decades. Only belatedly do we recognize infrastructural problems, and frequently, because of the cost, prefer to patch and shore up the existing system rather than replace it. However, the growing magnitude of these needs is real: witness New York state's $3 billion bond issue for repair of roads and bridges, passed in November 1988.

Since the numbers and costs involved are so large, the estimated projections deserve special attention. Americans spend somewhat more than $50 billion a year on upkeep and need a total of about $1.2 trillion for these projects over the next 16 years. The Joint Economic Committee of the Congress, in a substantial report on the infrastructure, predicted a shortfall in funding over that period of almost a half-trillion dollars ($443 billion); it was discouraging news since almost three-quarters of a trillion dollars ($720 billion) alone was needed for roads and bridges. The federal government spends only about half the amount of GNP on these projects today (2.3 percent) as it did in the 1960s (5 percent); per capita infrastructure spending adjusted for inflation has fallen to $120 from $207. Amitai Etzioni, who has written extensively on these problems, feels the erosion is so far advanced that he warns that the U.S. has become an "underdeveloping [country], a modern economy in reverse gear."[1]

Before the New Deal, the building of roads, bridges, and airports was most frequently a state or local project. Construction of those projects varied widely in size, quality, and commitment. By 1930 a comprehensive national highway system was clearly necessary. Nevertheless, not until FDR's New Deal was there major federal involvement in road construction. Building roads and dams created jobs in Tennessee, Arizona, and elsewhere, and these projects became unusually popular in Congress. Many of these structures still stand, monuments to Roosevelt's political acumen. However, the road system built in the 1930s was already totally inadequate when World War II broke out in 1939. In 1948 Congress appropriated funds for highway building that had military value, and President Eisenhower in 1956 pushed this building program into high gear. He was convinced the United States stood in jeopardy if it could not move military forces expeditiously and efficiently. The Eisenhower administration supported the building of a comprehensive interstate system to meet these needs. In fact, the highways were built so that small aircraft could land on them. The federal government promised to subsidize 90 percent of the costs and mandated the building of 41,000 miles of highways (2,000 additional miles were authorized later). Since the 1950s over $715 billion has been spent building the interstate system. But the increasing demands of a highly mobile society have tended to overwhelm the system. One can no longer imagine the country functioning without the interstate system, which makes it even more imperative that it be brought up to modern standards. Parts of the system in forty-six states remain unfinished, but already 40 percent of what has been built is over twenty years old and needs maintenance. Ten percent of the mileage is in need of immediate resurfacing and an additional 30 percent is only in fair condition, barely adequate to handle traffic at 55 mph maximum speed. No interstate was built to standards that can handle double-rig trucks or even the current amount of "normal" traffic. Older U.S. routes are worse off. Some two-thirds of the 260,000 miles of federal roads are rated as "poor or fair." Annual upkeep alone costs over $3 billion. Meanwhile, the combined fleet of cars and trucks is approaching the two hundred million mark. Highway phobia brought on by driving conditions in some of our metropolitan areas is a recognized and treatable psychological condition. It takes great skill, courage, and daring to manipulate the Cambridge, Mass., Fresh Pond Parkway, Philadelphia's Schuylkill Expressway, the D.C. Beltway, and of course the Los Angeles freeways. If needed repairs are not addressed, however, we may crumble to a stop altogether.

Although the federal government, for the most part, paid for the construction of the interstate system, routine costs of upkeep and repair were to be borne by the states. These routine costs have grown tremendously, and states have been unable to keep up their share. In 1976, therefore, when the system was already twenty years old, Congress finally voted money for repairs. At one time, we could build a mile of road for a million dollars; today the average cost to put a $1\frac{1}{2}$ inch layer of new asphalt on 2,000 miles is $160 million. The cost of building entirely new roads is astronomical. Poor agricultural states like Tennessee and Georgia that lack maintenance funds are forced to see their highway system crack and deteriorate in huge chunks.

Driving on a deteriorated highway is also a life and safety hazard, shortening the life of the vehicle and forcing up the cost of repairs. Increases in vehicle operating costs have been estimated at 35 percent, which is probably understated. Federal officials claim that 17,200 lives would be saved and 480,000 personal injuries could be prevented if $4.3 billion were spent on the repair of roads and bridges over the next decade and a half. Other needs, however, take priority in our system—health, welfare, defense. In 1983, Congress raised the federal gas tax a nickel per gallon. The five-cent tax was earmarked for improving interstate and U.S. highways and urban mass-transit systems. This tax levy increased by more than 50 percent (from $11 billion to $17 billion) the amount of money available for repairs to the infrastructure. However admirable, the revenue raised is now totally insufficient and inadequate.

Congress approved $7.5 billion in repair funds in March 1985 and $4.8 billion in September 1985. Initially $5.3 billion was allocated for what was deemed the most pressing problems of interstate highways: approximately $1 billion to mass transit to help reduce congestion and for repair; other funding went for major resurfacing, repair, and improvement of existing interstate highways; $960 million to the states for other road and bridge repairs including major repairs to primary U.S. routes. On February 13, 1991, the Bush administration proposed a five-year, $105 billion program of federal aid to the states for highways and mass transit. These proposals are much too little and too late. The monies are targeted largely for the last two years, and will provide only bandaid repair treatment. The sacrifice of mass transit to highway repair will accelerate urban decay. Congress is not likely to take kindly to these proposals.

In past years, much of the benefit of highway repair legislation has been eliminated by concessions to the trucking industry, which, in return for higher user fees, was given approval to drive outsize double-trailer trucks on the whole length of the interstate as well as on the 230,000 miles of federal and state roads. These double trailers, measuring more than 75 feet long and 102 inches wide and weighing up to 80,000 pounds, are highway crushers. Each trailer does as much damage as 4,500 cars. Furthermore, the large trucks are major road hazards. The failure to hire additional inspectors means that a sizable number of vehicles are deficient in safety and performance. Despite the popularity of trucker renegades portrayed in such movies as *Smokey and the Bandit*, these Goliaths imperil every driver on the nation's highways.

The Federal Highway Administration has reported that one-third of the nation's nonfederal bridges and 10 percent of those built with federal funds are "structurally deficient"; almost one-fourth of the 574,000 bridges are considered safe only for cars and light trucks. It would take almost $50 billion to repair or replace them. In many states, the condition of bridges is more than worrisome. In 1985 a span collapsed in Connecticut, causing a major accident. Hundreds, if not thousands of other bridges need repair or replacement. In New York a bridge on the Thruway collapsed in 1988, killing ten people. Falling bridges are more than matched by leaking dams. Most dams in the country are earthen and therefore very subject to erosion and washout. The Army Corps of Engineers classified 7.4 percent of the nation's nonfederal dams as unsafe. In November 1977, an earthen dam in Georgia broke, killing thirty-nine people. A follow-up inspection of private dams in Alabama, Georgia, Florida, North Carolina, and South Carolina found more than 50 percent of them unsafe.

Almost half the country's sewage treatment plants are near overload capacity and much of the nation's drinking water is threatened by pollution. In older cities with antiquated water systems, there is evidence of lead poisoning from old and corroded pipes. Many cities combined their sewer and street-drainage systems when they built them at the turn of the century. Today this flow of human waste into rivers and waterways is unacceptable, but it is estimated that $400 billion would be required nationwide to separate the systems. Older cities in areas of the country where economic conditions have deteriorated are least able to raise the revenues necessary for such major projects and are most affected by this problem. In 1986, the *New York Times* described its city's needs:

How to Quench New York's Thirst

New York City will have to spend hundreds of millions of dollars in the next 10 to 15 years—possibly billions by the year 2030—on new sources of water, a task force concluded in a report released by City Hall last week. It was the first public acknowledgment by municipal officials that even Draconian conservation measures will not serve to meet a growing demand.

The panel reviewed existing studies of the water needs of New York City and the upstate watershed communities served by the city's 18 reservoirs, but found widely varying estimates. If water needs were to increase at a rate of 0.4 percent a year, the lowest projection, the city would need to add a few hundred million gallons to the daily average, now 1.5 billion gallons. If needs were to rise to 1.6 percent, the highest estimate, the report said, "an immense project, equal to or greater than the entire existing system, would be necessary by the year 2030." Even at the 1.1 percent rate of increase that has prevailed in recent years, the system would have to be expanded by at least 50 percent.

The panel recommended "every reasonable" conservation measure, including metering and rate setting; better studies to determine long-range needs, and immediate steps to create a supplemental supply of 200 to 300 million gallons a day.

Noting that "the best reservoir sites within 100 miles have all been developed by the city," the task force warned: "To develop a major new source, the city would have to consider pumping the Hudson River, building reservoirs in the Upper Hudson Basin, drawing water from the Great Lakes or recharging Long Island aquifers to store up a drought emergency supply. Each option involves great cost, active opposition, and at least 20 years to develop.[2]

To conclude this litany of social and political failure, one need only add the sorry story of mass transit. Urban bus and subway systems have always been the poor relatives in our transportation system, but they have never faced a crisis so overwhelming as they do today. New York City, of course, is the outstanding example of mass transit in disarray. Subway cars were brutalized both inside and outside, and compared to subway systems in many parts of the world, New York City's system was (until very recently when major capital improvements were made) a disgrace. So ever-present is the threat of violence on New York City's subways that many individuals routinely take cabs to avoid subways, further congesting the already clogged surface transit system. Commuting into New York City is also unpleasant whatever means of transportation one uses. The West Side Highway has vir-

Table 9.1 U.S. Infrastructure Cost Projection, 1983–2000 (billions of 1982 dollars)

Component	Needs	Revenues	Shortfall
Highways and bridges	$720	$455	$265
Other Transportation	178	90	88
Water	96	55	41
Sewer	163	114	49
Total	$1,157	$714	$443

Source: *Hard Choices: A Report on the Increasing Gap between America's Infrastructure Needs and Our Ability to Pay for Them*, p. 5.

tually disintegrated, and any progress on the "Westway Development" has been brought to a halt. New York City is an extreme case, of course, but most of our large cities are approaching a critical point of no return. Mass transit in the U.S., however, will remain unregenerate until the federal government sees fit to inject massive amounts of aid. Over a half million people continue to commute daily into New York City, yet conditions today are worse than they were two decades ago. By contrast, the city itself is resplendent with beautiful new buildings, beautiful restaurants, and beautiful people.

The report prepared in 1984 by the Subcommittee on Economic Goals and Intergovernmental Policy of the Joint Economic Committee of the Congress, entitled *Hard Choices: A Report on the Increasing Gap between America's Infrastructure Needs and Our Ability to Pay for Them*, is worth studying. Although incomplete, the investigation is useful for what it says. Overall, the conclusion of the committee was moderately optimistic. Americans face, they said,

> a serious, but manageable problem related to the condition and adequacy of its basic infrastructure—surface transportation, water supply and distribution, sewer collection and treatment facilities. . . . Continued reduced levels of investment and/or continued levels of investment insufficient to meet priority needs will result in many undesirable consequences. Clearly, the nation will suffer a reduction in its economic development potential, productivity and jobs. Just as clearly its residents will suffer a loss in the quality of their lives and the choices open to them.[3]

The committee's analysis recognized a current and projected shortfall of $450 billion through the end of the century and an inability of state governments to meet the needs of the deteriorating and/or inadequate infrastructure. Not only did the committee recognize the need for a new dimension of state-federal cooperation, but also called for new and innovative financing mechanisms. The report pointed out that

> historically, the federal government has played a major role in supporting infrastructure investment. The Committee urged Congress to consider four basic changes in the current federal infrastructure role.[4]

First, the committee recommended creation of new financing schemes to assist infrastructure development. Second, it urged Congress to mandate development of a coordinated national infrastructure needs assessment program and unified capital budget evaluation. Third, it urged Congress to initiate a review of infrastructure standards. Fourth, the committee proposed that Congress mandate an early evaluation of statutory and administrative rules now governing the use of existing federal infrastructure assistance programs. Finally, the advisory committee recommended that these proposals be premised on "state and local government enhancing their own fiscal capacity."[5]

The examination of future infrastructure needs and revenues indicated:

For the 23 states studied, total infrastructure needs (highways, other transportation, water, sewerage) for the 1983 to 2000 period are projected to be about $750 billion in 1982 dollars. Revenue to meet these needs is projected to be about $460 billion resulting in a revenue shortfall of $290 billion.

For the country as a whole, infrastructure needs for the four categories addressed in this study are estimated to be $1,160 billion in 1982 dollars. Revenue to meet these needs is projected to be $710 billion leaving a financing gap of $450 billion.

The greatest regional per capita infrastructure needs are projected for the Midwest. The region forecasting the smallest total requirements is the West. The Northeast, South and South-Central project total needs of similar magnitudes. All regions project future needs that are in excess of historical expenditure levels. All regions expect revenue to be insufficient to meet future infrastructure demands.

The single most dominant need across the country is highways and bridges. Total capital needs for this infrastructure component for the 23 states were estimated to be $466 billion, or 62 percent of the combined needs for highways, other transportation, water and sewerage systems. Assuming the same per capita relationship holds for other states throughout the country, total highway needs are projected to be $720 billion over the 1983 to 2000 period in 1982 dollars.

On a regional basis, the greatest highway needs are projected for the Midwest. Annual per capita needs in the Midwest are projected to be $257, or 281 percent more than recent levels of capital outlay for highways.

Total sewerage treatment needs are projected to be $106 billion in the 23 states, or $163 billion nationally in 1982 dollars. The greatest needs are projected for the Northeast and Midwest. The per capita requirements in these two regions are substantially larger than their recent expenditure levels and about triple the needs of the South and South-Central.

Water needs are projected to be $62 billion in the states under study, or $96 billion nationally in 1982 dollars. Water supply is predominately a concern of the South-Central and West Regions where per capita needs are projected to be $44 and $31 respectively. Protecting supplies and renewing aging distribution networks are major concerns of the Northeast and Midwest.

Other transportation (i.e., ports, airports, railroads, mass transit) is a vital infrastructure component, but one in which the private sector has traditionally played a major role. Projected other transportation needs varied greatly from $3 per capita in the South-Central to $65 per capita in the Northeast. This variation is largely attributable to the relative importance to the various states and regions of "other transportation."[6]

The key to these proposals was the recommendation that Congress create a means of financing infrastructure needs through a unique new financial intermediary, a National Infrastructure Fund (NIF). The NIF would be federally chartered. In order to raise the needed capital, it would directly sell taxable bonds in the private market or through the Federal Financing Board and use this revenue to capitalize state infrastructure financing entities that in turn would support state or local government infrastructure programs. States could receive interest-free capital, and in turn could make below-market-rate loans to finance projects. NIF capital would be repaid by state and local governments from various taxes or user charges. State and local governments could continue to recycle this capital for other projects until the time when the bonds became due. The federal government would be liable only for interest payments on NIF debt.

Clearly, the report demonstrated the extent and seriousness of the problem, and suggested creative solutions, but no action has yet been taken!

ACID RAIN AND THE ENVIRONMENTAL CRISIS

In 1962 Rachel Carson, an American writer and marine biologist, wrote *Silent Spring*, a book that touched the emotions of postwar Americans and expressed passionate concern that we had done great damage to our habitat, and imperilled the future of our children.

> There was once a town in the heart of America where all life seemed to live in harmony with its surroundings. The town lay in the midst of a checkerboard of prosperous farms, with fields of grain and hillsides of orchards where, in spring, white clouds of bloom drifted above the green fields. In autumn, oak and maple and birch set up a blaze of color that flamed and flickered across a backdrop of pines. Then foxes barked in the hills and deer silently crossed the fields, half hidden in the mists of the fall mornings.
>
> Along the roads, laurel, viburnum and alder, great ferns and wildflowers delighted the traveler's eye through much of the year. Even in winter the roadsides were places of beauty, where countless birds came to feed on the berries and on the seed heads of the dried weeds rising above the snow. The countryside was, in fact, famous for the abundance and variety of its bird life, and when the flood of migrants was pouring through in spring and fall people traveled from great distances to observe them. Others came to fish the streams, which flowed clear and cold out of the hills and contained shady pools where trout lay....
>
> Then a strange blight crept over the area and everything began to change. ...There was a strange illness. The birds, for example—where had they gone?...only silence lay over the fields and woods and marsh.
>
> No witchcraft, no enemy action had silenced the rebirth of new life in this stricken world. The people had done it themselves.[7]

Rachel Carson was neither an economist nor a historian. She was a biologist who wrote sensitively about the environment that modern American society was polluting. Instead of presenting her analysis in cost-benefit terms, she sensed that most Americans would respond to a more emotional description of the threats to themselves, their families, and the very quality of their lives.

The present emphasis on the environment is barely thirty years old, but it is likely to be the most important issue for the remainder of this century. Americans have today a growing sense that they stand a fair chance of destroying themselves not only through nuclear war but through a mindless disregard of the air, water, and space around them; that cancer-producing chemicals are real, and that pollutants in the water supply and in the food chain are threatening life itself. In the 1990s every schoolchild knows about the "greenhouse effect" and the holes in the ozone layer.

For the greater part of our national existence, we paid scant attention to these matters. Vast stretches of the landscape were so sparsely inhabited that no place in the world seemed healthier than the United States. Rivers were clean and swift flowing, the air was pure and sweet, and the products that came from our fields and factories contributed to a high standard of life. Even now, one does not have to journey to the empty areas of the Southwest to feel this way; Americans have never had to face most of the problems of crowding that industrial societies all over the world find commonplace. We have been a nation of big skies and empty spaces, and we have preserved this mythology long after reality should have made us keenly aware of national limitations.

Yet our atmosphere is not big enough to contain the impurities which cars and factories now produce. Rivers are not swift enough to handle PCBs and PBRs; even the oceans are not deep enough to carry away the wastes that are dumped into them. And the land does not cleanse itself of pesticides and other toxins but churns them into the food chain of the diseased environment. What a terrible awakening this has been for a nation that for so long enjoyed a wilderness unspoiled!

The environmental problem that drew the attention of the country first was acid rain. In the vicinity of chemical and industrial plants, trees withered and died. Then it became clear that hundreds and thousands of miles away, even across our national borders in Canada, acid rain was killing life in many lakes, stunting and destroying forests and permanently altering the ecology of entire areas. The lack of scientific knowledge and difficulty of assessing fault has added to the problems in dealing with acid rain. Acid rain also has become a kind of metaphor for environmental problems in general.

The Air Pollution Control Act (1955) was the first major piece of federal legislation passed after a study by the California Technical Institute found a link between automobile exhaust and Los Angeles smog. Only $5 million was appropriated over a 5-year period to do research, training, and demonstration projects. In 1963, the Clean Air Act gave the federal government enforcement powers through the clumsy and cumbersome method of the Enforcement Conference. Two years later (1965) the Health, Education, and Welfare Department, through the Motor Vehicle Air Pollution Control Act, was given the authority to prescribe emission standards for automobiles, but the standards set were at best modest. In 1967, a four-day air inversion in New York City frightened millions of people; the Clean Air Act of 1970 followed. Still by 1977 so little had been achieved that Congress came to the conclusion that its original goals were unrealistic. The amended legislation of 1977 stretched out time required for compliance with these standards: the "healthy" air goals originally targeted for 1975 were postponed to 1982 and 1987; the 90 percent reduction in automobile emissions originally set for 1975 was extended to 1980 and 1981. Meanwhile, the Environmental Protection Agency was required to allow exceptions for technological innovation and compelled to issue full economic and employment impact statements with all new regulations. Although the EPA today can order severe penalties for violation, it has tended to avoid heavy-handed action since the start of the Reagan administration. In theory, the EPA can levy fines of up to $25,000 a day for each continued day of some violations and can punish violators with one year in jail. Subsequent violations can double these penalties. Each car sold by manufacturers in violation of EPA standards can earn a $10,000 fine, and unmet motor vehicle fuel standards can also lead to a fine of $10,000 a day. However, the Reagan administration did great damage to the EPA by appointing untrained and controversial bureaucrats and by holding its budget and staff levels, in real terms, to what they were in the early 1970s before the EPA was given major new responsibilities.

The Clean Air Act of 1990 is the first major piece of air pollution legislation in thirteen years. This statute sets standards for the control of smog in ninety-six areas. All but nine areas are to meet these standards by November 1999. Los Angeles, the most critically affected, has been given until November 2010. Beginning in 1995, all gasoline sold in nine metropolitan areas (Los Angeles, Baltimore, New York City, Chicago, Houston, Milwaukee, Hartford, Connecticut, Philadelphia, San Diego) must be cleaner-burning fuel that cuts emission of hydrocarbons and toxic pollutants by 15 percent. Other provisions toughen standards for toxic emissions and acid rain. The cost of these changes is estimated at $25 billion a year by early next century.

For many liberals, the solution to environmental problems lies in increasing the appropriations to EPA, just as for many conservatives the solution must be found in the private sector. Neither approach by itself, however, is sufficient. The problem of acid rain illustrates some of the difficulties. After two full decades of research and legislation, we do not know the exact causes of acid rain. What we do know are the consequences—dead and dying forests, stagnating lakes. Scientists have gone back and forth between the relative importance to the problem of sulphur oxides (SO_2) and nitrogen oxides (NO_2 and NO_3). At present, the best thinking seems to support a combination of photochemical oxidants, specifically, ozone and SO_2, NO_2 and NO_3, and oxygen (O_3), all of which have a toxic effect on plants. However, the complexity of what really happens cannot be easily identified; for example, some amounts of each of these chemicals exist naturally in the stratosphere, although the largest source is auto exhaust.

In March 1985, after a conference with Prime Minister Mulroney of Canada, President Reagan advocated a program of accelerated study of the causes of acid rain and pledged to come to "some solution."[8] By autumn, however, Reagan had retreated to a more noncommittal position, declaring that there wasn't sufficient scientific data on the causes of acid rain to proceed with vigorous policy initiatives. Since then, President Bush and the Congress moved to do something substantial on these issues in the Clean Air Act of 1990.

The costs of dealing with these problems are, as we have seen, very high, but so are the costs of doing nothing. Health care, defense, social security, for example, are familiar programs with substantial yet finite needs, however difficult the controversies that surround them. The costs of fixing the environment seem to have neither a beginning nor an end, only undefined horrors with price tags of undefinable dimensions—tens of billions? hundreds of billions of dollars? In order to survive, must we give up the automobile? Our industrial society? And then how would we live? How can "we" even act together? As one journalist put it in 1977:

> Existing laws and institutions are not adequate to deal with the acid rain problem. The Clean Air Act is designed to deal with air pollution in the vicinity of pollution sources. In contrast, acid rain involves consequences for water and soil in areas hundreds or thousands of miles away from these sources.[9]

Everyone is familiar with the long disputes over acid rain between eastern Canada and the United States. Now Mexico is building a huge smelter which may send acid rain north over the Southwest. Few indeed have been the legal settlements involving acid rain within the country, even fewer are the agreements involving international effects of pollution. Who pays? for what? These are not academic questions. But in addition to further study and research, consensus building and negotiation, programs must move along faster, even faster than the deadlines in the newest legislation.

Historically, attempts to control water pollution date back to the Refuse Act of 1899. Between 1899 and 1970, Congress passed a number of measures dealing with the problem: the Water Pollution Control Act (1948), the Water Pollution Control Act Amendments (1956), and the Water Quality Act (1965). Oil spills have constituted a major threat. In January 1969 an oil well in the Santa Barbara Channel off California blew out, creating an ecological disaster. Thousands of fish were killed, thousands of birds were covered with oil, and miles of beach were ravaged by the slick. The president of the responsible company, Union Oil of California, allegedly met the crisis with enormous insensitivity. He was initially quoted in the media: "I am amazed at the publicity for the loss of a few birds." (He claimed he actually said, "I am always tremendously impressed at the publicity that death of birds receives versus the loss of people in our country in this day and age.") Twenty miles of ocean beach lay covered in sludge, and the Santa Barbara Channel has been closed for oil exploration since the spill. Twenty years later Exxon spent over a billion dollars trying to clean up the damage caused by an oil spill in Alaska when one of its tankers was ripped open on the rocks.

In October 1971, the Senate Commerce Committee headed by Senator Muskie, from the pristine coast of Maine, drafted a 120-page bill intended to eliminate the discharge of all pollutants in the nation's water resources by 1985. This act, as did the Clean Air Act, mandated the EPA to set specific deadlines to achieve the goals set by Congress. The Safe Drinking Water Act of 1974 authorized the following:

1. Effluent standards for factories and waste treatment plants.
2. Stringent federal standards for discharge of toxins, such as carbon tetrachloride, bromodi-chloromethane, and lead.
3. Permits limiting discharges from every source of industrial or municipal pollution—the permits, based on effluent guidelines where they are available, are issued...by the federal government under the National Pollutant Discharge System (NPDES)....
4. Prohibitions on the dumping of any radioactive waste into the nation's inland and coastal waters.
5. Regulation of the disposal of radioactive waste in the ocean.
6. Grants to assist states in area wide waste treatment management planning and make loans to small businesses to help them fulfill water pollution control requirements.
7. Grants to state and regional governmental agencies to plan and carry out solid-waste management programs.
8. Control of pollution from non-point sources (e.g., runoffs from agricultural and silvicultural operations) by requiring the polluters to employ "best management practices" that reduce the amount and impact of the runoff.
9. Standards for chemical and bacteriological pollutants in the water systems...

This legislation introduced the concept of "best practical technology" (BPT), a concept not easily defined. President Nixon vetoed this bill because of its burden on the national economy and the Treasury, but Congress overrode the veto; in that sense the Clean Water Act was a milestone, even though its standards were difficult to define and implement.

Within a year, the energy crisis was to deal a serious blow to these early environmental efforts. Standards for air pollution were modified and target dates stretched out. Similarly, for water pollution "best practical technology" was stretched to "best adequate technology" (BAT) and then to "best pollution control technology" (BPCT) by 1984. However, the severity of the economic downturn caused by Middle East exploitation of oil markets squeezed the American economy powerfully in the 1970s, and the optimism about environmental progress of the late 1960s evaporated.

In a way, social welfare programs and environmental standards shared a similar quandary—any effort to rectify abuses disclosed a still more massive problem that needed even greater sums of money. Environmental problems were not solved and never disappeared; they instead revealed a society living beyond its environmental means and heavily discounting its future. For example, the National Water Commission estimated that it would cost $220 billion between 1972 and 1983 to meet the BAT standards for stationary and plant source water pollution set down in the 1972 legislation; the Council on Environmental Quality (CEQ) estimated a cost of $130 to $140 billion to achieve similar intermediate improvements in air quality. One estimate of the money spent in cleaning up pollution since 1968 has been placed at over $600 billion. Unfortunately, this amount is a tiny fraction of the money that eventually must be spent.

TOXIC WASTE

The state of Washington had the distinction of being enshrined in the lyrics of a popular song called, "Our State is a Dumpsite," for it had been chosen by the federal government for the disposal of nuclear waste. But nuclear waste is only a very small part of the overall toxic waste problem. Over the last century, since the Second Industrial Revolution's discovery of the widespread uses of chemicals for industrial purposes, even more especially since the end of the Second World War, Americans have not only enormously increased the production and use of chemicals but have also, in the old American tradition, dumped the waste products willy-nilly into dumps, lakes, rivers, oceans; any hole in the ground seemed O.K. Since the 1960s we have been discovering and unfolding an enormous sub-surface bed of toxic waste. Congressman James Florio (now Governor) of New Jersey made two comments in 1985: "The problem is worse than it was five years ago," and "It's much, much greater than anyone thought."[10] Even the head of EPA under the Reagan administration admitted that "there are far more sites that are far more difficult to deal with than anybody ever anticipated." The Office of Technology Assessment thinks that there may be 10,000 hazardous waste sites in the U.S. that pose a serious threat to public health. The cost of cleaning up these sites is estimated at $100 billion; since the costs have invariably exceeded the estimates, we may well be facing a cost double or triple this estimate. The General Accounting Office has identified thousands of waste sites that could require action. The EPA has 850 dumps on its top list, but over a five-year period it has managed to clear up only six sites.

Critics believe that every county in every state has at least one toxic dump site—steel drums rusting and leaking toxins into soil and water sources, or chemical by-products pumped into streams and lakes. Mistakenly, it was once believed that these wastes would be rendered harmless over time by nature; no one foresaw the increasing magnitude and consequences of the problem. Wastes buried years ago, thought harmless and long forgotten, seem to rise from the dead to claim the living.

Map 9.1   **Hazardous Waste Sites in the U.S., 1987**

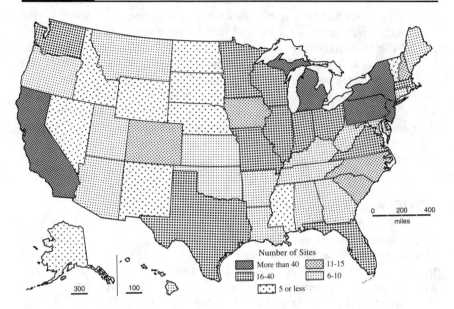

Source: *Historical Abstract of the United States,* 1988.

In 1980, Congress created the "Superfund," a $1.6 billion, five-year crash program administered by the EPA to clean up these thousands of leaking dumps. Much of Superfund I was spent studying problems or particular sites, in many cases a very expensive boondoggle. If the EPA had been better administered, certainly more could have been done. But the EPA under the Reagan administration was poorly run, and the President preferred to visualize the America of "amber waves of grain" than of dead lakes gurgling poison bubbles. In 1985, Congress and the President haggled over the amounts to be given to the Superfund, but neither amount—$10 billion (proposed by the House) or $5.3 billion (offered by Reagan) over five years—was meaningful given the enormity of the problem. Many of the sites are old-timers, but some are the outcomes of both legal and illegal current activities. One site in Pennsylvania, for example, resulted from the systematic and illegal dumping of chemical wastes into shafts that fed into an outlet tunnel for waste water from abandoned coal mines. After a three-years investigation and trial, three people were convicted, with one receiving a prison sentence and a fine of $750,000. Heavy rains from Hurricane Gloria had activated and brought to the surface 100,000 gallons of oily, smelly chemical wastes from this "cleaned-up" site which the EPA had declared safe. In another site, Baltimore's Annapolis Road, the EPA scraped off topsoil to find contamination fifteen feet below the surface. When environmentalists have examined the sites which the EPA is monitoring, they invariably have found the sites leaking and out of compliance with the regulations.

The truth is no one wants the sites, no one really knows how to clean up the sites, and no one seriously believes the problem can be put on hold. Cases of cancer, leukemia, kidney disease, and other illnesses can be traced to toxins bleeding into the ground water supplies. People have been moved from their homes that had been built over landfills containing these poisons. Times Beach, Missouri, may gain a unique distinction of being totally abandoned (the EPA agreed to pay off all property owners) because the oil spread over its ten miles of unpaved streets was laced with dioxin waste sludge, a powerful carcinogen. If other places have less dramatic stories, like the one of the polluted water system in Holbrook, Massachusetts,[11] they are no less real.

Sixty thousand of the 66,000 chemicals used in the U.S. are classified by the EPA as potentially hazardous to human health. If the chemical industry and the public have shown more awareness of the problem, their concerns have not yet translated into the kinds and amounts of monies needed for cleanup or effective treatment programs. Here is one description of a modern disposal waste facility; multiply this thousands of times, and tens of billions of dollars and you will have only begun to scratch the surface.

> A giant excavation 35 feet deep covers two acres. A floor of compacted clay approximately 40 feet thick has been laid below the bottom of the hole. On top of this virtually impermeable bed, workmen are placing a plastic liner to be topped by a plastic-grid system that will collect and direct any seepage into a series of sump pumps. Above the grid will be another plastic liner, another layer of clay and yet more plastic. A plumbing system will pump rainwater out of the area.
>
> Nearby, the company is spending $1.6 million to improve its large surface collection tanks, made of concrete lined with epoxy, that receive waste from steel-processing plants. New fiberglass liners are being placed inside the cylinders.[12]

Advanced technologies do exist and have been used in such western European countries as Germany and Switzerland, but the U.S. is only beginning the process of establishing modern waste disposal facilities.

CITIES

Is it too late to save our great cities? Even a few years ago the answer given by most economists would have probably been a qualified 'yes'. But today we are seeing a new revitalization. It is too early to call this trend a reversal of the downward decay since the 1940s, yet it is certainly something of a renewal. New transportation and communication technology has contributed to the weakening vitality of our cities, but these forces may also forge an era of urban renewal.

We are all familiar with the intractable problems of the city. Mitchell Gordon's *Sick Cities: Psychology and Pathology of American Urban Life*

Table 9.2   Population Changes in the Twenty Largest Cities, 1960 to 1980 (population in thousands)

1980 rank	City	1960	1960 % black	1970	1970 % black	1980	1980 % black	1980 % hispanic	1988
1	New York	7,782	14.0	7,896	21.1	7,071	25.2	19.9	7,353
2	Chicago	3,550	22.9	3,369	32.7	3,005	39.8	14.0	2,978
3	Los Angeles	2,479	13.5	2,812	17.9	2,967	17.0	27.5	3,353
4	Philadelphia	2,003	26.4	1,949	33.6	1,668	37.8	3.8	1,647
5	Houston	938	22.9	1,234	25.7	1,594	27.6	17.6	1,698
6	Detroit	1,670	28.9	1,514	43.7	1,203	63.1	2.4	1,036
7	Dallas	680	19.0	844	24.9	904	29.4	12.3	987
8	San Diego	573	6.0	697	7.6	876	8.9	15.0	1,070
9	Phoenix	439	4.8	584	4.8	790	4.9	14.7	924
10	Baltimore	939	34.7	906	46.4	787	54.8	1.0	751
11	San Antonio	588	7.1	654	7.6	785	7.3	53.8	941
12	Indianapolis	476	20.6	737	18.0	701	21.8	0.9	727
13	San Francisco	740	10.0	716	13.4	679	12.7	12.2	732
14	Memphis	498	37.0	624	38.9	646	47.6	0.8	645
15	Washington	764	53.9	757	71.1	638	70.3	2.8	617
16	San Jose	204	1.0	460	2.5	637	4.6	22.1	738
17	Milwaukee	741	8.4	717	14.7	636	23.1	4.1	599
18	Cleveland	876	28.6	751	38.3	574	43.8	3.1	521
19	Columbus	471	16.4	540	18.5	565	22.1	0.9	570
20	Boston	697	9.1	641	16.3	563	22.4	6.4	578

Source: *Statistical Abstract of the United States, 1990.*

(1965) dissected urban problems in the same way that Rachel Carson's *Silent Spring* analyzed environmental ones. In such intemperate chapters as "Water: Filthier and Farther," "No Place for Fun," "Help, Police!" Gordon left little to the imagination about what was wrong with our cities.[13] Twenty-five years later the urban problems of welfare, drugs, AIDS, crime, substandard education and housing, unemployment, inequitable taxes, and transportation and environmental woes still dominate the central cities. Three-quarters of the American people live in metropolitan areas and about a third still reside in central cities. However, a large portion of those who live in central cities are the poorest, least educated, and most socially dependent of our citizens. Moreover, the central city is not only the home of our minorities, but it is also a predominant place for vice, crime, drugs, and prostitution.

The largest five cities by 2000—Los Angeles, New York, Chicago, Boston, and Philadelphia—will be badly dysfunctional in key areas if resources are not funneled into their renewal. The tunnels out of New York now with the greatest difficulty carry four-and-one-half times the number of vehicles they were built to handle. It is possible to get into a traffic loop outside Logan Airport in Boston that will carry you in a circle, like a holding pattern for a plane, until the volume of traffic eventually is worked off. The Bonaventure Hotel in Los Angeles sits on a concrete island around which the freeways spin a massive spider web of cars. Chicago reverses many of its traffic lanes day and night to try to manage flow into and out of the city. Transportation is only one of the most visible of urban problems; combined with the specter of total gridlock in urban services, drug control, and dealing with the homeless, the totality of these crises is truly frightening.

Still, urban renewal projects such as Quincy Market, the South Street Seaport and Battery Park, Baltimore Harbor, Peachtree Plaza, the new St. Louis Center, and Ghirardelli Square make one aware of the lasting strength and vitality of great cities. Tens of billions of dollars are being put into the core of these central cities and the worst of the decay may be over. The next decade may see the genesis of improvement.

The new developments in these central cities are very different in kind and quality from those of the past. The golden era of American cities from 1880 to 1920 corresponded roughly to the period of the Second Industrial Revolution in the United States. Before that time, we were not really an urban society. Our first cities were built on major bodies of water—such were the seaports of New York City, Boston, and Philadelphia, as well as important river cities like Albany, Toledo, and St. Louis. The advent and spread of the railroad made possible the establishment of cities remote from major waterways. Steam power also removed the necessity for water-driven machinery and permitted factories to be built in cities close to transportation, marketing, or banking centers. Only seven of today's largest cities were incorporated by 1816; only thirty-nine by 1875. Most of these cities were clustered in the Northeast, Middle Atlantic, and North Central areas; the South, Southwest, and West had very few large urban centers.

The industrialization of the late nineteenth century changed cities. Old commercial centers were encircled by industrial and residential rings. Break-throughs in building techniques allowed developers to build three and four-story tenements near the factories. Moreover, the railroad allowed the wealthy to commute to work downtown, yet live beyond the urban blight. By the turn of the century, however, the very rich had staked out claims to new areas within the cities and were constructing mansions and taller business buildings, in part made possible by the introduction of the passenger eleva-tor and steel construction, applicable to apartments as well as factories. These wealthy individuals also demanded as necessities clean water and po-lice and fire protection and encouraged the establishment of other such amenities as restaurants, parks, and opera houses. The newest technology, then, allowed cities to accommodate much greater population densities. The United States could boast of fifty cities with over 100,000 people at the be-ginning of the twentieth century, whereas in 1860 only nine cities met this standard.

Cities also acted as magnets. As agriculture became more specialized and commercialized, and as the percentage of the population engaged in ag-riculture shrank, rural people sought escape, opportunity, and adventure in cities. Immigrants landed and frequently stayed in the cities. The heaviest ur-ban concentration of Norwegian immigrants, for example, was in Brooklyn, not in the Midwest. The census of 1920 pointed out that more than 50 per-cent of the population was "urban," i.e., living in places with more than 2,500 inhabitants.

Not that cities were without problems even then. The vertical stacking of dwellings as well as climbing land values produced urban slums and blight of unimaginable hardship and ugliness. However, the pre-Depression cities contained something of a balanced proportion of lower and upper in-comes which contributed greatly to the overall well-being of the city. The predominance of the street trolley and urban railway virtually assured that all residential, commercial, and industrial development could be confined within the expanded city limits. The costs of running a city and providing es-sential facilities were enormous, however, and the tax base fragile. The dec-ade of the twenties saw those problems increase, and the Great Depression signaled the end of the golden period.

The New Deal had no urban policy as such, nor has there ever been an urban policy in the United States above and beyond general funding for things such as highways or welfare programs. The uneasy equilibrium that sustained the cities rapidly shifted in the post–World War II period. Auto-mobiles broke the boundaries of a city's limits by extending almost indefi-nitely an outer perimeter for commuters and by making virtually all transportation into or out of the city dependent on the private automobile. Cities have never been able to manage the automobile revolution. In every decade since World War II, the exodus to the suburbs has grown; only lately has there been a minuscule trend in the opposite direction. The social bal-ance, the tax structure, and the political clout of cities all deteriorated rap-idly in the postwar era. In the cities, those unable to leave became the dominant populations. Because of the dwindling tax base, net deficits for urban budgets became depressingly familiar.

Meanwhile, the aspirations of American society became synonymous with the lifestyle of suburbia. The good life was no longer found in the city. Especially concerned were middle-income or upwardly mobile parents appalled by the violence of urban schools. In addition, they sometimes faced court-ordered busing for their children. Such families fled to school systems much more to their liking like those in Larchmont or Niskayuna, New York, or Newton, Massachusetts. There, involved parents in very active parent-teacher associations, with very attentive school teachers and administrators, could fashion the type of education that would prepare their youngsters for prestigious colleges. Government policies aided the exodus of middle income people from the cities. Low-cost mortgages, many guaranteed by the federal government, coupled with income-tax benefits for homeowners, as well as the prospect for capital gains in rising home prices, encouraged the growth of suburbs. Industry, when it could, followed. Manufacturers found suburban industrial parks cheaper than urban facilities, and employees could leave their automobiles in a suburban parking lot for much less money than an indoor garage in a downtown metropolis. In the cityscape which came into being after 1950, suburban shopping malls further eroded the money-making potential of downtown areas.

Since the end of World War II, the deterioration of the central cities has been appalling. New York City became the prototype of urban decay, and "Harlem, unsafe at any hour" became a byword. In 1975, the city faced bankruptcy when the large banks refused to continue the merry-go-round charade of continuing financial bailout. But New York City was not unique. Virtually every major city faced a similar, if not quite as acute, crisis. Public services of all kinds, especially transportation facilities, undermaintained and underfunded, were grinding to a halt. Educational facilities teetered out of control as underpaid and undertrained teachers faced a youth culture of drugs, violence, and crime—indeed everything except a commitment to learning. On either side of the continent, on a clear day, one could still see the blanket of smog hovering over either New York or Los Angeles. Housing too deteriorated rapidly in the central cities. Enormous slums flourished in postwar decades. So bankrupt was public policy that urban renewal became synonymous with expensive and ill-conceived "low-cost" public housing. St. Louis finally dynamited a number of high-rise apartments built by the Housing and Urban Development Authority, closed because they had become a public hazard. Added to these woes were the scandals that rocked HUD in the 1980s.

Beginning in the 1950s, we even began to describe our urban centers differently. The 'central' city took on less significance and was replaced by the SMSA (Standard Metropolitan Statistical Area) which comprised a central city of at least 50,000, the county it was located in, plus neighboring counties that were closely associated by daily commuting. By 1980, there were 318 SMSAs containing 74.8 percent of the population. The SMSAs of the South and West mushroomed, with cities like Phoenix (experiencing 63 percent growth in a decade) and Houston transformed into major centers. Phoenix, a desert town, expanded until it reached the limits of its water supply. Future growth will be restricted by lack of access to cheap water. Blooming flower beds and lush golf courses in the desert are a remarkable testimony to the extent of water subsidies provided by the federal government and are but one example of how misguided public policy has squandered water resources.

Another phenomenon of the postwar period has been the development of the "megalopolis" or "conurbation," continuous urban areas that stretch, for example, from Boston to Washington, San Francisco to San Diego, Cleveland to Chicago. These "strip cities" remind one of the Japanese landscape, where urban sprawl is continuous. "Boswash" is America's biggest urban region, extending from Strafford County, New Hampshire, to Stafford County, Virginia; it contains 20 percent of the nation's population. The interstate highway system built in the 1950s, of course, has aided this

Table 9.3	Fastest and Slowest Growth among Regions		
	1970 Population	1980 Population	Change 1970–80
Phoenix	863,357	1,409,279	63.2%
Florida Peninsula	5,730,764	8,290,959	44.7
Texas Gulf Coast	2,744,131	3,769,719	37.4
Salt Lake Valley	821,689	1,128,328	37.3
Eastern Slope	1,653,442	2,200,507	33.1
Centex (Central Texas)	1,555,989	1,994,053	28.2
Willamette Valley	1,234,001	1,547,821	25.4
Dalworth	2,434,793	3,020,312	24.0
Carolina Coastal	1,145,097	1,406,371	22.8
Soonerland	1,267,128	1,550,123	22.3
Nashville	818,216	1,000,725	22.3
Piedmont	5,280,515	6,359,479	20.4
Central Gulf Coast	2,868,144	3,447,126	20.2
Puget Sound	2,149,939	2,535,367	17.9
Southern California	10,887,954	12,647,607	16.2
Northern California	6,225,084	7,221,281	16.0
Central Alabama	1,358,439	1,547,604	13.9
Southern Virginia	2,255,466	2,526,187	12.0
Bluegrass	1,207,934	1,316,215	9.0
Twin Cities	2,235,444	2,431,154	8.8
Central Indiana	1,888,648	1,977,019	4.7
Missouri-Kansas Val.	1,685,260	1,758,957	4.4
Southern Ohio	3,227,179	3,363,971	4.2
Lower Great Lakes	20,265,576	20,827,980	2.8
Boswash	41,716,435	41,786,061	0.2
Upstate New York	4,689,370	4,617,434	-1.5
St. Louis	2,429,376	2,376,998	-2.2
Cleveland	8,370,354	8,141,391	-2.7

Source: U.S. Department of Commerce, 1983.

Map 9.2   **Percent Change in State Population, 1980–1988**

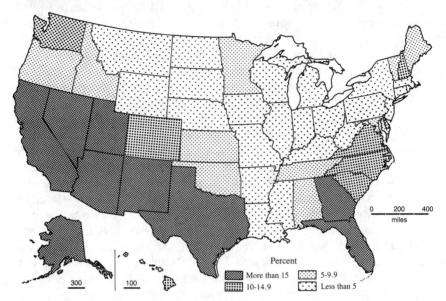

Percent

▨ More than 15 ▦ 5-9.9

▦ 10-14.9 ⬚ Less than 5

Source: *Statistical Abstract of the United States,* 1990.

sprawl. But even these massive highway expenditures have failed to prevent the loss of population in the North, Northeast, and North Central areas. Boston, Buffalo, Newark, New York City, Philadelphia, Pittsburgh, Cleveland, Detroit, Milwaukee, and St. Louis all suffered major declines. The popularity of the Sunbelt as well as improved economic and employment conditions led to the growth in the 1970s of Atlanta, Dallas, Ft. Lauderdale, Houston, Miami, Tampa, St. Petersburg, Anaheim, Denver, Riverside, Sacramento, and San Diego. Yet all of these 'new' cities rapidly took on most of the problems of the old urban areas.

The plight of the central city has become the burden of the poor, the elderly, and minority black and Hispanic groups. The exodus of blacks from the Deep South to northern cities that started during WWI accelerated in the post–World War II period. Northern cities offered many opportunities—employment, health care, personal freedoms, welfare—unavailable in the rural South. At the same time northern industry began moving south, drawn by cheaper labor, lower costs, and a friendlier business climate. Like previous waves of immigrants, blacks and Hispanics were subject to racial and class prejudices. At a time when the resources of the cities were coming under great stress, these arrivals exacerbated the problems. Forced to take the lowest-paid jobs (when they could get jobs), subject to housing discrimination, unable to afford decent urban housing, and untrained, uneducated, and unsocialized into city culture, minorities formed massive urban subcultures of poverty, despair, and violence. In the urban ghettos, unemployment figures for black teenagers in the early 1980s approached 50 percent; even when blacks and Hispanics got jobs, they were paid less than whites for the same work. Black women earned about 54 percent of the salary of white men (white women earned about 60 percent) in 1988, while black women earned 76 percent of the salary of black men, and Hispanic women earned 73 percent of the salary of Hispanic men.

The urban ghettos broke out in riots in the 1960s. During the peak of violence, twenty-eight American cities were under martial law. If the riots were foreshadowed by the militant civil-rights movement in the South, they also were indicative of the urgency of central-city problems. Blacks, angered by poverty, unemployment, racial prejudice, government neglect, and political impotence, no longer reacted with nonviolent sit-ins but with fire-bombings and lootings, often of their own neighborhoods. The torching of the central cities sent whites and white business fleeing. In the 1970s the exodus of whites from the central cities was greater than their combined natural increase and in-migration for the first time in history. In the major cities, these declines were very large. Detroit lost 50.7 percent of its white population; Atlanta, 42.7 percent; Chicago, 32.5 percent; New York City, 29.5 percent and Boston, 24.9 percent. By 1980, 81.1 percent of all blacks lived in metropolitan areas, and 57.8 percent in central cities; 83.5 percent of all Hispanics lived in metropolitan areas, and 88.2 percent in central cities; 73.3 percent of all whites lived in metropolitan areas, but only 25 percent lived in central cities. (See Table 9.2)

Nothing demonstrated more clearly the economic decline of the cities than the figures on income distribution. Incomes were higher in metropolitan areas than nonmetropolitan areas; higher in large SMSAs than small; and higher in the suburbs than in the central city. The median family income in metropolitan areas, $22,590 (1980), was 25 percent higher than the median family income outside the metropolitan area ($18,069), but the gap between the higher suburban and the lower central city median family income was 39.3 percent. Median annual income for white families was $23,815, 73.5 percent higher than the black family median income of $13,726. In large SMSAs, white families' median income was 55.1 percent higher than black families; in small SMSAs the income gap was even greater. In 1980, white income was 85.7 percent higher than black income in small SMSA central cities. Nor were these differentials decreasing. In 1980 61.6 percent of the nation's poor lived in metropolitan areas and 36.4 percent in central cities.

Between 1959 and 1980, the proportion of central city poor blacks rose 8.8 percent. In the past, the city encompassed not only diversified populations, but also diversified economic enterprises. Today cities are economically more homogeneous: the cities today specialize in finance, insurance, and professional services—occupations for which the poor have few qualifications. The poor earn their livelihood through menial low-paid and dead-end jobs: dishwashers and cleaners, hamburger flippers and garage attendants, yet they know that American society offers more, and increasingly they are reluctant to accept the standards of permanent poverty that they have inherited. Especially in the young, the tendency is often to strike out against an unfair society.

The political history of cities has usually been written in terms of the political machines and the bosses who dominated them—men like Tweed, Daley, and Curley. Today, however, the political economy of the cities is basically a problem of economic resources and governance, with the two elements very much intertwined. Although redefining urban areas as SMSAs has been a major perceptual breakthrough, it has not resulted in a re-creation of political boundaries more in line with the economic realities of metropolitan areas. As examples, the permanent boundaries of Philadelphia were fixed in 1858, of New York City in 1898, and Boston in 1912. In 1972, 264 SMSAs contained 22,185 local governments. Chicago alone had 1,172 local governments, and almost 95 percent of them had the authority to levy property taxes. Philadelphia had 852 local governments, almost two-thirds of which had taxing power. This nightmare of political fragmentation is compounded by social and economic problems, especially those of creating revenue for central-city areas.

To meet the soaring costs of its obligations, cities have tried every expedient to raise additional monies, but these attempts have been only modestly successful. Cities derive about one-third of their revenue from taxes, the rest from fees and intergovernmental transfers. However, almost 55 percent of all municipal tax revenue comes from the property tax. Although cities are absolutely dependent on assistance from state and federal governments, which amounts to roughly 30 percent of all municipal revenues, this aid comes in bits and pieces through massive bureaucracies, usually with strings attached.

The property tax is the best example of the revenue-raising problem. All taxes are unpopular, but the property tax that falls on home and business owners seems to bear a special onus. Homeowners see it as a heavy burden, despite the fact that property taxes are deductible from income tax payments. However, property taxes in central cities embody peculiar problems. Revenue from property taxes in the city is adversely constrained by two different tendencies: urban decay and insecurity make property values fall or increase much less rapidly than property values outside the city; also, the fear of driving middle-class homeowners and business into flight to join the exodus of homeowners and businesses that have already migrated makes cities reluctant to raise taxes for additional revenue.[14] Large numbers of abandoned, burned-out buildings, or buildings repossessed by government agencies that insured their mortgages, bear testimony to the shrinking tax revenues of many central cities. The South Bronx is notorious as an example of this decay. Some homeowners burned down their buildings to collect the insurance, and rent controls sponsored by the city have tended to debilitate the relations between tenants and landlords. Berkeley, California, another city with a rent control program, has watched parts of the city turn rapidly into slums.

As business activity declines in the central city, property values fall. Even imaginative city officials who have devised new fees for business, new forms of sales taxes, and new user charges for suburbanites have not made up the revenues lost when the property tax base shrinks. The sales tax in particular is mercurial. The suburbs draw customers away from the central cities frequently by offering a lower sales tax and easier free parking. Some cities have tried to levy payroll and commuter taxes, but these have not been successful. Cities are left to cut costs by reducing services, which make them less attractive for business, for living, and for entertainment. Moreover, essential services—fire, police, water, education, health—can not be reduced proportionally to declines in growth. City officials complain constantly that suburbanites enjoy only the advantages of being near a great urban center. Not only do they not share the responsibility for a city's functioning, but they add to its maintenance costs, especially in the upkeep of bridges, highways, tunnels, and museums. Each day the great game of Catch-22 is played out—the most affluent suburbs are rich because they are near great cities, but the great cities are impoverished because they cannot get at the wealth of the suburbs.

One can only hope that movements to turn this situation around will expand and proliferate. If national and state government policies have aided and abetted the growth of suburbs by providing highways and lowering taxes, these branches of government have an obligation to help rectify this situation. The federal government has advocated the formation of Councils of Government that contain the elected heads of all the local governments in metropolitan areas; as yet these have not been very effective. States in the South and West have allowed cities to annex their suburbs in order to increase their tax base: among them are Columbus, Denver, Houston, Memphis, Phoenix, Kansas City, San Diego, and San Antonio. Other cities have consolidated with their counties into single city-county jurisdictions—Jacksonville, Nashville, Indianapolis, Detroit, Cleveland, and Louisville. But the norm is still an enormous separation and duplication of essential services such as sewers and jails. In Schenectady, N.Y., the boundary between the city and its wealthiest suburb runs down Garner Ave. On Tuesdays, city trucks collect the garbage on one side of the street. On Wednesdays, town trucks collect the garbage on the other side. Both city and county maintain duplicate snow removal equipment. After a snowfall the county truck stops halfway down the road and the city truck begins.

In order to change the downward course of our major cities, we need to redefine a city according to today's realities. With some imagination and allocation of resources, new urban cores can be built which can serve as a nucleus for urban revitalization. The central role of government is crucial despite the importance of private initiatives. The urban crisis has been long in building. In the 1940s and 1950s the concern of urban renewal was providing housing for returning veterans and for the postwar baby boom. Other largely neglected urban problems were brought to light during the civil rights movement in the 1960s. The Great Society programs had awarded money to the center cities in the form of community block grants and categorical grant programs, e.g., grants for so-called "model cities," poverty, unemployment, pollution, and education, all administered by a half-dozen federal departments. Later, the Nixon administration proposed a "new federalism" to allow state and local governments more freedom to use federal funds. The President also consolidated many categorical grant programs into five "block grant" programs, and the Nixon administration in 1971 started a program for federal revenue sharing that cities could use "for priority expenditures with very loose restrictions." In October 1972, in response to the mayors of major American cities who told the President that they were facing major urban crises, Congress allocated $30.2 billion over a five-year period to states and localities, with one-third going to states and two-thirds to localities. Localities had to spend the funds on high-priority items, but the guidelines were fairly unspecific. Watergate and OPEC brought an end to the Nixon initiatives but not to revenue sharing of grants.

The Carter administration further increased federal revenue sharing to some $7 billion a year in categorical grants and $80 billion in block grants; cities received more than $30 billion directly. In 1977, President Carter initiated the Urban Development Action Grants program and tried to encourage private investment in urban areas. In 1979, eligibility requirements were broadened to include cities in the South and West. President Reagan retained this program reluctantly, but in 1981 sought to replace it with a revived "new federalism" (though Reagan was more concerned with reducing the power of the federal government than aiding the cities). UDAG grants have been praised by local governments and urban lobbyists and are especially popular with the Congressmen from northern cities, for political as well as economic reasons. The program, however, continued to be cut back by the Reagan administration, from $440 million in 1981, a one-third reduction from previous levels, to a budgeted outlay of $100 million in 1987. Private developers had to put up at least $2.50 for every dollar they received from the grants. Supporters of the grants claim that 400,000 new jobs have been generated. Although the most distressed cities have benefitted most, several states have received nothing.

Presidents Reagan and Bush have promoted their own program of "free enterprise zones" which would place greater emphasis on private initiative and the free market. The most distressed areas of the most depressed cities designated by HUD, up to twenty-five zones, would be encouraged to grant substantial tax breaks to industries locating or expanding in these urban zones. Although the proposal has made little headway in Washington, twenty-four states since 1981 have enacted their own legislation for enterprise zones in specific localities. Advocates claim that these tax abatements have stimulated new activity and employment in distressed areas. Indeed, states and cities have mounted enormous programs to attract business, and a number of states maintain permanent offices in western Europe and Japan for this purpose.

It is, however, much too early to declare these programs a success. The burdens of these subsidies are shifted to present taxpayers and businesses, who must pay higher costs; whether these 'freebies' are more than a lavish subsidy to private companies can only be determined from the long-run results. The permanent problems of the cities—social, political, and economic—are not likely to be solved in so simplistic a fashion. As the population ages and the baby boomers attain affluence and high levels of disposable income, some features of the central city will be remade. Already this is happening all across the country. But for the poor, only subsidized low cost housing which private markets cannot provide has a chance to prevent increasing squalor and homelessness.

NOTES

[1]Amitai Etzioni, *An Immodest Agenda: Rebuilding America before the Twenty-first Century* (New York: New Press, 1983), p. 186.

[2]"How to Quench New York's Thirst," *The New York Times*, February 16, 1986.

[3]Subcommittee on Economic Goals and Intergovernmental Policy of the Joint Economic Committee of the Congress, *Hard Choices: A Report on the Increasing Gap Between America's Infrastructure Needs and Our Ability to Pay for Them* (Washington, D.C.: GPO, 1984), p. 2-3.

[4]Ibid. p. 3.

[5]Ibid. p. 3.

[6]Ibid., pp. 8-9.

[7]Rachel Carson, *Silent Spring* (Boston: Houghton Mifflin, 1962), pp. 1-3.

[8]*The New York Times*, March 18, 1985.

[9]Ibid.

[10]*Time*, October 14, 1985: 76.

[11]Ibid., p. 84.

[12]Gordon Mitchell, *Sick Cities* (New York: Penguin Books, 1965).

[13]Ibid., pp. 307-310.

[14]*Business Week*, January 28, 1985: 82.

SUGGESTED READINGS

American Association of State Highway and Transportation Officials. *A Policy on Geometric Design of Highways and Streets.* Washington, D.C.: GPO, 1984.

Billington, David P. *The Tower and the Bridge: the New Art of Structural Engineering.* New York: Basic Books, 1983.

Carson, Rachel. *Silent Spring.* Boston: Houghton Mifflin, 1962.

Etzioni, Amitai. *An Immodest Agenda: Rebuilding America before the Twenty-first Century.* New York: New Press, 1983.

Gordon, Mitchell. *Sick Cities.* Baltimore: Penguin Books, 1965.

Jacobs, Jane. *Cities and the Wealth of Nations: Principles of Economic Life.* New York: Random House, 1984.

Lave, Lester B., and Arthur C. Upton. *Toxic Chemicals, Health, and the Environment*. Baltimore: Johns Hopkins Press, 1987.

Vogel, David. *National Styles of Regulation: Environmental Policy in Great Britain and the United States*. Ithaca, N.Y.: Cornell University Press, 1986.

10

The Social Environment: Education, Health Care, Women, Jobs

EDUCATION

In 1989 George Bush announced he would be an "education President" whose goal was to make American students first in the world in science and math. Yet in his 1990 budget, student loan money was sharply curtailed. This is only one aspect of the dilemma the United States faces as it moves into the Third Industrial Revolution and an intensely competitive global economy. Everyone is in favor of education, but no one wishes to allocate significant new monies to achieve higher standards or to change the current and largely deficient system in any major way, not even to lengthen the number of days American children are in school (presently about 180 days compared to 210–260 days for most advanced industrial countries). Why are we so mired in the present educational disorder?

The history of American education reflects the nation's broad social, cultural, political, and economic evolution. At every stage Americans developed curricula for meeting vocational needs and for cultivating ideals. Typically Americans placed great emphasis on openness, heterogeneity, democracy, pragmatism, and functionalism while trying to sustain broad religious and ethical values derived both from the Judeo-Christian heritage and the classical-humanistic elements of Western civilization. Such a commingling of goals has not been easy to attain. Conflicts between competing values in our time have become not only loud but divisive, and the educational system caught in between has seemed adrift and leaderless, without direction and support, and always starved for resources. Not infrequently such periods have coincided with social, political, and economic crises in the larger society. No period reflects this discordance more clearly than the one we are now living in; the debate on education in all its aspects has never been more acerbic. This current period of change and uncertainty has forced Americans to reexamine fundamental questions: What should educators do? Who and what should education serve? Who should be the educators? Who should pay? What portion of the national budget should be devoted to education?

Although Americans have differed in the past about educational philosophies, they have given unanimous consent to the value of education as a national priority. Americans have believed most fervently that education is the means for the nation's continued prosperity. The anti-intellectualism which surfaces from time to time in American life is usually limited to attacks on what special interests perceive as threats to their value system, e.g., the teaching of Darwinian evolution. Any thriving nation must, of course, constantly reassess the performance of its educational system. Opponents who see this as unnecessary tampering fail to understand the way educational change takes place. Innovation and experimentation are the ingredients which make the American system worthy of attention.

Through the interwar period (about 1914–1950), educational policy more or less followed a conservative course. The era of the great educational innovator, John Dewey, was waning, and no issues such as mandatory public education or equal educational opportunities for minorities surfaced during these decades. The fundamental concerns continued to be the retention of local control and funding, teachers and curriculum, and public versus private and parochial education. Even the Depression and world wars that brought much hardship and turmoil to students and teachers barely altered the philosophical underpinnings of the educational establishment. Though often disparaged by western European intellectuals, the American system was greatly admired by most of the world. It was said that anyone who wanted an education in the United States could get one.

The New Deal established a number of educational programs that were to have long-lasting effects. Federal incentives strengthened and expanded existing programs in agricultural education, in vocational training, and in vocational rehabilitation for the handicapped. During the Depression, the federal government provided free milk, subsidized school lunches, and sponsored programs such as those administered by the National Youth Administration to help keep students in school. By 1935, the federal government was accelerating a broad-based educational program to train workers in defense-related industries such as aviation, ship building, and radio communication. All the armed services paid directly for reserve officer training programs in colleges and universities throughout the country.

Even more revolutionary for American educational history was the passage of the "G.I. Bill of Rights" (Servicemen's Readjustment Act of 1944). Truly this legislation was a momentous innovation in educational history. To all veterans who wished to continue their education, the federal government underwrote tuition, books and supplies, counseling, and a monthly subsistence ($50 for one person, $75 for individuals with dependents) up to a total of $500 for a school year. By 1951 almost 8 million veterans had taken advantage of this opportunity. Millions who had never dreamed of having the means to study enrolled. Over 2 million young people went to college, and over 3 million received school training. More than 2 million benefitted from subsidized on-the-job training. To veterans of the war in Korea in 1953 and those of Vietnam in 1966, similar benefits were granted. This and subsequent legislation reflected a changed philosophy towards higher education—namely, that people previously denied a college education should be given opportunity and financial support. The timing too was appropriate—the benefits for higher education increased work opportunities and mobility to many who otherwise would not have gone beyond high school. In terms of social welfare and national wealth, the increased skills thereby resulting immeasurably increased by billions of added-value the country's net worth.

The four decades since the end of World War II have spurred, in turn, educational innovations and controversy. So rapid have these alternatives been implemented that although the educational system remains deeply rooted in and connected to its historical past, most observers recognize that great changes have taken place. An era of even more radical change has barely begun. A Third Industrial Revolution is advancing on a dozen technological fronts; its common thread is the explosion of knowledge. Our greatest need is to enhance our ability to handle this new world of uncertainties. The need for competent, trained people has added a new and special urgency to educational expansion and reform. What is overwhelming the educational system is the extraordinary increase in cost and enrollments. Education now takes officially almost 7 percent of GNP, though this number surely understates the real amount. In fact, we no longer know exactly how to define formal education, nor do we know how to count the many educational systems which are not administered by colleges and universities. Almost $100 billion is spent in employer-sponsored industrial educational activities, and these cost figures will certainly increase rapidly as industry tries to fill its labor needs. By the year 2000, Gunnar Myrdal predicted "practically all American youths would...demand and obtain not only secondary but also college education of some kind." It appears his prophecy has been fulfilled.

To a degree unimagined in 1945, the postwar era has been one of fundamental change in educational needs and goals. During this period education received new emphasis as a means for correcting social problems. The National Defense Education Act of 1958, for example, allocated $440 million over a four-year period for student loans. It also gave grants to the states to improve math, science, and foreign language facilities and to create vocational guidance agencies for students. The monumental Supreme Court decision *Brown* v. *The Board of Education of Topeka* (1954) made equal opportunity in education the law of the land. A decade later a number of Great Society programs were established in the hope of bettering education, particularly for minorities. The Economic Opportunity Act (1964) authorized the expenditures necessary for hundreds of antipoverty programs. The Elementary and Secondary Education Act of 1965 allocated $2 billion for schools at all levels. Aid was to be commensurate with the number of children from low-income households in the district. Monies went also to libraries and student loan programs. The Higher Education Opportunities Act of 1965 allocated $804 million for federal scholarships and federal loan insurance for student loans. Seven million deprived children received educational benefits and almost one million by 1967 had gone on to college. Through programs such as Head Start, youngsters were (and still are) offered help to acquire the necessary early training which will allow them to succeed in the educational system. Nearly a million adults received on-the-job training subsidized by the federal government. Despite the waning of the War on Poverty, the modest involvement of the federal government in education stayed.

National crises and insecurities seem to magnify the attention given to education. In 1949, the Atomic Energy Commission spent almost $80 million on grants to colleges and universities to promote fundamental research and training in areas deemed necessary to national security; today a comparable figure runs into the billions. The definition of national security has continued to broaden, providing federal grants worth billions of dollars to hundreds of colleges and universities. Worry about the power of the military-industrial complex is bolstered by evidence that government pays in excess of 60 percent of all defense research. By contrast, educational funding for minority groups has slowed appreciably.

A broad system of loans and grants to students under a variety of programs and terms has also become an entrenched feature of modern education. These tens of billions of dollars have enabled post-secondary educational systems to grow rapidly and have helped millions of students complete their education. During the 1980s, however, the Reagan administration severely criticized and acted to cut the expense of student loan programs. Noteworthy government programs include the enormously successful Fulbright and Smith-Mundt international exchange scholarships for students and faculty. More recently, private institutions and businesses have become even closer participants in the educational environment. The Ford, Rockefeller, and Carnegie foundations as well as several hundred others have discovered and funded needs bypassed, overlooked, or unsupported by government systems. The MacArthur Foundation gives grants to geniuses, and the Marshall Foundation sends exchange students to Germany. Half as big as the public expenditures on education are the programs supported and paid for by the business system. No study has yet surveyed systematically these educational clones and hybrid programs. They range from matching alumni employee gifts to colleges (Exxon, for instance, furnishes $3 for each $1 given), to contracts with university departments for specialized research as well as tuition refunds, outright gifts of cash or equipment (frequently offered by IBM and Apple Computer, for instance) to in-house training and education programs like General Electric's Crotonville and McDonalds' Hamburger University. The history of philanthropy in the United States is only now being extensively studied, but clearly it will show how much schools and students have benefitted from the American commitment to democracy through educational achievement. Hardheaded businessmen and financiers like Edward Lange and Felix Rohatyn have "adopted" classes in Harlem providing incentives for achievement. Ironically, the monies of anti-intellectuals like Henry Ford and J. Paul Getty support the humanities and the creative arts.

There are exciting experiments to upgrade teachers' salaries and status. One is happening in Rochester, New York, where a new salary range for teachers of excellence has been set at $50,000 and beyond—a breakthrough program which may serve as a national model. Students also need encouragement. Conservative intellectuals continue to complain about the inadequacies of American students (most notably Allan Bloom's *Closing of the American Mind* and E. D. Hirsch's *Cultural Literacy: What Every American Needs to Know*) but these criticisms are very limited and conventional.

Education in America reflects the larger society. It is good and bad, high-brow and common, brash and elitist, function-oriented and uncouth. Great universities somehow own great football teams, distinguished scholars, and scientists who win most of the Nobel Prizes. The American system of education is still the greatest democratizing force in a diverse culture, though it is no longer adequate for the emergent world of high technology. We do not educate well at the elementary and secondary levels and continue to have one of the highest rates of illiteracy of any major advanced country. There is no way that high-technology can be made so user-friendly that it can serve an illiterate population. In science and engineering, our classes are dominated on the graduate level more and more by foreign students as American students shy away from these more difficult subjects. We can reverse this trend by providing government support as we did in the 1960s after the launching of Sputnik. Americans should open immigration to advanced students, many of whom wish to stay in the United States. We cannot allow human resources to be wasted. The coming decades will see a heightened concern over what we want our educational system to achieve as our political and economic position in the world is diminished.

HEALTH CARE

By the mid-1980s, the problems associated with providing and paying for adequate health care for the American people had taken on critical proportions. Health was a $350 billion business that involved the federal government, state and local governments, private health insurers, hospitals, nursing homes, physicians, health-related services, and other personal health care deliverers. If the United States government has failed to adopt a national health system like those of European countries, it certainly has not lagged behind in its spending. The federal government spends almost double the percentage of GNP that the British government spends on its socialized medical program. Various private health insurance programs borne either by employers solely or by employers and their employees have spread widely and are a standard part of union contracts, public employees benefit programs, and educational institutions' payment packages. But individuals

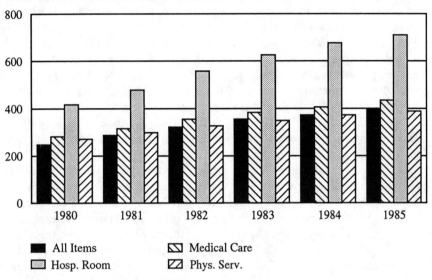

Figure 10.1 **Consumer Price Index for Health Care, 1980–1985 (billions of dollars)**

Legend:
- ■ All Items
- ▨ Medical Care
- ▦ Hosp. Room
- ▨ Phys. Serv.

Source: *Statistical Abstract of the United States,* 1987.

not covered are faced with the soaring cost of illness and are extremely vulnerable to catastrophic expenses.[1]

A summary of some of the major health care problems is useful. From a public standpoint the major issue is cost. Although medical expenses are rising less rapidly than they were a few years ago, they still outpace yearly inflation rates by 100 percent or more. Illnesses are now classified by 467 diagnostic-related groups (DRGs), and in nine regions of the country hospitals are reimbursed based on the average cost for treatment; this very radical bureaucratization of the fee structure is already having major repercussions on hospitals. If the system continues it will not only shorten hospital stays, but affect such things as hospital design and construction and the standards of patient care. Another far-reaching innovation is the increase in private contributions to Medicare costs, similar to the taxing of Social Security payments. Still other developments involve the growth of health maintenance organizations, acceptance for treatment on a prepaid group-benefit coverage, and, of course, the rapid spread of walk-in, storefront offices, e.g., the "emergicenters." Moreover, there seems to be a decided and permanent shift to outpatient treatment and shorter hospital stays. Care for the aged remains an intractable problem, however, for those who attempt to keep a ceiling on health care costs. Many fear these changes indicate a decline in the standard of patient care, but new technologies strongly suggest that this need not be so.

Until very recently, public health care concerns in America were largely limited to disease prevention and the flagrant threats to safety such as poor sanitation facilities, contaminated and/or adulterated foods, impure water, and imported food products at risk of contamination. Local boards of health came into being largely to control infectious diseases—smallpox, cholera, tuberculosis, and malaria. Not until the mid-nineteenth century did state boards of health emerge. Still uniform standards of training for doctors were virtually unknown before the First World War. Most American physicians before 1917 apprenticed in a way not so far removed from that of skilled blue-collar workers. Between 1900 and 1960 the federal government was only peripherally involved in supporting medical research. The post–World War II educational grants to G.I.'s enabled many young men to go to medical school who might otherwise not have been able to pay the costs.

In 1965, the creation of Medicare and Medicaid ushered in a new era. These two programs were meant to assure treatment on some minimal level for the aged and the poor. Since that time it is fair to say that the federal government's involvement in health care, like other areas where the federal government has become a partner, has outraced the imagination of the initial architects of the health program. The federal government controls research in medicine, construction of medical facilities, training and education of medical personnel, and the payment process of claims; now the widespread use of Diagnostic Related Groups (DRGs) will certainly increase the involvement of the central government. Still out-of-control are the enormous cost increases that have occurred since 1965. Nevertheless, supporters of federal aid to health programs press for even greater funds and the institution of some form of national health insurance. At least, they claim, a catastrophic health program for the treatment of chronic diseases requiring expensive treatments such as kidney dialysis is overdue. More cautious observers argue that the sheer extrapolation of present costs will be a burden to the economy. In two decades, costs have risen tenfold, from approximately $39 billion in 1965 to $360 billion + in 1985. In 1984, health care spending increased only 9 percent from the preceding year, but it was still higher than the 3.5 percent national inflation rate. This was, however, the first time in 19 years that the percentage of health care increases had been below double digits. By the late 1980s Americans paid about $1 billion every day for health care. Expenditures for Medicare and Medicaid were $92 billion, which represented 10 percent of the federal budget and its fourth largest item, exceeded only by national defense, interest on the debt, and social security programs.

The surge in health care costs is the result of many factors, but the direct reasons are closely linked to the demand for care, the system of third-party payment, and the increase in medical insurance rates. The increased demand for care is a phenomenon closely related to the Medicare and Medicaid programs enacted in the 1960s. Since it is naïve to believe that these programs could be withdrawn without creating a political furor, the rise in costs must be contained in some way without eliminating basic medical support for the aged and the poor.[2] Somehow Medicare's fee-for-service system, as it is presently constituted, will also need serious revision.

For a fixed premium, health insurers agree to pay the charges of medical care. Although the insured consumer is largely free from the possibility of catastrophic costs, the system offers only minor incentives to physicians,

Figure 10.2 **National Health Expenditures, 1970–1987**

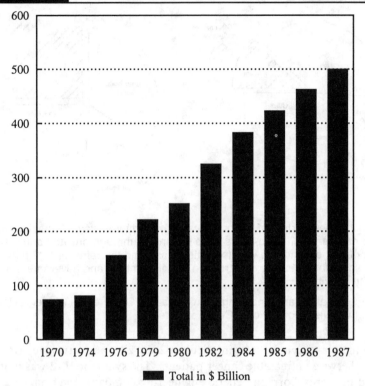

Total in $ Billion

Source: *Statistical Abstract of the United States,* 1981, 1990.

hospitals, or other providers to keep down costs. The inflation of medical malpractice insurance rates, for example, is unconscionable. Clearly market forces cannot be allowed to dictate patient-doctor and patient-hospital relationships. To be sure, if some terrible mistake has occurred during treatment of an illness, fault should be assessed, but neither justice nor equity is served by the protracted litigation and enormous jury awards now endemic in the courts. Malpractice litigation has created an uncontrollable system in which those who have been hurt most are least compensated. More than 30 percent of a court judgment typically finds its way to lawyers, and only slightly more than 25 percent to those injured. Moreover, to protect themselves from these ruinous suits, doctors are forced to carry astronomical levels of insurance coverage. Some health specialists estimate that medical fees might be reduced 15–20 percent if some kind of cap could be put on malpractice judgments. At the present time, however, the insurance industry has not devised a satisfactory solution.

Although the economics of health care is numbing, the technology of medicine has never been more exciting. New technologies and drugs are arresting deadly diseases and extending longevity. Steven A. Rosenberg and scientists at the National Cancer Institute reported preliminary success using

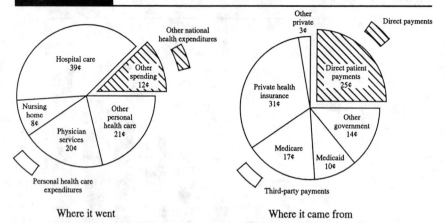

Figure 10.3 — The Nation's Health Dollar in 1986

Where it went

- Hospital care 39¢
- Other national health expenditures
- Other spending 12¢
- Nursing home 8¢
- Physician services 20¢
- Other personal health care 21¢
- Personal health care expenditures

Where it came from

- Other private 3¢
- Direct payments
- Private health insurance 31¢
- Direct patient payments 25¢
- Other government 14¢
- Medicare 17¢
- Medicaid 10¢
- Third-party payments

Almost three-quarters of national health expenditures were channeled through third parties. Nearly two-thirds were channeled through private hands. The bulk of that expenditure was for patient care, and the remaining 12 percent was spent for research, construction, administration, and government public health activity.

Source: Health Care Financing Administration, Office of the Actuary; Data from the division of National Cost Estimates.

the immune-system booster interleuken-2 (IL-2) in a new two-step treatment for otherwise untreatable cancer patients. The synthetic IL-2 was manufactured by Cetus Corp., a genetic engineering company. Intermagnetic General in Rotterdam, New York, produces the special magnets that go into magnetic resonance imaging devices, which are rapidly becoming a key instrument in diagnostic investigation. Machines breakup kidney stones through the use of sound waves; lasers repair detached retinas; a $3 kit will screen blood for the AIDS virus, and a $6 test will tell you whether you are pregnant. Genentech has received FDA approval for the production of TPA (tissue plasminogen activator) which dissolves blood clots in heart and stroke victims.

The helpfulness of these medical advances has ironically created new problems. The larger fact remains that the health system has prolonged life, yet at enormous dollar costs. The cost, for example, of extending life from eighty to eighty-three years absorbs a disproportionate amount of the money spent on health care. By the end of the century we may well be able to prolong the average lifespan well into the 80s if we are willing to allocate sufficient resources. But a democratic capitalist society has only so much money to spend on health care. We all know that life is precious, worth all the resources to prolong it. But whose life shall be extended, young or old, or at what stage or condition of life? We have few guidelines. This ethical and moral dilemma is unlikely to change, though thoughtful discussion of these questions is beginning. In their platform adopted in San Francisco in 1985, the Democrats promised to 1) "limit what health care providers can receive as reimbursements [and] 2) spur innovation and competition in health care policy." But these rhetorical statements offer no help for untangling the specific dilemma of providing at least minimal health care while keeping down costs. Planners hope that the new cost-cutting approaches, especially the use of DRGs, will cut the excess capacity of many hospitals and streamline the entire system. Regardless, the system may be financially strapped by the end of the century, leaving the federal government no choice but to impose still more bureaucratic regulations and controls.

Since 1960 one of the most dramatic changes in U.S. health care has been the privatization of hospital care for profit. To be sure, the movement is still in its infancy and 75 percent of hospitals are still nonprofit community facilities, but large chains such as the Hospital Corporation of America, National Medical Enterprise, Humana Inc., and American Medical International have grown at an extremely rapid pace. Indeed, some observers believe that the DRG structure will benefit the for-profit enterprises most. These companies claim that they can apply traditional management efficiencies to lower costs through economies of scale, especially in bulk buying of drugs and equipment and in the drastic lowering of administrative costs through centralized financial and accounting offices. Whereas nonprofits are more likely to provide an essential community service with costs as a secondary consideration, skilled administrators driven by profit considerations can cut costs to the bone. Some skeptics have asked whether we really want costs cut drastically for hospital care. Corporate marketing techniques, advertising, and sophisticated financing, however, now are a permanent fixture of the nation's hospital system.

Health maintenance organizations are still another innovation in the field. California led in the proliferation of HMOs, and the Kaiser-Permanente HMO has been a model for similar groups across the country. In exchange for a fixed monthly fee, an HMO provides full medical and surgical care, including hospitalization. Most HMOs stress preventive medicine and encourage prompt treatment of illness, a good strategy for the patient and one less costly to the provider. More than 13.5 million people participate in HMOs, and since 1973 any employer with more than 25 employees has been given the legal option to offer an HMO plan as an alternative to ordinary medical insurance. Although California still leads with over 4.5 million subscribers, membership in HMOs is spreading rapidly in the rest of the country. Changes in Medicare requirements have also encouraged 1.5 million health-care recipients to move to HMOs.

The most radical change, the DRGs, have been in effect universally since 1987. Over 75 percent of federal program expenditures are now tied to hospital care. Under the new system, a Medicare patient upon admission will be diagnosed according to a specific set of 467 categories, e.g., pneumonia: DRG. No. 89, angina: DRG. No. 140. Regardless of the severity of the particular patient's illness, payment will be made based on the "average" hospital stay for that particular illness. For that reason many doctors are concerned that the quality of individual health care may suffer. Pressure on the hospital to conform to the DRG guidelines will be enormous, and observers fear the system could boomerang on both admissions and discharges. The structure could certainly militate against the admission of very sick patients who are going to exceed the "average" DRG limits for their illness. Since early discharge is so desirable under the new system, will patients be sent home too soon? What the health care system does not need is more litigation, and the DRGs could just lead to a new epidemic of patient suits against hospitals. Clearly so fundamental a change will lead to many unexpected consequences, but whether it will succeed in paring the steady growth of health costs is very uncertain. If, however, these costs cannot be contained, the Medicare system will be out of funds in the 1990s. All health care participants—hospital administrators, doctors, staff—will then have serious decisions thrust on them: How long should be the length of stay? What types of treatment, tests, and procedures should continue to be offered? These matters are vital since hospitals cannot charge Medicare patients for any unreimbursed expense. This strategy of shifting the cost burden to the hospital makes sense from only the government's view. Although no foreign government has adopted so dramatic and drastic a policy to contain costs, the DRG system is not likely to be a complete success, nor a cure-all for the financial chaos.

The philosophy behind the DRG system is supported by the Congress and the Reagan and Bush administrations. Patients, the argument runs, should be cared for at home. Hospitals, although necessary, are cold and distant, and patients at home are better cared for and recover more quickly. This philosophy of care, however, runs counter to a general belief of the last sixty years that has asserted the superiority of hospital care. Although there is some validity to the faith in home care, there are many serious problems with this home-spun philosophy. In a society where more than 52 percent of all women between the ages of 16 and 50 work outside the home, the question of who is to remain at home to take care of the ill needs to be answered. Health care, of course, can be administered by either gender, but most men also work and are not any more available than working women for home care. The costs of sophisticated medical technology are not likely to be shifted to home-care control. Since 1981, the Congress has authorized states (subject to the approval by the Secretary of Health and Human Services) to pay for certain home- and community-based services, but both the bureaucracies of Medicare and Medicaid as well as private insurers are suspicious of transferring treatment to a location that cannot be easily monitored.

A special case in this evolving home-care structure is nursing care for the aging. As life spans increase, the cost of nursing-home care is fast outstripping both private and public funding, making home care more attractive. Still, home care as a replacement for institutionalized treatment of the aged is practical only in certain instances where the patient does not suffer from extensive physical disability. So far, the plight of the aged is falling between the DRGs with their limited stay constraints and an impractical, anachronistic home-care romanticism. Since private funds cannot pay for more than a tiny fraction of these costs, a great crisis in medical care may well first occur in trying to meet humanely the needs of an aging America.

Table 10.1	U.S. Age Distribution in 1990	

Ages	1990 Total	Percent Change 1980 to 1990
All Ages	250,410,000	9.9
Under 5	18,402,000	11.8
5–17	45,030,000	-3.1
18–24	26,140,000	-13.9
25–34	43,295,000	16.7
35–44	37,897,000	46.5
45–54	25,487,000	12.0
55–64	21,364,000	-1.8
65–74	18,373,000	17.4
75 and up	13,187,000	31.2

Source: *Statistical Abstract of the United States,* 1990.

America's aging population affects the demand for and the cost of health care. Most old people (85%) are still cared for at home. Older people suffer from more health deficiencies than younger people; they have more than double the number of physician visits; they account for more hospital admissions; and they stay longer in the hospital. After hospitalization, older patients are more likely to require longer rehabilitative care. They consume many more drugs, and eventually are unable to care for themselves. Often their lives end in nursing homes, after a final illness whose costs have been staggering. Pneumonia—the old man's friend—has been taken care of by antibiotics, but other diseases may be chronic and the deterioration slow but inevitable. Preserving humane treatment is one of the reasons why cost-containment is so difficult. The average cost per month of nursing home care is $1,500 ($18,000 to $20,000 per year) and steadily rises. Many of the elderly exhaust their own savings in nursing homes until they are impoverished enough to become eligible for aid. Medicare will pay only for 100 days of post-hospitalization, while Medicaid takes over only after personal resources are exhausted. Many proud elderly patients see Medicaid as welfare, which they resist. Nevertheless the necessity of care leaves elderly patients impoverished by the system, and Medicaid now pays for 40 percent of the nation's nursing-home bills, even though nursing home recipients of Medicaid constitute only 7.3 percent of its total recipients. Prior to 1980, some patients beat the system by transferring their assets to family or friends, but that loophole has been tightened, and more than thirty states have adopted programs to prevent the dispersal of personal assets if done to receive Medicaid payments. Initially, the crackdown was restricted to anyone who had transferred their estate within the two years prior to requesting help, but states are finding more ways to tighten the net around the middle class. Some states insist on personal payments for nursing-home care and have also placed a cap on the amounts nursing homes can charge for every kind of service.

Under Title XIX of the Social Security Act, the Federal-State Medicaid Program (1965) subsidizes health care for 22 million people—those with demonstrated need, welfare recipients, the disabled, the indigent elderly. Each state administers its own program under guidelines established by the federal government. The criteria vary widely. In some states, those eligible are well below the federal poverty line. Although states are required to provide coverage to those families receiving welfare under Aid to Families with Dependent Children, each state sets the standards for those who qualify for AFDC. In general, states must also provide for those covered by Supplemental Security Income, i.e., low-income aged, the blind, and the disabled.

In the heavily industrialized states where there is a long tradition of social welfare, the benefit programs are the best. In rural states and especially in the South and Southwest, the programs are the least satisfactory. The Senate Finance Committee estimated that between 15 and 32.5 million Americans are not covered by any health program, either public or private. In 1978, the American Hospital Association provided an estimated $3.9 billion worth of charity; four years later this figure had doubled to $7.8 billion. "Living longer, not better" is a bitter slogan for many Americans. Merely having the resources to pay for retirement years alone can be a critical problem.

In its numerous attempts to cut back costs, the government has tried a number of alternatives, such as delaying eligibility, increasing co-payments

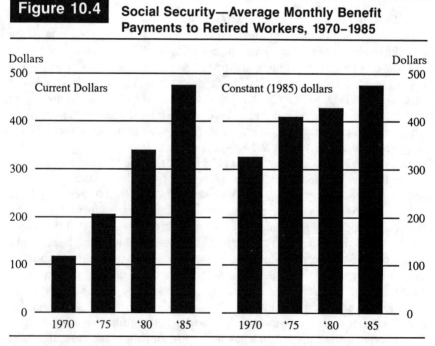

Figure 10.4   Social Security—Average Monthly Benefit Payments to Retired Workers, 1970–1985

Source: U.S. Bureau of the Census/*Historical Abstract of the United States,* 1987.

Table 10.2	Social Welfare Expenditures Under Public Programs	
	(in billions of dollars)	(as a percentage of GNP)
1970	145,856	10.2
1975	290,084	14.7
1980	492,528	19.0
1985	737,154	18.5
1986	782,786	18.4
1987	834,446	18.5

Source: *Statistical Abstract of the United States*, 1981, 1990.

made by those insured, and "voluntary" freezing of doctors' fees. The administration also has considered taxing employer-paid health insurance premiums. The federal government would also like to limit what are now open-ended matching payments to the states. But almost any proposals to cut back any health care payments find little support in the Congress and/or the opinion polls. Health care clearly is now thought of as an entitlement by most Americans, and observers see government, both federal and state, as permanent partners in this system. Even attempts to encourage private health insurers to market long-term health care policies have had very minor acceptance. Private insurers are reluctant to enter this market because they fear that only the people most likely to need costly long-term institutional care will take out policies. Most potential customers are not very interested because they erroneously believe that somehow the federal programs will cover them.

How far can private sector health care be extended? American consumers are paying a great deal for health care directly; employers pay benefits for 75 percent of their workers and their families, and health insurance coverage must be considered a substantial and permanent cost of doing business. Corporations have introduced a variety of measures to hold down costs, namely, wellness programs, regular check-ups, nutritional and other forms of counseling, executive exercise programs, and stress management workshops. Many companies have placed on their premises physical exercise equipment which is available to their employees and even to their families under certain conditions. Much more, however, can be done in these areas of prevention. In Japan, by comparison, a mobile clinic of a half-dozen medical trailers with a full complement of medical personnel routinely checks the entire personnel of the FANUC-Fujitsu robot factory in Japan.

In the long run, however, the great gains must come from a changed lifestyle—less junk food, more exercise, less stress, less poverty. We know, for example, that cigarette smoking is bad for health in general, especially for anyone with lung disorders, but the U.S. government continues to subsidize tobacco growing and to allow cigarette advertising, more than two decades after the U.S. Surgeon General's first warning on smoking. We also know that poverty has detrimental effects on health, and there is too much poverty in our affluent society. Nevertheless, there is a growing awareness of the need for maintaining good health. Of the six major income security programs, two, Medicare and Medicaid, involve health subsidies.

Over the last sixty years, the treatment of disease and the delivery of health care have been among the most revolutionary changes in our society. We are at the beginning of a new frontier in health that brings to bear new information, new technologies, and new abilities that will all but eliminate such diseases as cancer and heart disease. The future possibilities are indeed awesome as we unravel the mystery of the brain and implant man-made organs. But this happy future is as much dependent on the ability to find economic solutions to health care problems as it is on the genius of medical discoveries.

WOMEN AND WORK

The last decade saw the beginnings of an American social revolution that is gathering momentum and leading to new definitions of work, marriage, family, and legal rights. These massive changes have only just begun, and we will not see the end of them in our lifetimes. It is worth focussing on the implications of some of these changes for the future, and what we must do to accommodate this most significant social revolution of the last 250 years.

Over the last decade Americans have created almost 20 million jobs, whereas most countries in the industrial world have either barely held their own or seen jobs disappear. Two-thirds of these new jobs have been garnered by women. And with this new flood of entrants into the job market has come a redefinition of roles for all women in American society. This new development goes far beyond the impact that "serving women" of the 19th century or working immigrant women made at the turn of the century, and more profound than the millions of women who temporarily joined the labor force in World War I and in even larger numbers in World War II.

Women are an important and previously wasted resource in boosting the economy. In 1950, some 29.6 percent of women were in the work force, but by 1995 the Bureau of Labor estimates that over 60 percent will be working. No imaginable cause can reverse this trend. The recent surge in numbers correlate to the baby boomers who reached employment age in the 1970s but also to the new consciousness among women, coupled with their ability to control childbearing. These circumstances made it possible for women to attain a new economic independence. Although women still receive roughly only two-thirds the average wage that men receive, and although there remain other forms of discrimination against women, the principle of economic and occupational equality is now accepted unconditionally by most employers. Overall growth of the labor force is already slowing, but the percentage of women working continues to increase.

As the economy becomes less dependent on heavy manufacturing and more dominated by service industries, a higher percentage of qualified women will find vital roles. Clearly, mere physical strength is becoming less relevant to the operation of the shop; in finance and service industries, in management and entrepreneurship, muscle alone is irrelevant. Only a few Western industrialized countries such as the U.S. are in the van of these developments; Norway and Sweden probably have the highest percentage of women working for wages (80 percent), followed by the U.S. For other non-Communist, especially nonindustrialized countries, the percentages are much smaller. The potential supply of women wage-earners in the U.S. is still large. Undoubtedly the percentage of working women can and will, as we have said, continue to increase. This development will be accompanied by the upgrading of skills and positions for women, which is probably even more important for its potential impact on the American economy.

Many women joined the labor market to preserve or enhance their standard of living, or that of their families, against the ravages of inflation. Moreover the double income is a key to greater discretionary income. Two decades ago, 13 million families (28 percent of total American families) had earnings exceeding $25,000 in 1985 dollars. As of 1989, 29 million families or 46 percent were in this category.

The movement of women up the career ladder is also important. Most professions are still male-dominated at the top—only 5 percent of top business executives are women. Overall, men continue to dominate the top fifty professions listed by the federal government. On the other hand, no job is now off limits to women. Symbolic though it may be, within the past decade we have had the first woman Supreme Court justice, Sandra Day O'Connor, the first woman astronaut, Sally Ride, and the first woman Secretary of Transportation, Elizabeth Dole. Of course, we have also seen the first woman candidate for the Vice Presidency, Geraldine Ferraro, even though fewer than 5 percent of congressional representatives are women. The division between the occupations of the pre–World War II world and the emerging one is distinct. Some tradition remains: women still account for 71 percent of the nation's classroom teachers but fewer than 2 percent of school district superintendents. To be sure, women are pressing hard to break these barriers—25 percent of medical school students are women, and women account for one-third of the students in law and business schools. Still the majority of jobs held by women are low-paid clerical, teaching, sales, and caring positions. If there are twelve times the number of women accountants than there were in 1972, only 38 percent of accountants are women. Everywhere women still face discrimination in promotions and access to upper-level, high-paying jobs. The Department of Labor predicts that even by the end of the century women overall will have increased their earnings to only 70 percent of men's salaries.

If the slow pace of advance frustrates many women, there is the hope that women have not been in some positions long enough to reach the top rungs, and that they are positioning themselves well to reach these goals in future. In 1983, 86 percent of women aged 20-24 with college degrees were in the work force. As older workers depart, these women will take over leading positions. The problems of child custody (most divorce settlements still give

Table 10.3	Percentage of Women at Work in Male- and Female-Dominated Occupations		

Male-Dominated Occupations		1980	1988
Managers		26.1	44.7
Sales Supervisors		25.7	33.5
Physicians		12.6	20.0
Lawyers		12.8	19.3
Truck Drivers		2.2	2.1
Carpenters		.7	.7
Engineers		4.0	7.3
Janitors		27.5	37.2
Farm Operators		10.6	15.0

Female-Dominated Occupations			
Nurses		96.5	94.6
Prekindergarten and Kindergarten Teachers		98.4	98.6
Health Technicians		70.8	82.6
Cashiers		86.6	82.6
Financial Records Processor/Bookkeeper		90.5	91.0
Telephone Operators		91.8	89.8
Teacher Aides		96.2	95.9
Child Care Workers		98.8	96.3
Secretaries		99.1	99.1
Waitresses		89.1	82.6

Source: *Statistical Abstract of the United States,* 1990.

custody of the children to the mother) and child care (better, safer facilities, especially for day care) are becoming less stressful for working women but are still very expensive propositions relative to the income many women earn. The number of child care centers to meet these needs will in all likelihood increase. Some women will choose to stay at home with young children, but they too will rejoin the workforce after their children are older.

In 1983 Congress passed the Equal Pay Act, which stipulated that women be paid the same as men for the same job. Women have sponsored their own movement for "comparable worth," a more far-reaching plan than the Equal Pay Act. Great Britain, Australia, and Canada have passed comparable worth legislation. Advocates for comparable worth in the state of Washington won a case involving public employees that may cost the state $500 million in back pay to 15,000 people. Simply stated, comparable worth would pay women and men the same wages for jobs that require similar skills, effort, and responsibilities. Not only might secretaries make as much as truck drivers, but child care workers might earn the same as upper-level bureaucrats, the reasoning being that they bear a greater burden of responsibility.

If equal pay causes conservatives to worry, comparable worth seems like the end of the world. Comparable worth is not going to gain an easy victory. Businessmen hate and resist what they perceive as interference in the market's determination of pay scales. Comparable worth may have even more obstacles than one confronts with the usual problems of discrimination.[3] The National Committee on Pay Equity, the organization devoted to furthering comparable worth, believes that comparability can be determined by evaluation studies that assign point values to such items as responsibility, skill, and effort of each job, and that most companies and public employers already make such comparisons. The argument runs that male employers decided fifty years ago to pay women less, and that this wage differential has been perpetuated to the present day.

At the present time everyone's rhetoric about comparable worth obscures much of the issue, but even the rhetoric is making some employers much more sensitive to the issue of equal pay. Many employers will try to avoid the issue of comparable worth by raising women's wages. The U.S. Chamber of Commerce and the National Association of Manufacturers have contended that comparable worth drives up wages, which must be passed along to consumers in price hikes. Such a development would make U.S. products less competitive in world markets. Most of all, comparable worth would hinder an employer's right to set pay strategies: "What employers do not want is some court or government agency playing God." Yet neither in Britain nor Australia has the sky fallen where "work of equal value" is administered by three-member industrial tribunals; nor in Minnesota, where legislation gave pay-equity wage hikes to 9,000 of 29,000 state employees. State payroll costs in Minnesota have risen about 5 percent, the state budget less than 2 percent. If these increases are small, they are not negligible. In an important article in the *Harvard Business Review* (May-June 1985), George Sape argued that however one felt about the concept, the underlying problem of discriminatory pay disparities will not go away. He suggested five basic steps that employers concerned about recent court decisions might take: 1) examine each element of the compensation system for possible discrimination; 2) review key job evaluation determinations for bias; 3) audit the impact of pay practices on men's and women's salaries on a regular basis; 4) eliminate job segregation; 5) take corrective action. As more women enter the work force and move up into positions of greater authority, it seems inevitable that managerial change of this type must occur.[4]

The women's revolution has an even darker side than wage discrimination, and that is the feminization of poverty. Simply put, more women are getting poorer and are bearing greater burdens of child care in America. Thirteen million women, of whom 4.2 million are nonwhite, are stranded in poverty. In a single decade, 1973–1983, the numbers of families in poverty headed by women jumped almost 50 percent (8.2 million to 12 million); over 40 percent of families headed by women were poor. "The trend is that women, particularly those maintaining families, are disproportionately poor at the same time other groups are moving out of poverty."[5]

These shocking numbers are the side effects of a social revolution—high rates of divorce, soaring rates of teenage pregnancies, low-paying jobs for

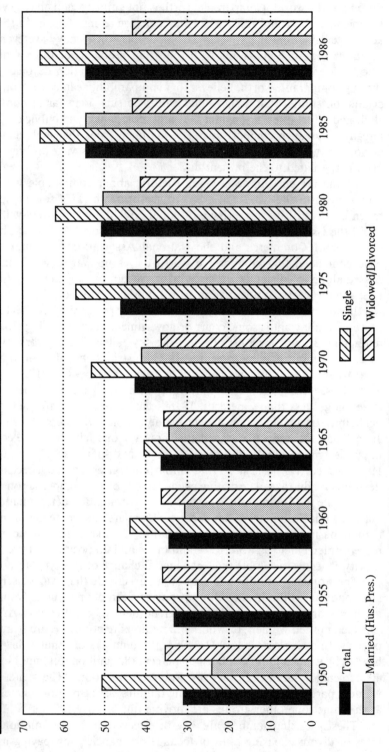

Figure 10.5 Marital Status of Women as a Percentage of Civilian Labor Force

Legend:
- Total
- Married (Hus. Pres.)
- Single
- Widowed/Divorced

Source: *Statistical Abstract of the United States*, 1987, p. 382.

Figure 10.6 Comparison of Mean Income (Male/Female)

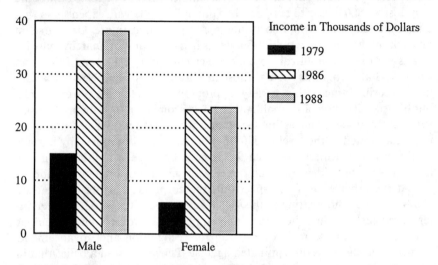

Income in Thousands of Dollars

■ 1979
▨ 1986
▦ 1988

Source: *Statistical Abstract of the United States,* 1990.

women which do not include child care and health benefits, and longer widowhood and retirement. Since the end of World War II, divorce rates have more than tripled and teenage pregnancies make up more than 12 percent of all pregnancies. In New York City, the number of teenage and out-of-wedlock pregnancies is close to 50 percent. Elderly women live 5 to 8 years longer than men. The prescription for poverty is easily written—any one of these categories will do. No-fault divorce settlements, a badge of the women's movement, has turned out to be a means of impoverishment. Changes in administration of state and federal legislation also have cut back many benefits.

The Reagan administration firmly believed that welfare benefits encouraged dependency and "unsocial" behavior such as out-of-wedlock children and welfare cheating. The belief that rapid economic growth would, like the rising tide, lift all people to affluence, does not in fact apply to these groups mired in poverty. Far too simplistic is the notion that the best way to cut back poverty in general is to help people move from publicly supported jobs to unsubsidized employment. The culture of poverty, especially women's poverty, is self-perpetuating. Only modest success for the improvement of poverty can be predicted. Lack of education, minimal job skills, multiple children without support, and poor health all become part of the vicious circle that prevents improvement. Clearly the country must face these problems, but typically the concerns of the poor are given short shrift in Washington. The "Lifestyles of the Rich and Famous" grab more attention than the lifestyles of the poor.

Projected cost figures for the kinds of support that would make for meaningful change are available, but Americans have to decide that these schemes are worth the investment. There are even studies that show these antipoverty programs save money. For example, a family of three on welfare may cost $4,800 a year to support, but providing child care expenses so that a parent could work would cost only one-third of that figure. Of course, in an environment in which public finance is in a condition of anarchy, only interests with strong political power can get temporary relief and long-term support. State programs such as those in Massachusetts and New York have been experimenting with a variety of programs to break the poverty cycle, but of necessity these are small, vary widely from state to state, and are insufficiently funded. One estimate is that it would take a sustained multiyear program funded at the level of $10–15 billion annually to make any inroads on the problem. Unless there is a fundamental change in political attitudes in the 1990s, these ideas have no conceivable chance of implementation.

At the other end of the spectrum, the corporate heights, women are climbing but are not getting to the top. Women executives who have been interviewed feel on the whole that only superficial manners and amenities have changed. In the real competition for recognition and advancement, women continue to be discriminated against. They expressed a belief that in order to advance to a higher-level job, a woman had to be much better than the man she is competing with. Moreover, the corporate pinnacle is still very much a bastion of males. The number of entry-level jobs occupied by professional women is close to 50 percent; in middle management, the percentage of women has reached one-quarter in many companies; but above middle management the numbers dwindle to tiny single-digit percentages. One estimate suggests that not more than 1,000 women hold top management jobs out of the 50,000 total. Only 367 women sit on the boards of directors of major companies, whereas 15,500 men are directors. Considering that historically this women's revolution is not more than two decades old, the achievements have been spectacular. It is encouraging that many of the skills needed to manage the industries of the Third Industrial Revolution are accessible to either gender. But for women with ambitious goals, the climb will only become less difficult, not easy or automatic.

The resource that may offer the greatest support to women overall may be their still unfocused power in the political process. Women are potentially the greatest political force in America but have yet to develop an efficient organization. This will not be easy, but not impossible. Women have already demonstrated potent political force at the state and local levels. In fifteen years, the number of women elected to state legislatures more than tripled— from 301 in 1969 to 993 in 1984. In 1983, Rhode Island elected nine women to its state's senate. North Dakota has a woman Speaker of the House, and about 30 percent of New Hampshire's legislature is female. Four lieutenant governors are women, eleven are elected secretaries of state, one is a state treasurer (Texas). Six mayors of major cities, including San Francisco and Houston, have been women; 7 percent of all U.S. city and village mayors are women. Three governors, those of Kansas, Oregon, and Texas, have been women. In local politics 10 percent of city council members are women, and 30 percent of school board members are women. In the higher political ranks, women are still only thinly represented. Only thirty-one women are in Congress, and a mere 13 percent in state legislatures. But more female candidates are running for every office.

Political preference among women is highly dispersed, with more registering as Democrats (46 percent) and many fewer (28 percent) as Republicans. The Democratic party has made the greater effort to attract women voters: their vice presidential candidate in 1984 was a woman; they have adopted party planks supporting the passage of the Equal Rights Amendment; and they have encouraged equal pay for work of comparable worth. But building a dependable women's coalition is far from easy in the United States, a situation complicated by the sizeable percentage of women who have Republican loyalties. Because women make up 53 percent of the voting-age population and for the past two decades have outnumbered men at the polling place, their political strength intoxicates politicians. In 1980, nearly six million more women voted than did men, and in 1982 it is believed that women provided the margin of victory in three important elections of governors in New York, Michigan, and Texas.

Carol Gilligan of Harvard, in an important study entitled *In a Different Voice* (1982), makes clear the fundamentally different ways in which women approach problems.[6] With primary emphasis on love, caring, and relationships, they stand at the other end of the spectrum from the men, who see violence, competition, and law as the most important elements in society. These differences have challenged traditional political perspectives. Women on the whole have a different political wish list than men. Education, environmental concerns, health care, protection against personal violence, social programs, and peace initiatives such as a nuclear freeze all rate more highly with women than with men.

Most older Americans have a vision of family, widely promoted by politicians, religious groups, and advertisers, that existed at least a century ago, if ever. However comforting this image is meant to be, the reality is far different. Only 12 percent of American households conform to the middle-class picture of a working breadwinning father, full-time housekeeper/homemaker wife, and dependent children. In more than 60 percent of households, both father and mother work. Two-thirds of women who are single parents work; 33 million children have full-time working mothers; one-third of mothers with babies under seven months are working. Usually women take maternity leave and then return to work. Women end up with the children in most divorce settlements. Women still run the house. And 85 percent of women interviewed in one study answered that integrating career and family life was a problem. Historians of the women's movement claim that all the home conveniences have raised the standard of living and the quality of life, but have done little to lessen the workload of women.

The problem of caring for the children looms largest for all women of all income levels, though the women in poverty, as we have pointed out, have the most difficult time. Census statistics estimate that over 5 million children under age five are in some type of day-care program. About one-third are looked after in their own home (29.7 percent); home-based programs ac-

Table 10.4	Women in the Workforce					
	1970	**1975**	**1980**	**1985**	**1987**	**1988**
Women in the Workforce (millions)	31.5	37.5	45.5	—	—	49.3
Share of Women Age 16 and Older as a Percentage of Total Workforce	43.3	46.3	51.5	54.5	56.0	56.5

Source: *Statistical Abstract of the United States,* 1990.

Table 10.5	Women as a Percentage of All Workers by Occupation	
	1980	**1988**
Managerial/Administrative	26.1	39.3
Sales	45.3	48.9
Professional/Technical	44.3	49.8
Service Industries (Including Health)	58.9	60.5
Clerical	80.1	80.1

Source: *Statistical Abstract of the United States,* 1981, 1990.

count for 41.3 percent, and 14.7 percent are enrolled in day-care centers. Nursery or preschool account for 6.4 percent and kindergarten/grade school programs an additional 1.2 percent. An additional 6.7 percent are cared for by a parent at work. If adequate day-care facilities were available, it is estimated that an additional 1.7 million women would join the labor force. Not only do we not know what strengths and weaknesses those children raised in these "care" facilities will have when they grow up, but we can imagine a society not far distant in the United States when this experience will be the norm.

When women decide to work, they assume additional costs (day care being one of the heaviest) that must be subtracted from their salary. Women usually spend more on clothes, household expenses, transportation, and amenities like vacations than if they stayed at home. Women are not immune from the stresses that go along with working careers; notably lung cancer incidence related to smoking has soared. The increased incidence of rape, battered women, and child abuse all may be directly or indirectly related in part to these changes in society. Still, the tide of women entering the labor force shows no sign of receding. Studies indicate that women's mental health has improved despite the pressures of these changes. Employment has by far the largest and most consistent ties to good health, while marriage ranks second, and parenthood a weak third. The stresses from jobs and from coordinating family and work schedules certainly exist, but they are offset by the health-promoting aspects of work and careers. Women are living longer than men, almost eight years more as against four years a short time ago, and although women go to doctors more frequently, they have fewer serious medical problems than men. Medical breakthroughs in contraception, treatment of breast cancer, and pregnancy have been among the striking gains of the past decade.

Stereotypes of women such as the beautiful but dumb blond à la Marilyn Monroe or that of the scatterbrained Lucille Ball in "I Love Lucy" are passing quickly, but thousands of years of gender discrimination will not be totally erased so soon. Only a few countries on this globe are party to women's liberation. More women in the world wear the *chador* and live in *purdah* than share the benefits of open relations between the sexes. In the United States marriages continue to move towards more equitable relationships. There is a growing sense of self-esteem among women, and a growing acceptance of women working in all occupations and professions; "my mother the fireman" is no longer a joke. Women doctors, lawyers, and financial managers are carving out new areas of competence as they bring their special insights to these professions. When a Brooklyn judge referred to a lawyer as "little girl," he brought down on his head a formal censure. Most media presentations still portray women as sex objects, but such portrayals of women will change as they emerge as an economic force. If women indeed speak "in a different voice," all of us are going to have to learn to listen to that voice.

WORKERS AND THE WORKPLACE

Former Japanese Prime Minister Nakasone believes that the world is on the verge of a new industrial and consumer revolution. These dramatic developments in information processing and other technologies are producing radical changes in traditional patterns of industrial life, crucially affecting the future of those who work.

Current research on labor unions points to important changes in union strength and performance and to the growth of nonunion labor. Although membership in labor unions has fallen sharply, the premium of union over nonunion wages has continued to widen. This differential varies, of course, from industry to industry, but is especially alarming in government, where the difference exceeds 20 percent. The Linneman-Wachter data point out that unemployment in goods-producing industries has increased only in the union sectors of these industries, which suggests that many companies were helped into difficulty by the high cost and inflexibility of their wage agreements and are therefore not inclined to hire additional union labor. The widespread belief that unions are accommodating employers who face new competitive pressures, especially those from abroad, by granting wage concessions is not supported by the evidence. Organized labor granted concessions in only those industries where union wage premiums had been both prolonged and significant. Then too wage concessions may be regarded as temporary measures by union members. Union leaders who represented Chrysler employees were naturally under great pressure during the mid-eighties to win back all the concessions that had been granted the company during its earlier life-and-death struggle to survive. Naturally the union hoped to acquire additional adjustments for inflation. Economist Michael L. Wachter argues that the rigidity of union wage scales in the U.S. stems from labor law and government regulation: wages and conditions, spelled out in the labor contract, are long-term commitments open to few modifications. This lack of flexibility, however, forces employers to use cost-saving strategies such as moving jobs to nonunion plants wherever possible.[7] We appear to be at a point where two major changes are taking place: the permanent decline in union membership and power, and the restructuring of the labor market to meet the needs of the Third Industrial Revolution. In the years ahead, workers will face a revolutionary transition.

In March 1986, the President's Commission on Organized Crime reported that four major unions were deeply infiltrated by organized crime elements. The nation's largest union, the International Brotherhood of Teamsters, had "been firmly under the influence of organized crime since the 1950s," and the commission recommended that the government consider removing union officers and placing union activities under court supervision. In addition to the Teamsters, organized crime controlled the New York-New Jersey waterfront through the Longshoreman's Union. At least twenty-six locals of the Laborers International Union of North America had a "documented relationship" with organized crime. Hotel union locals in New York and New Jersey are heavily infiltrated by organized crime. So thorough was the corruption that organized labor seemed most unlikely to clean its own house as it did in the 1950s.

Union membership as a percent of the total workforce has fallen from 35 percent in 1960 (18 million members) to 20 percent in 1984 (21 million members) to 17 percent in 1988, and continues to fall. A Gallup poll in 1981 recorded that only 55 percent of its respondents approved of labor unions, the lowest rating since 1936. Only in some of the service industries and in government is there substantial union growth. Everywhere else, unions are widely viewed as restrictive, noninnovative, and self-serving, if not crime-ridden and anachronistic. It appears that unions will play only a small part in the new labor arrangements which are coming into being.

Twenty-five years ago, only one in three workers was a woman, whereas in 1988 the number has passed 50 percent. One-half of the labor force is between 16 and 34. Twenty-five percent of workers are college graduates; in 1959, only 10 percent had gone to college. Among younger couples, two wage earners is common. Younger, more educated, and/or female workers are less likely to join a labor union. New workers have little sense of the history of the labor movement and do not identify with it. They have little regard for the aging union oligarchs who meet in Florida each year to decide the national and international policies that are paid by rank-and-file dues. Workers are not only younger, they are more sophisticated, more materialistic, and more independent-minded. American workers have almost no class consciousness when compared to their European counterparts.

In addition to the changes in the labor force, the demands of the economy have created greater need for service-oriented occupations. Between 1955 and 1984, blue-collar manufacturing employment fell from 41 percent of total nonagricultural employment to 26 percent, while employment in private sector service industries grew 11 percent. We should emphasize that the manufacturing share of GNP has remained relatively the same; only employment has fallen. These trends are likely to continue. U.S. companies hounded by international competition are being forced more and more to operate as true multinationals by sourcing, assembling, manufacturing, designing, and/or selling abroad. A new lobbying group, the Committee for Production Sharing, involving 140 multinational corporations, opposed the protectionist legislation sponsored in the House of Representatives in March 1986. Unless there is a complete breakdown in international policy, an increasing number of companies must adapt to this way of business in order to remain competitive. Moreover, types of occupations are expected to change through the mid-1990s as employment patterns depart from historical trends and adjust to the needs and demands of the Third Industrial Revolution.

The analysis of these data by Silvestri and Lukasiewicz tells us a great deal about how the overall economy will look by the end of the century. The percentage of executive, administrative, and managerial workers will increase by 22 percent, 7 percent faster than the rate for total employment. The need for salaried management specialists will also spur a growth sector, including computer-related occupations, engineering, and health specialties. The fastest growth sector of all, 29 percent, will be technicians and related support workers for these salaried managers. The number of salesworkers will continue to increase at a rapid rate, but much slower than in the decade 1973–1983.[8]

Jobs for administrative support workers, including clerical ones, will grow more slowly than average. Such workers, however, will still remain the largest group in the work force, with 20.5 million workers by 1995. This group is rapidly becoming the major corps of the public service unions. Automation, particularly the office of the future, will place many new strains on this occupational group. New complaints, if not new diseases, are already being connected to stress and fatigue from video screens as workers spend more and more of their time hunched in front of terminals.

The number of service workers will increase more than any other broad group, accounting for 3.3 million of the 16 million new jobs that must be created during the next decade. Precision production, craft, and repair occupations are expected to grow, but less rapidly than total employment. Operators, fabricators, and laborers will increase by only 7 percent, although this modest growth will reverse the last decade's decline in the number of these workers.

In large part what is happening in the U.S. manufacturing industry is similar to what occurred in U.S. agriculture fifty years ago. Manufacturing in the U.S., though less competitive on a global basis, is becoming much more productive, i.e., manufactured goods are becoming less expensive relative to other goods and needs and are absorbing smaller amounts of both employment and capital investment. As automation, robotics, global sourcing, and internationalization expand, these tendencies will increase. As more sophisticated automation is introduced and new technologies become widely used, the United States could regain the competitive edge it has lost in recent times. Although the traditional industries such as automobiles, steel, and shipbuilding may shrink in importance, the benefits of low-cost labor that sent U.S. companies abroad is likely to be replaced by new manufacturing systems where innovations from knowledge industries can once again be used to create jobs at home and produce dependable, reasonably priced goods.

The most rapidly growing occupations are not going to generate the largest number of jobs because they will use fewer workers. However, computer programmers, computer systems analysts, electrical and electronics engineers, technicians and technologists, plus health practitioners make up

Table 10.6	Occupations with (estimated) Largest Job Growth, 1984–1995 (numbers in thousands)				
Occupation	Employment 1984	1995	Change in Employment 1984–95 gain	%	Percent of total job growth 1984–95
Cashiers	1,902	2,469	556	29.8	3.6
Registered nurses	1,377	1,829	452	32.8	2.8
Janitors and cleaners, including maids and housekeepers	2,940	3,383	443	15.1	2.8
Truck drivers	2,484	2,911	428	17.2	2.7
Waiters and waitresses	1,525	2,049	424	26.1	2.7
Wholesale trade saleworkers	1,248	1,617	369	29.5	2.3
Nursing aides, orderlies, and attendants	1,204	1,552	348	23.9	2.2
Salespersons, retail	2,732	3,075	343	12.6	2.2
Accountants and auditors	882	1,189	307	34.8	1.9
Teachers, kindergarten and elementary	1,381	1,662	231	20.3	1.9

Source: *Monthly Labor Review,* November 1985.

			Change in Employment 1984–95		Percent of total job growth
Occupation	Employment 1984	1995	No.	%	1984–95
Paralegal personnel	53	104	51	97.5	.3
Computer programmers	341	586	245	71.7	1.5
Computer systems analysts, electronic data processing (edp)	303	520	212	68.7	1.3
Medical assistants	123	207	79	62.0	.5
Data processing equipment repairers	50	78	28	56.2	.2
Electrical and electronic engineers	390	597	206	52.3	1.3
Electrical and electronic technicans and technologists	404	607	202	50.7	1.3
Computer operators	241	353	111	46.1	.7
EDP equipment operators	70	102	32	45.0	.2
Travel agents	72	103	32	43.9	.2

Table 10.7 Fastest Growing Occupations, 1984–95 (numbers in thousands)

Source: *Monthly Labor Review,* November 1985.

half of the fastest-growing occupations. Similarly the twenty most rapidly declining occupations are in those industries such as apparel and textiles which have already been lost to international competition. By 1995, these two industries will have lost 350,000 jobs. Continuing declines will also affect those in railroad transportation and agriculture as well as private household workers. In the future there will be less need for stenographers, industrial truck and tractor operators, telephone station installers and repairers, and statistical clerks.

To a remarkable degree, the occupational projections echo even larger changes in society. Computer-related occupational areas are going to soar. Computer systems analysts are projected to grow 69 percent from 1984 to 1995, a total of 212,000 new jobs. Computer programmers will also grow by 71 percent, adding 245,000 jobs. Computer operators will increase by 46 percent and add 111,000 jobs, and data processing equipment repairers will increase 56 percent, a total of 28,000 jobs. If anything, the projections in this area may be exceeded as new developments in the uses for computers proliferate, and the technology becomes even more user-friendly.

Some critics believe that the growth and use of high technology will be threatened by an educational lag. Our educational smorgasbord tends to produce more lawyers than engineers, but the market forces which already are paying starting engineers with bachelor of science degrees the equivalent salary of starting Ph.D.s in universities must also attempt to draw young people into teaching. The most acute shortage may be in recruiting and retraining teachers of engineering, since they will be drawn to industry by lu-

| | Table 10.8 | Fastest Declining U.S. Occupations, 1984–95 (numbers in thousands) |

Table 10.8 Fastest Declining U.S. Occupations, 1984–95 (numbers in thousands)

Occupation	Employment 1984	(projected) 1995	Percent decline in employment
Stenographers	239	143	-40.3%
Shoe sewing machine operators and tenders	33	22	-31.5
Railroad brake, signal, and switch operators	48	35	-25.4
Rail car repairers	27	21	-22.3
Furnace, kiln, and kettle operators and tenders	63	50	-20.9

Source: *Monthly Labor Review,* September, 1987.

crative offers. Still, the number of engineers are projected to increase 36 percent in the coming decade to fill 280,000 new jobs. Almost 40 percent will be electrical and electronics engineers, though the demand for mechanical and civil engineers will remain high. America's defense requirements alone constitute the largest single market for these skills, but industrial needs and those of the infrastructure will also create demand. Cutting back defense costs will greatly ease the shortages of engineers in other fields, but there will likely be no large peace dividend.

Health-related jobs are projected to increase by 26 percent but so great and so varied are the changes taking place in this sector that it is hard to pinpoint specific areas of change. Registered nurses are expected to show the largest growth, an increase of 452,000 jobs, 33 percent over 1984. The next largest increases will be for nursing aides, orderlies, attendants, and licensed practical nurses—overall, an increase of 454,000 new jobs. This growth area reflects the aging of the population as well as the shift in care from hospitals to nursing homes and outpatient care facilities. Americans will continue to allocate a substantial percentage of GNP to health services. Although a national health insurance program seems unlikely in the near future, some form of increased catastrophic insurance may be a distinct possibility within the coming decade. Finally, nurses and other workers will be paid more.

Demographic shifts will also affect the occupational changes in education. For some institutions, namely the small expensive private colleges of the Northeast and Middle Atlantic regions, their high costs may be less of a problem than the very sharp decline in the size of the cohort graduating from high school and intending to go to college. This decline of up to 30 to 40 percent, will of course, adversely affect the size of college and university faculties, which are projected to decline from 731,000 in 1984 to 654,000 by 1995; after that date a shortage of faculty in specific fields is forecast. Openings for secondary school teachers will grow only by 5 percent; only kindergarten and elementary school teachers will have a growth rate of 20 percent, an increase of some 281,000 jobs. Even preschool teachers will have only an average growth rate because of the leveling out of the rate of women's participation in the labor force. Virtually all jobs connected with the support of educational systems, e.g., librarians, will grow minimally. Nevertheless, there is some hope that teaching will remain attractive to some in this affluent society; retraining displaced persons and upgrading job skills may create some jobs for the educational professions. Still the overall number of those in higher education will be reduced. Unless some way can be found to subsidize continuing education, it will never boom, even though the potential is enormous. A system of education vouchers such as those used in Germany would greatly enhance the development of industrial skills.

Because manufacturing employs fewer people, many new jobs have been generated in the office-clerical fields. Over the coming decade, growth in this sector will be relatively slow compared to its rapid expansion over the past twenty years. With a projected total figure of over 20.5 million workers, this sector overall will still add 700,000 more jobs. Within this very large group there will be continuous shifts; as certain clerical functions are replaced (e.g., stenographers) other clerical areas will grow rapidly (e.g., credit checkers). Temporary help will become especially commonplace, both because of its flexibility for employers and employees as well as its short-run economic benefits. Employers can avoid paying benefits and employees do not have to be saddled with union dues and regulations.

Service occupations will continue to increase, but they will not add very many jobs, nor in many cases much quality of work. Although financial analysts may be part of the new service society and will be rewarded handsomely, opportunities for waiters and waitresses, as well as food preparation workers will show only slow growth over the decade (excepting fast-food chains) and will probably encompass many of the least satisfying jobs in the society. Too frequently these are, and will remain, the jobs with the lowest pay, the smallest personal satisfaction, and the fewest opportunities for job advancement. Note, however, that the aggregate numbers already in all these service categories, from food handlers to flight attendants, are very large.

In the trades, traditionally a large sector, the number of workers will remain large, although growth will only be modest. The need for carpenters and electricians will be small, with the latter being in greater demand. All the manual-skill jobs connected with manufacturing employment will increase only a slow 10 to 15 percent, with precision skills essential for high technology industries such as electronics, aircraft, and machine tools in greatest demand. Transportation jobs, especially for truck drivers, will show good growth. Aircraft pilots and flight engineers are the fastest growing occupation in this sector, while railroad workers will continue to decline in number.

All projections, especially those that attempt to forecast a decade hence, carry inherent errors, but unless the society and the economy is overwhelmed by crisis or catastrophe, the occupational structure will probably look about as described, with most Americans working in service occupations. What is disturbing is the very large group of unemployed youth, a high percentage of which comes from minorities. Many youth are functionally illiterate and will find it even more difficult than they do at present to enter and succeed in the occupational system. This enormous waste of human talent carries with it only the most serious economic consequences for our country.

Ever since the Hawthorne experiments in the 1930s, liberal observers have been predicting that the "human relations" approach to employees rather than top-down management would one day create a partnership between employer and worker. Over the past five decades, there have been many significant changes in this relationship, but the results still are far from the envisioned land of labor tranquility and shared power. It is not likely that the historical antagonisms which have dominated the relationship between employer and employee will change dramatically or quickly, but that alternate ways of working such as "flex time" (allowing workers to choose starting and quitting times within a range of available hours) that have spread within the past decade should continue to expand, especially in those occupational and industrial sectors where growth and profitability continue to rise. Overall the tensions between management and labor, especially organized labor, should lessen, but only slowly. In some instances (for example, airlines and construction) where an industry is determined to increase its profitability and feels trapped by earlier agreements, the relations are likely to become more adversarial. Within the airline industry, the uncertainty generated by deregulation has resulted in cost cutting and fare reduction, but other industries face similar problems caused by foreign competition, changing demand for their products, and the absolute need to automate their facilities and lower costs by reducing labor requirements. Market pressures will still be the governing force in the private sector. In the public sector, these kinds of pressures do not exist, and politicians, because of their concerns that public service employees will vote against them, can continue to pay labor a premium.

As the power of unions shrinks, a vigorous employees' rights movement will take up the slack. As employers aggressively cut labor costs, workers are resorting to a variety of means to protect their interests. These developments are occurring at every level—plant, national, and international. Workers have turned to the law and the courts and have made impressive gains, at least on the local level. Twenty-five states, many of the very same states that passed right-to-work laws, have passed right-to-know laws requiring companies to divulge information on hazardous substances used in the workplace. Twenty-one states have passed laws protecting corporate and government whistle-blowers. Nineteen states have laws prohibiting mandatory retirement at a certain age; Claude Pepper, who died at eighty-eight as a congressman from Florida, sought a federal statute to extend this prohibition nationwide. Thirty states have seen their courts erode employers' hitherto unchallenged belief that they have sole discretion to hire or fire. Three states have laws which require notice of plant shutdown and mandate severance pay for affected workers. Senate bill S2527, passed in July 1988, requires 60 days' notice of plant closings or mass layoffs.

The individual privacy of workers has been increased by the passage of the Federal Privacy Act (1974), which limits the data about individuals that governments can disclose to employers. Other laws that protect workers are those that limit the use of polygraph tests for job applicants (20 states); giving employees access to their personnel files (9 states); restricting the use of arrest records in the hiring process (12 states). Labor organizers recognize that successful tactics include voicing the concerns of local workers. Since much of the labor force is increasingly nonunion, judicial opinion and recent legislation has accommodated nonunion employees by extending to them typically union protections. As John Dunlop, former Secretary of Labor said, "I think the notion that an employer can get out of bed and fire anybody for any old reason is repugnant to a society of employees, whether they are organized into unions or not." American workers, unionized and nonunionized, are beginning to benefit from employee rights, vested rights, and job rights that are protected by government and the courts.

Certainly the national government has extended widely the parameters of its 'Magna Carta' with labor, the National Labor Relations Act of 1935. In addition to twenty-four state laws that set standards for health and safety in the workplace, the Federal Occupational Safety and Health Act of 1970 (OSHA) has created additional standards for the work environment. Other laws protect employees in specific ways: the Federal Mine Safety and Health Act (1977); the Civil Rights Act (1964); the Employment Act of 1967 that prohibits age discrimination, amended in 1978 to strike down laws that called for mandatory retirement before 70; the Equal Pay Act (1963), which embodied the principle of equal pay for equal work for women. States have taken the lead in protecting workers on sensitive issues involving marital status, sexual orientation, and comparable worth, and it is likely that the federal government will extend protections in some of these areas in the future. Laws further safeguarding pension rights and retirement income are also likely to be passed. These changes may well be linked to other legislation that could lessen the adversarial nature of business-labor negotiations.

Education, family, recreation, marriage, geographic mobility, health, length of employment, as well as job skill, will play important roles in the decisions of workers in the immediate future, when the shortage of labor will give them more choice and flexibility. Many of the problems and issues which women have experienced as they have moved into the work force will become generalized for all workers. For most people, traditional patterns of work will remain a truly significant part of their being, but for others there will be new choices that will redefine how "jobs" can be done. We will surely live in a more colorful and heterogeneous world of work that will demand more flexible attitudes and less rigid institutional forms.

NOTES

[1]Victor R. Fuchs, *The Health Economy* (Cambridge, Mass.: Harvard University Press, 1986), pp. 11–31.

[2]Robert J. Buchanan, *Health Care Finance: An Analysis of Cost and Utilization Issues* (Lexington, Mass.: D.C. Heath and Co., 1981), pp. 25–45.

[3]*Business Week,* January 28, 1985: 82.

[4]George Sape, "Coping with Comparable Worth," *Harvard Business Review,* 3 (May 1985): 152.

[5]*Business Week,* January 28, 1985: 84.

[6]Carol Gilligan, *In a Different Voice* (Cambridge, Mass.: Harvard University Press, 1982).

[7]Michael L. Wachter and Susan M. Wachter, eds., *Toward a New U.S. Industrial Policy* (Philadelphia: University of Pennsylvania Press, 1981).

[8]George T. Silvestri and John M. Lukasiewicz, "A Look at Occupational Employment Trends to the Year 2000," *Monthly Labor Review* 110 (September 1987): 46–63.

SUGGESTED READINGS

Battistella, Roger M., and Thomas G. Randall. *Health Care Policy in a Changing Environment.* Berkeley: McCutchan Publishing Corp., 1978.

Bloom, Allan. *The Closing of the American Mind.* New York: Simon and Schuster, 1987.

Boyer, Ernest. *High School: A Report on Secondary Education in America.* New York: Harper and Row, 1983.

———. *College.* New York: Harper and Row, 1987.

Buchanan, Robert J. *Health Care Finance.* Lexington, Mass.: Lexington Books, 1981.

Butts, Freeman, and Lawrence Cremin. *A History of Education in American Culture.* New York: Holt, 1953

Fuchs, Victor R. *The Health Economy.* Cambridge, Mass.: Harvard University Press, 1986.

Gilligan, Carol. *In a Different Voice.* Cambridge, Mass.: Harvard University Press, 1982.

Hirsch, Eric Donald. *Cultural Literacy: What Every American Needs to Know.* Boston: Houghton-Mifflin, 1987.

Kreps, Juanita. *Women and the American Economy: A Look at the 1980's.* Englewood Cliffs, NJ: Prentice-Hall, Inc., 1976.

Murray, Charles. *Losing Ground: American Social Policy, 1950–1980.* New York: Basic Books, 1984.

Somers, Anne R., and Herman M. Somers. *Health and Health Care: Policies in Perspective.* Germantown, Md.: Aspen Systems Corp., 1977.

Wells, Robert V. *Uncle Sam's Family.* Albany: State University of New York Press, 1985.

Wilcox, Claire. *Towards Social Welfare: An Analysis of Programs and Proposals Attacking Poverty, Insecurity, and Inequality of Opportunity.* Homewood, Ill.: Richard D. Irwin, 1969.

BOOK IV

The Third Industrial Revolution and the New Global Order

11

The Third Industrial Revolution and Our Economic Future

THE COMING REVOLUTION: NEW TECHNOLOGY

We are at the beginning of a Third Industrial Revolution that will reshape not only our industrial processes but also bring with it great changes that will affect all our lives for the next half century.[1] By comparison with the eighteenth century changes which cumulatively signalled the First Industrial Revolution and the revolutionary impact of autos, photography, electrical power, and industrial chemicals which established the Second Industrial Revolution in the United States roughly between 1880 and 1920, what is happening in microprocessors, telecommunications, biogenetics, lasers, energy, and space-age materials may be more significant by far than the earlier revolutionary period.[2] What will disturb Americans is that although their country reaped the largest share of benefits from the Second Industrial Revolution of Edison, Ford, and Eastman, it is not at all certain that the United States is as well positioned to take full advantage of the innovative technologies now coming into being.[3] Many young Japanese executives indeed believe that their country has already won the preeminent positions and will dominate the future.

Many technologies are largely already in evidence: microchips, CAD/CAM systems (computer aided design/computer aided manufacturing), fiber optics, lasers, holography, ocean mining, biogenetics, and bioagriculture, to name the obvious areas. Almost daily, however, the list grows. One might want to include robots, picture phones, home information systems, or, in the near future, superconductors. Five areas of change are linked together: electronics, manufacturing, biogenetics, telecommunications, and new materials.

The microprocessor is as revolutionary an invention as the wheel, the combustion engine, and the light bulb. Just over two decades ago Intel incorporated the entire central processing unit of its computer onto a single silicon chip. By 1980 VLSI (very large-scale integration) was in use, consisting of one million components fabricated and interconnected on a single silicon chip about one-tenth the size of a postage stamp. Visionaries in the industry speak of one billion components on a chip as being technologically feasible. The microprocessor heralds the advent of a new age of intelligence, and it is being connected to an enormous number of devices. As we become more accustomed to its potential, the imagined uses will proliferate like the biblical sands of the sea. Few today can even vaguely grasp the enormous potential of the microcomputer.

When a company introduces CAD/CAM into its design and manufacturing departments, their whole make-up changes. Engineers sit in front of computer screens with a menu board and an electronic pencil. On the screen these workers design equipment in a matter of minutes. A single piece outlined in soft green on the screen can be fitted into a more sophisticated piece of equipment whose various components are outlined in red, yellow, and blue. This artistry (for it is not only new technology but also a new art form) is a great step forward in economizing the time-design-manufacturing cycle. The computer can easily refer the design on the screen to the shop floor where machines can carry out the instructions. Instead of crowded, hurried environments reminiscent of Charlie Chaplin's *Modern Times,* a few operators work leisurely in bays outfitted with computer consoles, FM radios, and bags of doughnuts. Plates of steel weighing a half ton or more move into position and are cut by torches instructed by the computer. Hundreds of companies such as Boeing and G.E. have already moved far in the use for CAD/CAM in design and testing. The data generated by designers and engineers as they fashion products on a CAD system's video screen will provide much of the information necessary for flexible manufacturing systems (FMS). The manufacture of tools, the ordering of raw materials, the programming of robots, the scheduling of production runs, and the final inspection of products via the computer are all possible today. *No* company may be able to survive without such technology. Japanese corporations are the acknowledged world leaders in the completely automated factory of the future, though U.S. companies are closing the gap. Flexible manufacturing systems will diffuse around the globe.

In the 1960s the integrated circuit evolved into large-scale integration (LSI) and very large-scale integration (VLSI), offering manufacturers the ability to compress hundreds or even thousands of transistor circuits onto minute silicon chips. The first personal computers specifically designed for business use were introduced in 1981 and completed this initial cycle of the information revolution. Currently, in PCs alone, customers have over 200 billion dollars in hardware, software, and training. High definition television has also created much excitement. Companies are scrambling to implement advanced computer-chip technology in the hope of reaping huge profits through a new generation of products. Microelectronics will continue to revolutionize the future.[4] We can forecast the magnitude of the Third Industrial Revolution from the increasing dependence on new knowledge, a process that has already become institutionalized in key industries. The computer is so important to this revolution that many writers have labeled what is happening as an "information revolution." The march of the com-

The Advent of the Computer

The computer is a post–World War II development. The initial idea of a computer was conceived in the 1930s at the Massachusetts Institute of Technology (MIT), and a differential analyzer for electrical engineers was even built. In 1937, IBM built to Harvard professor Howard Aiken's specifications the first large scale automatic Mark I digital computer. A decade later, in 1947, Aiken completed Mark II, and IBM built the Selective Sequence Electronic Calculator (SSEC), which contained 23,000 relays and 13,000 vacuum tubes and could perform about one multiplication per second. The first all-electronic computer, the ENIAC (Electronic Numerical Integrator and Computer) was completed in the winter of 1944–1945 and owed much to the breakthrough efforts of John W. Mauchly and J. P. Eckert, Jr. ENIAC could perform 5000 additions and 300 multiplications per second, an enormous increase in speed compared to all machines of that period. Still ENIAC contained about 19,000 vacuum tubes and had a high-speed memory of only 20 words of 10 digits each. ENIAC was moreover controlled by hundreds of switches, plugs, and cables.[5] Mauchly and Eckert built the first commercial computer, UNIVAC, which became operational in 1951; one year earlier Remington-Rand had taken over the Eckert-Mauchly organization and launched its entry into the commercial computer industry. In the 1950s, developments shifted from the universities to industry. IBM, Sperry Rand, Control Data Corporation, General Electric, Philco, Honeywell, and others marketed computers of various sizes and capabilities. Very rapid growth in both the technology and the industry characterized this early period. Higher level languages, namely, FORTRAN (1956), ALGOL (1958), and COBOL (1960) were introduced. Of greater importance was Bell Laboratories' invention in 1947 of the transistor, which by the late 1950s was incorporated into the computer. The transistor was only a tiny fraction of the size of a vacuum tube, was solid-state, and much faster. It enabled a computer to multiply in 1/100,000 of a second two ten-digit numbers.

puter seems inexorable. Witness one such application: Thinking Machines received a $12 million contract from the Defense Advanced Research Projects Agency to develop the first supercomputer capable of speeds of a trillion operations a second.[6]

Thinking Machines' CM-2 computer uses 64,000 processors. Its new machine will have as many as a million processors that work in parallel. A government panel has stated that such performance would be necessary to solve twenty "grand challenges," those thorniest scientific problems such as creating precise models of the earth's weather patterns.[7]

Biogenetics

Biogenetics, only a few years old, is a revolution in knowledge and technology which is changing our world. Scientific breakthroughs of the kind we are experiencing with biogenetics have happened only once or twice before—perhaps with Isaac Newton in the seventeenth century or with Albert Einstein in the early years of the twentieth century. The miraculous unraveling of the DNA mystery has resulted in a vast new range of technological innovations and industrial applications including medicine, waste disposal, and genetic engineering in plants, animals, and humans. Already companies are producing artificial strains of interferon to fight diseases, bacteria that will eat sludge, and artificial insulin. For years Eli Lilly dominated the market for natural insulin, which it gathered from the pancreases of animals from all over the United States. The biogenetic insulin, "Humulin," which Lilly now makes, is only the forerunner of many new drugs created biogenetically. Companies such as Genentech, Biogen, Cetus, and Amgen will be common names in the 1990s. Genentech already has patents on three engineered drugs, the most famous being TPA (tissue plasminogen activator), which has gained an important place in cardiac treatment.

For the billions of hungry masses, no change was more important than the "Green Revolution" in the 1960s. All over the world, new, more productive strains of traditional grains have brought relief to underfed populations. What the Green Revolution was to the 1960s, the biogenetic revolution in agriculture will be to the 1990s. In place of the gradual changes of nature or the use of fertilizers and irrigation in the field, biogenetic agriculture enables scientists to produce in laboratories the improvements they wish. In 1980 Agriculture secretary John R. Block announced that scientists at the University of Wisconsin had, "in a pure research breakthrough, introduced a gene for protein production from a French bean into a sunflower, . . . [it is] the beginning of a whole new era in plant genetics." The "sunbean" may well be the Abraham of a new genealogy—plants that will be resistant to disease and drought, capable of growing without fertilizers and able to produce substitutes for oil. Soon genetic engineers may be able to "design and grow a single plant that has edible leaves like spinach, high-protein seeds like beans, a highly nutritive potato-like tuber, nitrogen-fixing roots, and a stalk that yields useful fiber."[8] Almost a decade beyond the creation of the sunbean, plant and animal research has gone far beyond Block's vision. Yet this future has both exciting and frightening elements.

Bioengineering

Bioengineering will forge a revolution which will have immediate industrial consequences. Biogenetics and bioagriculture have evolved from the scientific breakthroughs resulting from the unraveling of deoxyribonucleic acid (DNA) and the new world of gene manipulation. DNA is the genetic material of life. The DNA molecule encodes all the traits that parents pass to their children. Scientists have performed genetic engineering on a primitive level for well over a century, and genetic manipulation by breeders has been practiced for hundreds of years. Modern genetic engineers are directly manipulating the genetic material at the cellular and molecular levels; they do not have to wait for years for the results of a cross (controlled breeding) between organisms to become apparent. Recombinant DNA technology or gene splicing allows selective genes from a donor to be "inserted into a vector's DNA, amplified, and incorporated into the genetic material (genome) of a suitable host. The host, then, will carry and express its own DNA and the donor's DNA."[9] In little more than a decade and a half, developments of recombinant DNA have set the stage for the most momentous changes in human, plant, and animal life. Techniques for isolating fragments of DNA with the desired gene from the donor, for selecting a vector for the desired gene, and for propagating the recombinant DNA molecule along with its spliced-in gene have all moved ahead at breakneck speed. And all of this is but the beginning as these new skills in biotechnology are incorporated into business. We can already count more than 200 biotechnology companies in the United States.

For humans this biogenetic revolution means that probably half of all new drugs over the next twenty years will be genetically manufactured. Artificial insulin (Eli Lilly), Activase (Genentech), and many others already are. Billions of dollars are being invested in new research programs to produce these artificially engineered drugs. Health care costs, including the manufacture of drugs, are major items in national expenditures; over 12 percent of GNP is spent on health care in the United States. Glaxo, a multinational drug company, sold $1 billion of Zantac, an ulcer-treating drug, in 1989.

Many people are very frightened that gene manipulation and bioengineering might be applied to manufacture humans à la *Brave New World*. Although the potential for this kind of misuse is real, many more significant positive contributions for the control and use of genetic diseases will surely come first. No one suggests that gene manipulation and alteration should not be supervised with the greatest care and control—this is no area for government deregulation and free market forces. Already, questions are looming about whether we have allowed too much freedom in gene manipulation of plants and animals. The overwhelming new knowledge and skill can tell us how to produce "geeps," goats crossed with sheep, as well as rust-immune wheat. The current idea in the United States that government regulations are always counterproductive must yield to a common-sense view of government that posits it as a necessary and unbiased regulator in these emergent and potentially dangerous fields. Thousands of new possibilities in drugs, plants, and animals with billions of dollars of revenue at stake are too great a risk to leave solely to market forces.

Lasers

Lasers are a third area of explosive growth. Just slightly more than a quarter century ago T. H. Maiman produced the first operational laser in his laboratory. Today there are already many different and specialized kinds of lasers: ruby lasers, gas lasers, dye lasers, semiconductor lasers, etc., and their impact is just beginning. At present, lasers are widely used in medicine. Lasers can stop bleeding by sealing blood vessels during heart surgery and intrauterine operations. Laser angioplasty is being developed to treat coronary artery disease and may become widespread as an alternative to bypass surgery. Lasers have been used to remove oral cancer and to study the dynamics of proteins, nucleic acid, and other molecules.

In industry, laser links through fiber optic cables are part of the telecommunications revolution. Laser printers are an invaluable part of computer systems, just as laser scanners have revolutionized food retailing and all commercial operations where inventory controls are important. All holograms are made by lasers. Currently, credit card security systems make use of lasers to protect against fraud. Lasers as integrated optical devices will be widely used in the manufacture and operation of the next generation of microelectronics and computer chips. Fiber optic communication systems are becoming commonplace worldwide. And lasers in chemistry, as Schneider and Haus point out, have made an enormous contribution in measuring and monitoring environmental conditions, such as global wind and circulation problems as well as other meteorological data. Finally, lasers, they believe, may "provide the solution to creating controlled thermonuclear reaction."[10]

Application of laser technology is emerging at a breakneck speed. In ocean engineering and computer technology, in the welding, aligning, and calibrating of machinery, in the detection of leaking gases and the inspection of defective silicon wafers, lasers have demonstrated their usefulness in countless ways. Any device that can both weld a detached retina and bore a tunnel has an enormous future. By the early '80s, a laser was developed that would bore tiny holes one-fifth the diameter of a strand of hair. Unfortunately, the company that produced this scientific toy had not carried out any market research, and its laser remained just a curiosity. Today, however, the laser has proved its value in a large number of industrial, defense, and medical applications.

Second cousin to the laser is three-dimensional photography or holography. When it was discovered in the mid-'60s, holography was an intellectual puzzle. What was it good for? Today that answer has been found, and the uses for holography are growing rapidly. In five scientific areas holography has established its utility: microscopy, interferometry, optical memories that store large volumes of binary data in the form of holograms, commercial display (e.g., three-dimensional imagery and advertising), and medical holography (an alternative to x-rays). Industrial uses are proliferating daily. Holography has been used in oil prospecting to map a salt dome in the Gulf of Mexico. Holography is enhancing the effectiveness of radar, and acoustical holography has been used to determine whether a long-sought Leonardo da Vinci fresco was hidden under a more recent one on the wall of the Palazzo Veccio in Florence painted by the Renaissance artist Giorgio Vasari. These important breakthroughs betoken for U.S. industry the beginning of thousands of new applications.[11]

Fiber Optics

Fiber optics has been around the United States for some time as a scientific curiosity, but as a tool of communication its use is rapidly spreading. In the future, chips will use photons of light instead of electrons, improving the strength of telecommunication signals and increasing tremendously the number of messages that can be handled simultaneously. Some engineers suggest that one optical chip may be able to contain 10,000 or more "gates," those logical devices which will permit the unscrambling of messages easily and instantaneously. The age of stringing millions of miles of wire for telephone service is passing quickly as cellular systems emerge. Satellite communication is now well established. The *Wall Street Journal* is now transmitted by satellite, and the little box attached to the television screen is evidence of the ferocious competition that is making satellite-transmitted channel TV one of the hottest plays in town. Before this century is out, telecommunications of all kinds—audio, video, optical—will be commonplace. Even the Justice Department has paid its dues to the revolution in our midst by freeing AT&T to enter this new field. The seven new regional telephone companies that split from AT&T as well as the new long-distance competitors, MCI and Sprint, are fashioning a new industry. On that same day the Justice Department dropped an antitrust suit against IBM, Thompson C.S.F., the great French electronics giant, announced that it was putting millions of dollars into its campaign to make the home television set a data-retrieval center. The mini-tel in France is more advanced than anything we have in the U.S. at the present time, but a large number of American companies are experimenting with these same devices. That little box will soon give television subscribers an information system that entire nations could not afford a generation ago. Television will still continue to bring you "General Hospital," "Roseanne," and the latest episode of "L.A. Law," but it will also give you the flights from Kennedy, the Dow Jones ticker, the commodity futures, the weather, your heart profile, and the latest movies.

Energy and Superconductivity

In the wake of this Third Industrial Revolution will come solar-thermal energy, superconductivity, new space-age synthetic materials, and maybe a virtually endless supply of cheap energy from hydrogen energy systems. In many areas much work has already been done. The capturing of solar energy is moving along, though the economic constraints are still severe and the present costs uneconomic compared to the low costs of traditional fossil fuels. There may indeed be 500 years of coal underground, but human beings are increasingly reluctant to endanger their lives at the face of a coal seam, especially when the resulting product contributes to pollution.

Solar energy has long been an attractive alternative to traditional energy sources. Scientific calculations of the amount of energy transmitted from the sun assures us that if only a tiny fraction of this amount could be harnessed, we would have an almost unlimited energy supply. The amount of energy emitted from the sun is 23,000 times the amount of energy used by the entire global population. Major technologies can utilize solar energy. Among the discoveries: 1) The heat content of solar radiation can provide moderate and high temperature heat for industrial processes, and high-temperature heat for generating electricity. 2) Photovoltaics can convert solar energy directly into electricity. 3) Biomass technologies can exploit the chemical energy produced through photosynthesis to produce energy-rich fuels and chemicals and to provide direct heat for many uses. 4) Wind energy systems generate mechanical energy, primarily for conversion to electric power. 5) Finally, of a number of ocean energy applications the most advanced is the ocean thermal energy conversion, which uses temperature differences between warm ocean surface water and colder deep water to produce electricity.[12] A new viable, economically competitive energy source would further accelerate the Third Industrial Revolution and cut dependency on imported oil.

The Japanese have taken out over 1000 patents for items related to superconductivity. There are indeed many problems yet to be solved before superconductivity becomes commonplace in the transmission of power, but its enormous potential is clearly recognized by the scientific community and by many industrial leaders. In the development and production of space-age materials, Americans have a large lead over all their competition and must not lose this lead if they are to prosper. With the end of the Cold War, Americans should reap larger benefits from their staggering investment in space.

However promising the future of these and countless other new technologies, the arrival of the Third Industrial Revolution does not automatically mean prosperity and success for the United States. Unless education is reformed and fundamental human and social needs addressed, Americans will not be prepared to take advantage of these global changes. Other countries will optimize scientific and technological discoveries in the same manner that Americans took up and developed further penicillin, jet engines, and interchangeable parts just a few decades ago.

THE NEW AUTOMATION

Japanese companies at present are the acknowledged world leaders in completely automated factories. The Japanese have been quicker to accept robotics in industry than any other country and have more than 20,000 sequence, playback, numerically controlled (n/c), and intelligent robots in automobile assembly lines, electronic factories, and other places. By the end of this century, the United States must have 50,000 robots or more to be in a leadership role. This is not an impossible goal but an almost essential one if the United States is to regain its leadership in industrial manufacturing.

The robot stations at Fanuc Fujitsu produce robots which make other robots. This cloning is something revolutionary in the history of organization and production of goods. A robot can be defined simply as a reprogrammable, multifunctional manipulator designed to move material, parts, tools, or specialized devices through programmed motion for performing a variety of tasks. Typically, most robots have four characteristics: *a programmed and reprogrammable ability,* i.e., they perform a task or tasks until their programs are changed; *manipulators and controllers* designed to move the parts handled by the robot: grippers, effectors, or hands, whether mechanical, magnetic, or vacuum; *controls* such as computers and microprocessors; and *a power source*—either pneumatic, hydraulic, or electric. Major research and development in companies and universities is being done to add sensors of all kinds—sight, touch, sound, and artificial intelligence—to enhance robot performance. The Japanese have a small program which enables businesses to lease on a short-term basis small robots that perform only a few functions. The businessman, rather than making a very costly investment which might not work out for him, can take the robot and experiment with it in his business. In many cases, indeed, he discovers uses that are valuable. The United States could do well to imitate programs of this kind. Robot technology will dominate many areas of production by the end of this century.

What more can a robot do? "Jason Jr." assisted scientists by allowing them to look into the hold of the Titanic, but robots will make their greatest inroads in manufacturing. In both the United States and Japan, the robotic welding of automobile bodies was an early success. Robots also moved quickly into those areas where danger to the worker was clear. Spray painting, for example, with its high toxicity has led to the replacement of humans by robots, as has the handling of radioactive and other dangerous materials. Clearly the concern over health hazards in areas such as these will further the rapid and continuing substitution of robots for people. Especially in the United States, where industrial litigation is endemic, no manufacturer can resist the temptation to "robotize" a potentially dangerous operation if it is at all possible.

In the popular mind, the introduction of robots and other high-tech innovations is synonymous with elimination of jobs and increased unemployment. Initially however the reverse is true. Employment at the Fanuc robot plant in Japan, for example, increased even more through the introduction and manufacture of robots. In other companies, there are similar results. The manufacturing, maintenance, and programming of robots will expand jobs and create an entire new industry. To be sure, in the long run, job displacement will occur, and even from the outset there is certainly bound to be a great deal of job incongruence. In the longer run, by lowering unit costs and increasing productivity, high tech will increase the real standard of living as new technology has always done over the last two and a half centuries. We lack specific numbers as to the speed, concentration, and diffusion of high tech into the economy, and this lack of certainty increases speculation about its future economic results. Possibly only 4 to 7 percent of skilled production jobs, for example, will yield to robots in the 1980s, but high tech in some form will soon be part of almost all processes. A McDonald's hamburger may be cooked conventionally, but the store's inventory control will be computerized. A farsighted program to ease the employment dislocation caused by high tech is not only likely but virtually mandatory for any mature nation's social policy. Management and labor, certainly unionized labor, are already bargaining hard on both job security and job retraining issues. None of the present U.S. government job retraining programs for new technologies or social welfare plans aspire to these needs. However, the lack of a creative social policy ought not to inhibit the introduction and spread of high technology, lest we lose precious time to foreign competitors. A United States Congressional staff report vigorously stated the view that:

> As long as there is some place in the world where there are no impediments to the introduction of the new technology, any attempt to restrict the ultimate adoption of the technology will prove self-defeating, with unemployment and negative income effects from a loss of business to outside companies greater than if a pro-high-tech (or at least a neutral) public policy were followed.

> The Robotics Revolution is beginning and those who fully participate will reap gains while those who shrink from participation will suffer losses in incomes and jobs. Market forces will provide the inducements or signals necessary to bring about the resource allocations needed, but government can help by providing a positive tax environment that permits investors and workers a good return on their investments in human and physical capital. It can and should reduce regulations that hurt productivity and have little discernible offsetting social benefit. It can support research and development spending on robotics and its effects. It can encourage retraining programs. It can play a leadership role in reducing the human concerns over robotics that can potentially block adoption.[13]

THE COMING REVOLUTION: NEW MANAGEMENT

Management of Technology (MOT) and Consumer Relations

The management of technology (MOT) will be a far-reaching problem for American managers, workers, and industry in general. In the post-World War II boom, American industry neglected two essentials: product quality and the need to value the consumer. The decline in the reliability of U.S. products was illustrated on a grand scale by the precipitous fall in the quality of the American car. Even worse, we now know that some automobile executives were well aware that only if new capital investments were made and plants built, could American consumers be kept as customers. These oligopolistic auto companies decided instead to pile up short-term profits; they lost quickly large segments of the market to foreign imports. To a considerable degree, the mistakes of the automobile industry were repeated in many manufacturing areas. Products poorly designed and built were meant to be thrown away and replaced not with something better but with something superficially new. Quality control advocates like W. Edwards Deming, rejected at home, took their ideas abroad. Deming became an industrial hero in Japan, and the annually awarded Deming prize became one of the most prestigious and coveted awards in Japanese industry. Only belatedly in the mid-1980s did the importance of quality standards become a widespread concern in U.S. companies. Most U.S. managers after the Second World War sported an MBA degree, but most American business schools did not teach the management of technology or manufacturing. Instead they concentrated heavily on finance and the management and manipulation of financial assets. American industry seemed willing to bear the hidden costs of large numbers of manufactured rejects when throughout the rest of the industrial world quality and efficiency resulting in zero rejects was becoming the standard. Lessons of this kind come at heavy cost; the price paid was the loss of competitiveness and market share. Especially in some of the new consumer electronics industries, this disregard for quality brought disaster. America saw its share of virtually every branch of consumer electronics slip away. Initial scientific breakthroughs and early product development usually took place in the United States, but TVs, microwave ovens, VCRs, and computer chips were all captured by Japanese entrepreneurs, improved on, and sent back to the United States as finished products. By the end of the 1980s, each year saw a trade deficit with Japan of over $100 billion, almost all of it attributable to imports of autos and electronics.

The alienation of the consumer was due to a combination of industrial arrogance and the decline of civility in American life. Consumers were thought of as disposable, faceless; their concerns and demands things to be manipulated and taken advantage of. From the manufacturer to the retailer, service eroded. Consumers were treated in many instances as stupid complainers, not worthy of the attention of highly paid managers. What right did a customer have to complain that his car was a "lemon," or (as actually happened) that a washing machine danced across the room when clothing flipped over an inner lid and unbalanced the mechanism? When confronted with the complaint that socks were flipping out of the wash tub and into the motor one service manager insisted, until the washer was redesigned, that housewives loading the machine were nervous and that the malfunction was related to their personal instability! No one, no matter how horrendous the error, seemed able or willing to assume responsibility. The consumer left American products sitting on shelves and bought foreign ones. Even today, American consumers complain most about the level and inadequacy of service, from clerks who are rude and incompetent, to multimillion dollar executives who seem more interested in golden parachutes than in satisfying customers. Of course these are blanket criticisms and do not represent all manufacturers, but to a great degree this philosophy (consumers don't count) colored the attitudes of American business in the seventies and early eighties. To be sure foreign projects also fail, but German and Japanese goods in many areas—autos and machinery in particular—gained a well-deserved reputation for quality. Japanese service and attention to customers have become a byword for civility.

The process of manufacturing has changed dramatically in recent times, and will change even more fundamentally with the Third Industrial Revolution. Though most goods themselves will not be high tech, their production will increasingly be affected by the latest and most advanced processes. Machines will be programmed to prevent human error. Workers will be placed in small square, rectangular, or oval work stations holding eight to twelve people who can control the flow and tempo of production, shutting down the operation immediately if something goes wrong. In only a few industries today does the long linear production line persist, and in even these few cases it will be used less frequently over the next decade. The overwhelming emphasis on quality necessitates that the correction loop become shorter and shorter. Many industries must create sterile environments in manufacturing so that state-of-the-art quality goods can be produced. Of course, the overall operation of the enterprise—design, purchasing, inventory, billing—will be modernized endlessly by use of computer software. The paperwork in the back room and front offices will also be computerized. Word processors, fax machines, and teleconferencing will be commonplace as their costs continue to fall. Unfortunately, in many areas Americans must play catch-up with the Japanese. To be sure, the key to success will still rest on the competence of individuals and the overall strengths of our capitalist system.

Management of Human Resources

The Third Industrial Revolution will change the management of human resources, especially in the United States. Managers in particular will face grave problems and new excitement as they struggle with the transition from the technologies of the past to those of the future. As the new technology starts phasing in rapidly, David Newman notes that "a degree of uncontrollability has been introduced into the modern organization; an inherent unmanageability." Patterns of production, marketing, and finance have become entrenched during the last fifty years and have produced an orthodoxy of management style and culture. As we enter the new century new rules will apply and "management" will take on new meanings. In the United States

> earlier schools of management thought and conventional wisdom have viewed individuals in various ways: as raw units of production; as recalcitrant and incorrigible specimens to be driven and tightly controlled; as necessary components of task forces to be harnessed and motivated by skilled leaders and as such to be manipulated; and as higher beings with an innate capacity for self-control, self-development, and self-motivation.[14]

"Knowledge workers"—those who will dominate every one of the high-technology areas we have mentioned—will need patterns of interaction and involvement, new forms of recognition and reward, and new types of leadership to respect. In every country management orthodoxy is or will be tested. Managers in the areas of new technologies will have to be creative as never before. For the company's survival (or its equivalent organization), managers will have to think more in terms of finding niches for specialized products and customized batch processes rather than long manufactured runs of homogeneous items.

The proliferation of opportunities and markets which the Third Industrial Revolution offers brings with it new managerial strategies. To a great extent, customizing products and markets is now possible because of the computer. Traditional manufacturing necessitated large homogeneous throughputs to gain the cost benefits from the enormous capital investments in plant. Although massive amounts of capital will be necessary to enter a new industry, from research to production the computer will foster new markets for customized needs. Henry Ford wanted to produce cars of any color so long as the color was black; AT&T produced only black telephones for decades. Today, a customer can walk into a showroom, select a car, and order any number of customized features like upholstery, external finish, and so on. These desires can be forwarded by computer link to the factory, and as the shell car moves forward, the options can be added to it without any significant additional cost. Another development is the growth of businesses that cater to specialized needs. Paychex, Inc. provides payroll services for 100,000 small businesses. The production of software programs for professionals such as lawyers and travel agents will multiply, as will the demand for temporary help and consultants. We face a polychromatic world of great possibilities. In many instances, product cycles will be dramatically telescoped because these new technologies, for years to come, will be subject to constant alteration and elaboration. New products will be born before old products reach obsolescence. But most of all, managers will direct people in ways we do not yet know and cannot yet teach. Managers will have to learn on the job. Take a long look at a company's traditional organizational chart with its serried boxes of line and staff positions; the management structure of the future is not likely to look as neat again, nor as hierarchical. Propelled by an enormous amount of managerial experimentation, new organizational forms may emerge and transform everything we now have. Even in Japan, young people today will not wait quietly for ten or fifteen years for a leadership role, and traditional Japanese management will be under great pressure. In the United States, workers will not accept the rigid control system of the past. In many ways this system has already greatly changed over the past twenty years, but it will change even more in the coming years as the management pyramid flattens and the workplace becomes more consensual.

NOTES

[1] A portion of this material appeared in J. Finkelstein and D. Newman, "The Third Industrial Revolution: A Special Challenge to Managers," *Organizational Dynamics* (Summer 1984): 53–66.

[2] H. J. Habakkuk, *American and British Technology in the Nineteenth Century* (New York: Cambridge University Press, 1967); Serge Leontiev, "The New Automation," *New York Times,* February 8, 1983, p. 68; John Naisbitt, *Megatrends: Ten New Directions Transforming Our Lives* (New York: Warner Books, 1982).

[3] Alfred D. Chandler, Jr., *The Visible Hand* (Cambridge, Mass.: Belknap Press, 1977); Alfred D. Chandler, Jr., *Strategy and Structure* (Cambridge, Mass.: MIT Press, 1962); Joseph A. Schumpeter, *Capitalism, Socialism and Democracy,* 3d ed. (New York: Harper and Row, 1950).

[4] R. A. Powell, "Microelectronics," in *Windows on a New World,* Joseph Finkelstein, ed. (New York: Greenwood, 1989), pp. 1–19.

[5] Gerald W. Brock, *The U.S. Computer Industry* (Cambridge, Mass.: Ballinger, 1975), pp. 10–11.

[6] *New York Times,* November 29, 1989, sec. D, p. 4.

[7] Ibid.

[8] *New York Times,* October 25, 1981, p. 47.

[9] Arnold E. S. Gussin, "Biotechnology," in *Windows on a New World,* p. 121.

[10] Joseph W. Haus and John Schroeder, "Lasers: Now the Age of Light," in *Windows on a New World,* p. 85ff.

[11] Herman Kahn, William Brown, and Leon Martel, *The Next 200 Years* (New York: Morrow and Company, 1976); Dirk Hanson, *The New Alchemists: Silicon Valley and the Microelectronics Revolution* (Boston: Little Brown, 1982).

[12] *McGraw-Hill Encyclopedia of Science and Technology,* vol. 16 (New York: McGraw Hill, 1989), pp. 569–570.

[13] U.S. House of Representatives, *Robotics: Hearings before the Subcommittee on Investigations and Oversight of the Committee on Science and Technology,*

97th Cong., 2d sess., June 2 and 23, 1982; Robert J. Miller, ed., *Robotics: Future Factories, Future Workers* (The Annals of the American Academy of Political and Social Science, v. 470) (Newbury Park, California: American Academy of Political and Social Science, 1983).

[14]Joseph Finkelstein and David Newman, "The Third Industrial Revolution," in *Windows on a New World,* p. 229.

SUGGESTED READINGS

Bell, Daniel. *The Coming of Post-Industrial Society.* New York: Basic Books, 1973.

Chandran, Rajan, Arvind Phatak, and Sambharya Rakesh. "Transborder Data Flows: Implications for Multinational Corporations." *Business Horizons* (Nov/Dec. 1987): 74–82.

Chaudhuri, Adhip. "Multinational Corporations in Less-Developed Countries: What Is In Store?" *Columbia Journal of World Business* (Spring 1988): 57–63.

"Competitive Alliances: Forging Ties Abroad," *Management Review* (March 1987): 57–59.

"Europe's High Tech Gap," *Economist* (February 4-10, 1989): 13, 72.

Globerman, Steven. "Government Policies Toward Foreign Investment: Has a New Era Dawned?" *Columbia Journal of World Business* (Fall 1988): 41–49.

Hale, David D. "The Global Economy: Today and Tomorrow," *Government Finance Review* (February 1988): 5–18.

Hanson, Dirk. *The New Alchemists: Silicon Valley and the Microelectronics Revolution.* Boston: Little Brown, 1982.

Jelinek, Mariann. *Institutionalizing Innovation.* New York: Praeger, 1979.

Kahn, Herman, William Brown, and Leon Martel. *The Next 200 Years.* New York: Morrow, 1976.

Manufacturing Studies Board. *Toward a New Era in U. S. Manufacturing: The Need for a National Vision.* Washington, D. C.: National Academy Press, 1986.

"The Mechanization of Work," *Scientific American* 247: 3 (September 1982).

Noble, David F. *America by Design: Science, Technology, and the Rise of Corporate Capitalism.* New York: Knopf, 1977.
———. *Forces of Production: A Social History of Industrial Automation.* New York: Oxford University Press, 1986.

Munkirs, John R. "Technological Change: Disaggregation and Overseas Production." *Journal of Economic Issues* (June 1988): 469–75.

Quinn, James Brian. *Strategies for Change: Logical Incrementalism.* Homewood, Ill.: Richard D. Irwin, Inc., 1980.

Reich, Robert B. *The Next American Frontier.* New York: Times Books, 1983.

Thompson, James D. *Organizations in Action.* Hightstown, NJ: McGraw-Hill, 1967.

Toffler, Alvin. *Powershift: Knowledge, Wealth, and Violence at the Edge of the 21st Century.* New York: Bantam, 1990.

Whichard, Obie G. "U.S. Multinational Companies: Operations in 1986." *Survey of Current Business* (June 1988): 85–96.

———. "U.S. Multinational Companies: Operations in 1987." *Survey of Current Business* (June 1989): 27–39.

Woodward, Joan. *Industrial Organization: Theory and Practice,* 2d ed. New York: Oxford University Press, 1980.

12   The New Global Order: Foreign Direct Investment

Throughout most of the period since the end of World War II, especially the 1950s and 60s, the United States has dominated worldwide foreign direct investment. However, beginning with the oil shock of 1973 that situation has reversed, and the U.S. became the recipient of large investments from Great Britain, the Netherlands, and more recently Japan. Although the 1980s saw unusually rapid growth in worldwide foreign direct investment, from approximately $55 billion in 1980 to $137 billion in 1987, world output rose only by 20 percent and the volume of world trade by 28 percent. The past decade marked a reversal of U.S. fortunes as it became the largest recipient of foreign direct investment. On November 26, 1990, Matsushita acquired MCA for $6.60 billion, the largest acquisition by a Japanese company in the U.S. During this period, Japan became the leader in direct investment abroad.

What has been happening to and inside the U.S. in recent years is most important. The world's 600 largest multinationals are responsible for the creation of one-fifth of the world's total value-added in manufacturing and agriculture. Most multinationals are comparatively small but each one of these 600 MNCs has annual sales in excess of $1 billion and plays a very important role in the global economy. Since 1985, foreigners, especially the Japanese, have increased their acquisitions in America or have expanded or established businesses in the U.S. The reasons for this surge in investments, up 60 percent in 1988 over 1987 and four times the amount spent in 1984, are both varied and complex. Some foreign companies feel they must have a position in the American market, the richest and still the largest consumer market in the world. (With the creation of a free trade union composed of the U.S., Canada, and Mexico, this bloc will soon become the largest market, worth an estimated $6 trillion.) U.S. political stability and the appreciation of foreign assets make U.S. assets relatively attractive and cheap: witness Mitsubishi's purchase of Rockefeller Center for approximately $850 million, a fraction of what a similar piece of real estate in downtown Tokyo would cost. The lure of overseas profits push MNCs into staking out international

Table 12.1	Ten Largest Japanese Acquisitions in the U.S. in 1989		

Target	Acquirer	Effective Date	Value ($ billions)
MCA, Inc.	Matsushita Electric Ind.	—	$6.60
Columbia Pictures	Sony Corp.	Nov. '89	3.41
Firestone Tire	Bridgestone	May '88	2.65
Inter Continental Hotels	Seibu Saison	Dec. '88	2.27
CBS Records	Sony Corp.	Jan. '88	2.00
CIT Group	Dai-Ichi Kangyo Bank	Dec. '89	1.28
Gould, Inc.	Nippon Mining	Nov. '88	1.05
Rockefeller Group	Mitsubishi Estate	May '90	0.85
Union Bank (Calif.)	California First Bank*	June '88	0.75
Lyphomed, Inc.	Fujisawa Pharmaceutical	Oct. '89	0.67

*Owned by the Bank of Tokyo

Source: *Wall Street Journal,* November 27, 1990, A–3.

claims. Exporting countries can frequently skirt around another country's protective or exclusionary legislation by establishing factories within that country's borders. Honda U.S.A. now produces 100,000 cars; by the end of the 1990s, some observers believe that Honda will be producing more cars here than it makes in Japan. The existing know-how of all kinds—scientific, industrial, managerial, marketing—and well-developed finance, advertising, and insurance systems also have made the United States very attractive for investors.

The new global economy emphasizes consolidation and bigness. In the U.S., foreign investors acquired in 1988 two companies worth $6.5 billion and $5.2 billion respectively. Still domestic mergers and acquisitions among U.S. firms in 1988 were two-and-a-half times larger in value than overseas takeovers, over $60 billion in all. These domestic mergers happened six times more frequently than foreign acquisitions. Mammoth deals in pharmaceuticals, media, and food industries helped set a new record of $144 billion for the combined value of the fifty largest annual acquisitions, mergers, public offerings, and recapitalizations.[1] The Conference Board, however, argues that appreciation or depreciation of the dollar has not played a significant role either in increasing or decreasing foreign direct investment. Moreover, the Conference Board contends the criterion of pricing at book value oversimplifies the true nature of domestic and overseas investment decisions. A more accurate estimate would thereby increase the stock of U.S. investment abroad by as much as $600 billion, which would lower the debtor position of the United States substantially. Correspondingly such an adjustment would also increase the true value of foreign investment here. To be sure, statistics on foreign direct investment do not reflect the much larger quantities of bank borrowings, security issues, trade credits, and the equity position of host-country residents, all of which must be measured to determine the complete status of foreign investment.

MARKETING IN THE INDUSTRIAL REVOLUTION

Marketing experts tell us "the world's economy remains local in marketing characteristics. Furthermore global business success comes from combining product advantage with advantage in business and marketing systems across multiple geographic lines." Marketing is often ignored by academic economists, but all business managers know that the marketing of their products both at home and abroad is highly complex and fraught with the possibilities of failure. In the United States, marketing in the '90s will be fiercely competitive, and companies will fight to the death to protect their brand names and their profit margins. A range of new smart products produced by the marriage of software and sensors to traditional goods will compete for dollars. In addition, the aging of America will necessitate the growth of products that are more age-appropriate. Bottled water and low-cholesterol health foods will soar in demand, while Club Med vacations and Nautilus machines will lag. Abroad, the opportunities for the sale of consumer goods will be substantial as affluence increases and consumers in places like Eastern Europe try to catch up with the shortages of goods. Marc Particelli of Booz, Allen and Hamilton, Inc. offers nine suggestions for those firms who wish to market abroad in the 1990s: "Find out if there is op-

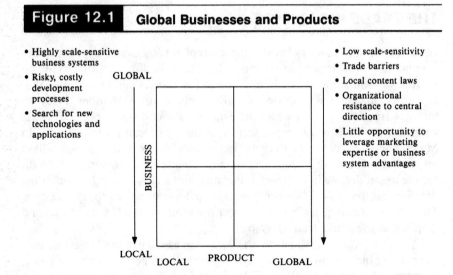

Figure 12.1   Global Businesses and Products

Source: Booz, Allen & Hamilton, Inc./Conference Board, June/July 1989.

portunity outside the country; Don't think that the product will carry the day when moving offshore; Pick your spot and spend enough; Do not necessarily go it alone; Be patient and persistent; Get started; Establish a presence; Know and respect your competition; Look for differences, not similarities."[2]

U.S. managers in many leading corporations are being trained to work more effectively in the international arena than managers of the past. Learning language skills, cultural values, and nuances in taste, design, color, and quality are now as important as acquaintance with tax laws and manufacturing standards. U.S. companies have a discrete advantage with their proficiency in electronic data interchange systems (EDI), which can provide a competitive edge in linking distribution, customers, suppliers, and competitors. So long as the technology is used to support customer relations and not replace them, this advantage may be considerable.

The rise of MNCs and the spread of global affiliates affects strongly the dynamics of international trade. For example, we know that in 1986 U.S. firms abroad purchased 31 percent of total U.S. exports and supplied 17 percent of total imports. Almost 80 percent of this overall trade was between U.S. parents and their affiliates. The other side of the coin was that foreign-owned affiliates in the U.S. accounted for 22 percent of total exports and almost one-third of its imports: "U.S. multinationals' share of world markets—combining exports by both parents and foreign affiliates—appears to have remained relatively stable, at around 17-18 percent since the late 1960s." Despite temporary setbacks in highly competitive areas such as consumer electronics, "the state of the global economy will be one of the most exciting elements of the future."[3]

THE TRADE IMBALANCE

Each month, the country awaits the current trade account figures to see whether the trade deficit has risen or fallen; these preliminary figures are almost always incomplete and later revised. The figures announced on January 17, 1990, showed a deficit of $10.2 billion for December 1989, an increase from the previous month. This news was disappointing to those who were looking for an improvement in the American trade position. In March and April 1990, the deficits declined to $9.5 billion and $8.3 billion respectively. The Bush administration and Congress have taken great credit for the recent decline in the trade imbalance, but a closer examination of the data suggest that this deficit problem will continue to persist for a long time. The search for causes leads us to inspect the health of the U.S. economy and its place in the world trading system.

For most of the last decade, the Japanese have been the largest beneficiary of the increase in world trade in manufactured goods. Japanese autos, consumer electronics goods of all kinds, and semiconductors have come to dominate world markets, especially those in the U.S. Although the United

Table 12.2 The Dollar and U.S. Trade

U.S. Trade Balance by Major Sectors ($ billion)

	Jan.-Apr. 1988	Jan.-Apr. 1989
Consumer goods	-22.0	-19.9
Automobiles	-18.9	-19.6
Industrial supplies	-10.5	-12.8
Other goods*	8.4	13.1
Capital goods	3.3	3.4
Food, feed, and beverages	1.6	4.0
Total deficit	-38.1	-31.8

*Includes military equipment, shipments valued at $10,000 or under, undocumented exports to Canada, and U.S. goods returned.

Source: *Department of Commerce*/World Economic Monitor, Conference Board, Summer 1989.

States ran trade deficits with Europe early in the 1980s, the estimated surge in exports from $61.6 billion in 1986 to $100 billion in 1989 has all but eliminated the Western European problem.[4] Not so with Japan, as the trade deficit persists. The debate on how to confront the issue of Japanese trade has exhausted many a trade negotiator and split academic economists. A recent publication of the prestigious Twentieth Century Fund on this subject produced a majority and minority report.[5] The liberal majority, in this instance led by Herbert Stein, favored traditional free trade. They argued that the trade deficit and poor showing of U.S. products abroad is symptomatic of the overall weakness of the U.S. economy, burdened by the large federal deficit, the low savings rate, and the low rate of productivity. They reject outright the idea that the United States should adopt some kind of an "industrial policy," which the minority proposed to support certain industries. "We have problems, but they are not made in Tokyo or Brussels, they are made here," Stein said. The minority opinion, vocal, persuasive, and possessing experts with equivalent credentials, argued that Japan practices a managed and directed capitalism which gives Japanese companies impressive advantages over their American competitors. Already the Japanese have built up such a staggering lead in some areas that it is virtually impossible for U.S. companies to reenter these markets competitively. The enormous capital buildup by Japanese companies will enable them to outperform competitors for the next two decades and widen the distance between themselves and American competitors.[6] When the General Electric Company announced that it would build the world's most powerful commercial jet

Table 12.3 — Top Ten U.S. Exports and Imports, 1988

Exports	Value ($ billions)	Imports	Value ($ billions)
Aircraft	20.3	Motor vehicles	47.5
Vehicle and tractor parts	13.2	Crude petroleum	25.8
Office machine parts	12.6	Motor vehicle parts	14.7
ADP machines and equipment	11.6	Petroleum products	12.0
Shipments valued at $10,000 or under*	10.4	Office machine parts	11.5
Electronic components	10.4	Electronic components	11.5
Motor vehicles	9.1	Telecommunications equipment	9.7
Undocumented exports to Canada	8.3	Special transactions†	8.4
Organic chemicals	7.8	ADP machinery	8.3
Measuring and checking instruments	7.4	Footwear	8.0

*Over half of which to Canada

†Mainly U.S. goods returned or reimported

Source: *Department of Commerce*/World Economic Monitor, Conference Board, Summer, 1989.

engine together with the French company Snecma, it also added that it was negotiating with a Japanese company to share in the project cost, estimated at between $1 and $2 billion. This engine would be designed for the new 767X, which Boeing hopes to build with Mitsubishi, Kawasaki, and Fuji Heavy Industries.

Table 12.4 — Top Ten U.S. Markets and Suppliers, 1988

Market	Percent of exports	Supplier	Percent of imports
Canada	22.0	Japan	20.3
Japan	11.7	Canada	18.5
Mexico	6.4	Germany	6.0
United Kingdom	5.7	Taiwan	5.6
Germany	4.4	Mexico	5.2
Taiwan	3.8	Korea	4.6
Korea	3.5	United Kingdom	4.1
Netherlands	3.1	France	2.8
France	3.1	Italy	2.6
Belgium	2.3	Hong Kong	2.3
	66.0		72.0

Source: *Department of Commerce*/World Economic Monitor, Conference Board, Summer 1989.

Analysts who have studied this trade imbalance problem point to few gains for American firms in the high value-added end of the market. Despite improved gains for agricultural products and in low-valued shipments, massive efforts for improvement have failed to close the gap. Closely tied to this problem is the value of the dollar. In the short run, the decline of the dollar in foreign exchange led to initial improvements. Now, however, the dollar continues to fluctuate because of world economic and political instability, and its partial recovery negates the gains Americans have made in the service sectors. "The deterioration in services resulted in an overall balance-of-payments deficit in excess of the deficit in merchandise trade."[7] We face therefore a very difficult problem of adjustment. Foreign companies, especially those in Japan and Pacific Rim countries, have been able to absorb a good share of the price increases caused by currency manipulation of the dollar while retaining their market shares. A headier growth in Western and Eastern Europe, aided by American investment, may benefit the U.S. economy more than any attempts to reduce further the value of the dollar. Still "even if all the barriers to trade were swept away, the U.S. would still record a bilateral trade deficit (albeit a somewhat smaller one) with Japan, just as it has since 1965."[8] Although Japan remains the most intractable of our trading partners, we must recognize that all peoples belong to a vast currency, financial, and trading system. We will all sink or swim together.

THE INTERNATIONAL EFFECTS OF HIGH TECH

Microchips, lasers, and other new technologies are already bringing special problems to the international arena. In a world where capital is scarce, the Third Industrial Revolution brings only hard choices. Not one of the new technologies comes cheap, nor can one count on long product cycles over which the costs of development can be absorbed, profits generated, and capital recovered. Quite the contrary: uncertainty dominates these new areas. There are no assured long periods of profitability. Moreover, the markets for these new technologies are fiercely turbulent. Investment decisions, quantitative and qualitative, will be crucial for managers. By the end of this century, all the major U.S. industries now in retreat, such as textiles, chemicals, iron or steel, shipbuilding, automobiles, and heavy machinery will continue to face heavy competition. However, information services connected with the new technologies will expand rapidly: business services of all kinds (legal, accounting, data processing, finance, insurance); wholesale and retail trade; health, education, and social welfare; hotels and real estate; entertainment and travel. In many of these industries, moreover, the service component—office work and paper handling—will be transformed by new information technologies. But in many areas there will be displacement and reduction of wages and status. Many service industries will, however, create well-paying jobs. Organized labor in the U.S., through its sizeable impact on pension funds, will exercise growing influence over company and management decisions. Although union membership will continue to diminish, no one should doubt that managers and politicians will be under enormous pressures to save jobs, to slow the initiation of profound technological change, and to sacrifice competitiveness in the market place for human welfare needs. If, however, public policymakers continue to demand large infusions of capital from abroad to ease budget deficits, it will in the long run make the cost of capital for economic growth more expensive and make U.S. industry even less competitive.

Controversy will grow acutely. The Third Industrial Revolution has a treadmill quality to it: to stay alive, one must keep moving. However, it also has an even riskier quality: to stay competitive companies must jump ahead into the unknown, and the cost and effect of these discontinuities are difficult to calculate. What strategy should companies and countries adopt? If the far horizon of the Third Industrial Revolution is glistening bright, the way to it is through a minefield. Even the very largest and richest countries and companies will have to make choices. Nations will be hard pressed to keep up with the latest technological advances while at the same time maintaining necessary social welfare programs.

Over the past forty years, the growth of multinational companies has been one of the telling factors in the surge of international trade and development. Companies have luxuriated in the freedom to move and produce abroad, taking full advantage of the opportunities and flexibilities in world markets. But multinational companies and their managers will find their freedoms both enlarged and hedged by national and international conditions such as the breakdown of the GATT negotiations in December 1990. The multiple ramifications of all these new knowledge-based industries will cause nightmares for public and private planners accustomed to the relatively leisurely difficulties of the past. Here again, the multinationals of the developed industrial countries of Western Europe, the United States, and the Pacific Basin will find themselves enmeshed in combinations and confrontations both amongst themselves and with all others. Just as companies became multinational because they have strengths—in marketing, products, and technology—so they must replace outdated thinking and join, harness, control, and exploit these unprecedented emerging opportunities of the Third Industrial Revolution. If they fail to grasp how much this environment is a sharp discontinuity from the past, they are not likely to succeed.

NEW PROTECTIONISM?

The Third Industrial Revolution will encourage latent protectionist forces. Governments will be under even greater pressures to protect their work force from the onslaught of new products and processes in which their own industries may have fallen behind. American companies and unions regularly demand protectionist help now, and many industries are consequently shielded in this way. To be sure, many of these demands are defended as temporary measures to allow "time to catch up" and devise ways to counter unfair competition. There is, however, very little time left. The pace of change is becoming so rapid that many industries will be unable to adjust. Some may, if they fall behind greatly, not be able to get back in the game. Western Europe's push toward an integrated European Community in 1992 is a strategy to combat its relative lag. U.S. investment in Western Europe, and to a limited extent its growing economic interest in Eastern Europe, also reflects these changes. The surge in interest in high technology among European Community members underscores also the European awareness to meet competitive challenges from both the U.S. and Japan. Agreements, partnerships, and cross-licensing arrangements between firms like Siemens, Philips, and B.A.T. and U.S. companies will become as commonplace as American agreements with Japanese counterparts. Companies situated in the newly industrialized countries (NICs) like South Korea are somewhat better positioned to face the uncertainties of the Third Industrial Revolution since the NICs do not have the incubus of troubled "sunset industries" and vested union interests. These countries, most notably South Korea, Taiwan, and Singapore all embrace the fierce worldwide competition from which Europe and the United States have tried unsuccessfully to protect themselves.

For fifty years since the New Deal there have been sporadic attempts to renew protectionism, but the Third Industrial Revolution brings added pressures for "information protectionism," the protection of, say, computer software or recorded music copyrights, an issue which the U.S. has not faced before. A recent news story highlighted a recent instance of this spreading problem:

> Representatives of Brazil and India said today [December 7, 1988] that a need to make advanced technology more widely available to combat hunger and disease was behind [their] reluctance to accept rules to protect patents, copyrights, and other intellectual property. The two countries also cautioned against cutting barriers to trade in banking, insurance, and other services because of fears that the third world could be overwhelmed by competition from the industrial countries.
>
> Officials of the United States and other developed countries said that linking technology protection to the fight against hunger was a red herring.[9]

The issues of information protectionism range from concern over the transfer of scientific knowledge to the threat of invading individual privacy. The so-called transborder data flows (TBDF) caused by the linking of computers and advanced electronic telecommunications systems, notably by satellites, are adding a new dimension of controversy between countries. The division of the world into the technological have and have-nots underlies much of the debate on the regulation of TBDFs.[10] At present the rich, developed, industrialized countries, especially the United States, are in favor of the broadest freedom and the fewest restrictions; other less developed but nevertheless industrialized countries—Canada, Germany and now possibly France—see limitations on the transfer of information as necessary. Information itself becomes an asset and can be sold, traded, taxed, subsidized, monitored, and regulated like any other commodity. At present, there is a worldwide race to build the computers and telecommunications equipment that can switch data instantaneously all over the world, but whether this equipment will be internationally standardized or manufactured by national standards alone is too early to tell. The ramifications of these decisions are universal but particularly important for the future of the U.S. economy. And of course, the markets for information are enormous. International companies, especially U.S. ones, have slowly begun to recognize that respecting the history and culture of a country are as important as profit, and that these high technologies must not transgress the rights of smaller nations. As an economic leader, the United States must be an advocate for the needs of the entire globe. We would be ill-served if we withdrew our efforts to regain our technological preeminence because we were scared off by these challenges.

INDUSTRIAL POLICY AND NATIONAL SECURITY

National policy will be affected by the Third Industrial Revolution on at least two sensitive issues: industrial policy and national security. As we have mentioned, all countries, including the United States, have some loosely devised "industrial policy." Our "policy" is an aggregation of laws, values, and political compromises that are mediated by the government, which acts as a broker. However, industrial policy is complicated by rapid technological change in the global economy. Dean Lester Thurow of MIT's Sloan School has declared that major investment decisions in the United States have become too important to be left to the private market alone. He advocates the formation of a national corporate investment committee that would redirect investment from fading industries to high-tech "sunrise" industries. The European Community, which is more sympathetic to these ideas, hopes to establish a dynamic industrial policy for the '90s. Government intervention, however, would be a mistake if it came to mean the short-sighted rescue of traditional industries.[11] The formation of a comprehensive industrial policy is complicated by the size and heterogeneity of U.S. industry, which presents insurmountable obstacles to any simple program. We will, however, see many versions of cartels such as Sematech, the loose research arrangement among chip producers formed to meet Japanese competition (though IBM and Apple refused to participate). Given the threat that these domestic cartels pose to the traditional independence of American companies, their implementation will be ponderous and many may very well fail.

We have few guidelines to regulate a technology that has multiple uses. Clearly computers, microchips, lasers, and biogenetics have varied applications; a computer, for example, can track a storm or an MX missile. For national security purposes, the U.S. government issues lists of all technology that may or may not be exported. Many times the list is obsolete on publication or overtaken by events (OBE) because of changes in policy and/or technology. What is and is not of military use cannot easily be resolved.

Discoveries and inventions have proliferated so rapidly in this Third Industrial Revolution that they are making obsolete and meaningless many of those security guidelines that have been painstakingly developed since World War II. The 1990s will bring a more exclusive list of protected items but the U.S. will still be on the alert against countries acquiring the know-how that could be used to manufacture a nuclear bomb or chemical weapons.

EPILOGUE

In looking at the Third Industrial Revolution we are looking at our future. New technologies will determine how we make things and how we live. New breakthroughs in knowledge and faster, more sophisticated supercomputers will transform the American economy and the global village we are part of. For many Americans, their daily concerns remain their jobs, their families, and their future. With reasonable national policies to slow inflation and public debt, employment should remain at high levels, especially over the next several decades. Those families that are strong and cohesive will be able to cope more effectively with the issues of technological change and uncertainty. For most Americans the future is as remarkably bright and expansive as it has been for more than 200 years.

But what of the other America? The United States Center for Disease Control projects 365,000 cases of AIDS and 263,000 deaths nationwide through the end of 1992. These figures are probably too low if New York state's projections are correct. State Health Commissioner David Axelrod anticipated a fourfold rise in caseloads in New York state from 20,000 to 90,500 and a sevenfold rise in deaths from 10,000 to 71,000 by 1994. This disease is a human tragedy but it also translates, as do all human problems, into billions of dollars of cost to a society that inevitably must shoulder the burden.

Millions of people in the United States do not have the resources for coping with the difficulties of modern society. Unfortunately their numbers will increase as the new changes spawn further economic dislocation and alienation. For the able, these uncertainties are challenges and opportunities; for the less competent the prospects are catastrophic. How many individuals are in need of some kind of assistance is difficult to measure accurately. Estimates include not only all those who for whatever reason cannot function physically or mentally in society but those millions who are temporarily impoverished by economic setbacks. Those who are functionally illiterate—the victims of our present educational system—are part of the numbers. Just as we need to upgrade our level of competence in the sciences and engineering, so we need to rescue those who currently do not reach a fourth-grade level of literacy, the minimum necessary to function in our society. The burden of illiteracy destroys personal incentive and deprives the economy of competitive individuals.

The sick, aged, homeless, alcoholic, and the addicted attest to the destruction which modern industrial society brings with it. To be sure, every society has always had its unfortunates, but the unraveling of significant portions of American society since World War II has created a new urgency to help these people. We need, for example, to build much more low-cost housing than presently exists, but building houses is not enough. Add to that the problems of the homeless, which are generally more severe than the problems of those on the poverty level.

In our society, alcohol is the drug of choice, and the lavish drying-out establishments are only for the affluent. In every American city one can see the ravages caused by drunkenness. The drug problem symbolized by crack, heroin, and cocaine fills most Americans with horror, and its pervasiveness is second only to alcoholism. Moreover, hard drug addiction tends to leave permanent damage. These drugs are everywhere, in our schools and communities, like roaches in the tropics. We are at present, despite government rhetoric, losing the fight against drugs. At stake, however, is the future well-being of the American people and of the commonwealth. A drug-ridden society cannot survive let alone win the competitive challenges of the Third Industrial Revolution. For two centuries, the United States was driven by a mighty dream of material achievement and success for everyone. We have not reached this goal, but we could lose much more than our high material standards of life if we do not succeed in redefining what makes up a meaningful and purposeful life.

The "other America" also includes those minorities who are excluded from the American feast. They bring more assets than we presently acknowledge, and society must accelerate their progress by removing as quickly as possible the vestiges of prejudice and racism. Since World War II we have made impressive gains, but nowhere are we in sight of universal fairness and equality of treatment for all Americans. The Third Industrial Revolution has need for every competence and ability; successful countries will not tolerate the narrow standards of the past. For Americans the choice is clear: either to adapt and move forward or fall behind to more dynamic nations.

The performance of the American economy has been an enormous achievement. Using the plentitude of land and natural resources, gifted people from every land fashioned a system of production and distribution which brought a high level of real income to five out of six inhabitants but not without a heavy price to the environment, native Americans, and minorities. For some it brought affluence and material comfort known in the past only to aristocrats and royalty. But such economic success must be tempered with consideration for the other qualities of human existence. As we push further into this new industrial era, ought we not use these great breakthroughs and advances to make life not merely richer in material terms, but gentler, more creative, and happier? We have never in our history, or in the history of the human species, had a better opportunity.

As it enters the 1990s, the U.S. is poised on a plateau, uncertain of the direction it wishes to proceed. The Third Industrial Revolution, the political transformation of Eastern Europe and the Soviet Union, and the impending integration of the Western European economies are monumental changes. Still, it is far from certain whether the U.S. will do more than muddle along as it has been doing, bogged down by problems it has accumulated over the last sixty years. Political stalemate at the federal and state level prevents decisive action. Lawrence H. Meyer and Associates (LHM&A) of St. Louis, an economic forecasting firm, has drawn up three possible models for the United States in the 1990s: a continuation of present trends, and two upward growth scenarios, one high, one modest.[12] Every significant economic indicator—GNP, productivity, interest rates, investment, corporate profits and living standards—fared better in the simulations of growth, reflecting the benefits of a vigorous policy of borrowing and investing for productive purposes. By muddling along, productivity would increase at the current rate of 1.2 percent a year and climb only slightly over the decade, while the federal deficit would remain at roughly 3 percent of GNP. Each of the other simulations provide significant gains, though the favored one, labelled "Borrow and Invest," comes out far ahead. The "Borrow and Invest" scenario projects a gross national product (GNP) in constant 1982 dollars of $7.3 trillion by 2008, a trillion more than what would be gained by muddling through. Very significant reduction in the national debt would occur; in contrast, muddling through would mean an interest bill of $625 billion versus $105 billion (constant 1982 dollars). "Borrow and Invest" would shrink the debt itself from 42 percent of GNP to 12.9 percent. Real interest rates would decline dramatically to 1 percent, competitive with the Japanese cost of capital. Gross private investment would soar to nearly 20 percent, and living standards would increase annually and over the decade; annual per capita disposable income would grow to $17,000, 11 percent higher than the muddling through figure. Consumers would spend $500 billion more than the baseline figure, though the percentage of consumption to GNP would decline 4.2 percent to 60.4 percent. Corporate profits would balloon 70 percent above the plateau figure to $518 billion in 1982 dollars. This model presupposes an extraordinary amount of foreign indebtedness ranging from 11.5 percent to 28.7 percent of GNP. Net foreign investment in U.S. assets would rise from an estimated $130 billion a year in 1990 to more than $457 billion, but the increased debt would be used for investment and increased production.

Since most Americans are not likely to want to risk such high levels of borrowings and sale of assets, some compromises are likely though at a heavy cost. A weaker dollar and greater volume of exports to balance the current account deficit, for example, will cost a great deal. Balancing the budget is essential and would yield enormous fiscal dividends if it could be done while lowering income taxes. The St. Louis firm would achieve this miracle by across-the-board spending freezes, a peace dividend resulting from the end of the Cold War, cutting farm subsidies, and putting social programs such as Medicare and other entitlement programs possibly on a means-tested basis. By making cost-of-living adjustments in social benefits programs trail the consumer price index by two percentage points, the government could save $93 billion over the next five years.

The benefits of the invest and grow model are captivating, but the means and the social costs LHM&A suggests are too severe in a democratic country where drug control, health care, poverty eradication, child care, housing, and the infrastructure have been underfunded for decades. More destructive for the long term would be addressing critical social problems with bandaid action. Still, most of the other LHM&A growth options remain available, even allowing for greater spending on neglected social and educational problems.

What can be done realistically short of the draconian measures suggested for cutting social welfare programs? We can and should raise federal taxes; even a small increase would produce very large sums, and if these resources were allocated efficiently, they would provide major benefits. An import tax on oil and a surcharge for gasoline could raise billions of dollars for much needed work on highways. For years, Americans have paid less for gasoline in both real and nominal terms than the rest of the world except for such places as Dubai. Why gasoline should sell at the same approximate price in real terms as it did forty years ago is an affront to both economics and the environment. A value-added tax (VAT), small and controlled, could lower consumer consumption and raise a great deal of productive capital. A small increase in the income tax would also produce vital revenue, and some increase in the estate tax would not be unfair. An indexed capital gains tax is long overdue. The so-called peace dividend, reaped by improving East-West relations, could easily produce $50 billion a year without any threat to our fundamental security or international obligations. We must finally pay the piper for the profligacy of the '80s, but we must not in the process destroy our future.[12]

The key to the future is to increase the flow of savings into the economy. We should encourage savings by restoring tax exemptions for individual retirement accounts (IRAs), which were an enormous success, and establish scholarships similar to the GI bill for students who enter fields with manpower shortages: engineering, hard science, health care, and teaching. We should encourage the lengthening of the school year from 180 to nearly 220 days by funneling incentive payments to school systems which move toward this goal. Funds must be provided for the ongoing technical upgrading of the work force (especially in the blue-collar manufacturing trades) through a voucher system. Immigration should be opened to people with skills and training that would benefit our economy. We ought to allow individuals to save at least $10,000 before subjecting this money to taxation. Several countries already have such incentives. These measures could do a great deal to reverse the downward drift we face.

The economies of the world rest on a wobbly three-legged stool; those supporting legs are the U.S., Japan, and Western Europe. Our leg needs to be strengthened forthwith since it is clear that what really happens in our future will be determined by what we do now.

NOTES

[1]*Fortune,* January 29, 1990: 136.

[2]*Conference Board Management Briefing: Marketing* 4:3 (June-July 1989): 1–2.

[3]Ibid., p. 4.

[4]*New York Times,* January 15, 1990.

[5]Twentieth Century Fund, *The Free Trade Debate: Reports of the Twentieth Century Fund Task Force on the Future of American Trade Policy,* background paper by Gary Clyde Hufbauer, December 18, 1989 (New York: Priority Press, 1989).

[6]*New York Times,* January 18, 1990.

[7]Conference Board, *World Economic Monitor* (Summer 1989): 2.

[8]Ibid., p. 4.

[9]*New York Times,* December 7, 1988, sec. D, p. 2.

[10]Rajan Chandran, Arvind Phatak, and Rakesh Sambharya, "Transborder Data Flows: Implications for Multinational Corporations," *Business Horizons* (Nov/Dec 1987): 74-82.

[11]Michael Porter, *The Competitive Advantage of Nations* (New York: The Free Press, 1990).

[12]*Fortune,* December 18, 1989: 52–66.

SUGGESTED READINGS

"Battle for Bigger Market Shares for Communications and Information Equipment," *Industries* (August 1986).

Clark, Rodney. *The Japanese Company.* New Haven: Yale University Press, 1979.

Conference Board Management Briefing: Marketing 4:3 (June/July 1989).

Conference Board Economic and Business Environment Program, *World Economic Monitor* 4:3 (Summer 1989).

Conference Board Economic and Business Environment Program, *World Economic Monitor,* 4:4 (Fall 1989).

Finkelstein, Joseph, ed. *Windows on a New World: The Third Industrial Revolution.* New York: Greenwood, 1989.

Henderson, D. F. *Foreign Enterprise in Japan.* Chapel Hill, N.C.: University of North Carolina Press, 1973.

Japan Economic Journal, August 1984–October 1986.

Naisbitt, John. *Megatrends 2000.* New York: Morrow, 1990.

Pepper, Thomas, M. E. Jarvin, and Jimmy W. Wheeler. *The Competition: Dealing with Japan.* New York: Praeger, 1985.

Porter, Michael. *The Competitive Advantage of Nations.* New York: The Free Press, 1990.

Reich, Robert B. *The Work of Nations: Preparing Ourselves for 21st Century Capitalism.* New York: Knopf, 1991.

Valery, Nicholas. "High Technology." *Economist,* August 23, 1986: 44–62.

INDEX

A

Absentee Ownership and Business Enterprise (Veblen), 6

Acid rain,
environmental crisis, 178–183
President Bush, 181

AFL-CIO, organized labor, 85–86

Agricultural acts, 123

Agricultural Adjustment Act of 1933, 14–15

Agricultural Trade Development and Assistance Act, 78–79

Agriculture,
Agricultural Trade Development and Assistance Act, 78–79
America in the '70s, 122–125
during world War II, 41–42
mid-century America, 76–79
and New Deal, 14–17
postwar America, 55–57, 78
United Farm Workers (UFW), 123

Aid to Families with Dependent Children (AFDC), 102, 141

Air Pollution Control Act (1955), 179

Airline Deregulation Act, 148

Alcoa, antitrust regulation, 157–158

Allied Expeditionary Force, Eisenhower and, 50

Allstate Insurance, 162

Amalgamated Clothing and Textile Workers Union, 127–128

America in the '60s, President's Commission on National Goals, 92–93

America in the '70s,
agriculture, 122–125
effect of the international economy, 116–119
energy crisis, 119–120
labor, 125–129

America in the '80s, Reagan boom, 141

American Express, 162

American Motors, 83

American Tobacco, 157

Amgen, and biogenetics, 238

Anderson, Martin, 141

Anti-trust regulation,
Alcoa, 157–158
American Tobacco, 157
in the business system, 155–159
Celler-Kefauver Amendment, 158–159
Clayton Anti-Trust Act, 156–159
Federal Trade Commission Act, 156
Liggett and Meyers, 157
McKinley Tariff, 155
Miller-Tydings Amendment, 157
National Industrial Recovery Act, 157
Reynolds, 157
Sherman Anti-Trust Act, 155–158
Webb-Pomerene Act, 156
Wheeler-Lea Act, 158

Apple Computer, 201

Army Corps of Engineers, 174

AT&T,

The American Economy from the Great Crash to the Third Industrial Revolution was copyedited and proofread by Michael Kendrick. Production editor was Lucy Herz. The maps were drawn by Jim Bier. The index was compiled by Gary Belkin. The text and tables were typeset by Point West, Inc. The book was printed and bound by BookCrafters Inc.

Text design by Matt Doherty.
Cover by DePinto Graphic Design.